LEADERSHIP AND PUBLIC SECTOR REFORM IN ASIA

PUBLIC POLICY AND GOVERNANCE

Edited by Professor Evan Berman, School of Government, Victoria University of Wellington, New Zealand

This series brings together the best in international research on policy and governance issues. Authored and edited by experts of the field, these books present new and insightful research on a range of policy and governance issues across the globe. Topics covered include, but are not limited to, policy analysis frameworks; health care policy; environmental/resource policy; local government policy; development policy; regional studies/policy; urban policy/planning and social policy.

Titles include:

Corruption, Accountability and Discretion
Nancy S. Lind and Cara Rabe-Hemp

The Experience of Democracy and Bureaucracy in South Korea
Tobin Im

Governmental Financial Resilience: International Perspectives on How Local Governments Face Austerity
Ileana Steccolini, Martin Jones and Iris Saliterer

The Global Educational Policy Environment in the Fourth Industrial Revolution: Gated, Regulated and Governed
Travis D. Jules

Governing for the Future: Designing Democratic Institutions for a Better Tomorrow
Jonathan Boston

Asian Leadership in Policy and Governance
Evan M. Berman and M. Shamsul Haque

Different Paths to Curbing Corruption: Lessons from Denmark, Finland, Hong Kong, New Zealand and Singapore
Jon S. T. Quah

Institutional Reforms in the Public Sector: What Did We Learn?
Mahabat Baimyrzaeva

New Steering Concepts in Public Management
Sandra Groeneveld and Steven Van de Walle

Curbing Corruption in Asian Countries: An Impossible Dream?
Jon S. T. Quah

LEADERSHIP AND PUBLIC SECTOR REFORM IN ASIA

EDITED BY

EVAN BERMAN
School of Government,
Victoria University of Wellington,
New Zealand

and

EKO PRASOJO
Faculty of Administrative Science,
University of Indonesia,
Indonesia

emerald
PUBLISHING

United Kingdom – North America – Japan
India – Malaysia – China

Emerald Publishing Limited
Howard House, Wagon Lane, Bingley BD16 1WA, UK

First edition 2018

Reprints and permission service
Contact: permissions@emeraldinsight.com

British Library Cataloguing in Publication Data
A catalogue record for this book is available from the British Library

ISBN: 978-1-78743-310-6 (Print)
ISBN: 978-1-78743-309-0 (Online)
ISBN: 978-1-78743-444-8 (Epub)
ISBN: 978-1-78754-684-4 (Paperback)

ISSN: 2053-7697 (Series)

CONTENTS

NOTES ON CONTRIBUTORS

Loo-See Beh is Professor at the Faculty of Economics & Administration, University of Malaya. Her research focus is on public administration and human resource management. She has published widely in leading journals and various publications. She has been a Resource Person and Associate Member with several organisations, including Malaysian Qualifications Agency, Royal Malaysian Police, Malaysian Tax Agency, and the Asian Development Bank Institute.

Evan Berman is Professor of Public Management at the School of Government, Victoria University of Wellington, New Zealand. He is recipient of the Fred Riggs Award for Lifetime Achievement in International and Comparative Public Administration from the American Society for Public Administration and other awards. He has published extensively on public administration leadership in Asia, performance, human resources and other topics. His publications include works on Public Administration in East Asia (2010) and Public Administration in Southeast Asia (2011). He is past University Chair Professor, and currently Adjunct Chair Professor, at National Chengchi University (Taiwan) and Distinguished Professor at Louisiana State University. He is also Coauthor of the popular textbooks, *Human Resource Management in Public Service* (Sage, 2016, 5th ed.) and *Essential Statistics for Public Managers and Policy Analysts* (Sage, 2018, 4th ed.).

Alex Brillantes is Professor of Public Administration at the National College of Public Administration and Governance in the University of the Philippines. Brillantes earlier served as Commissioner of the Commission on Higher Education, Executive Director of the Local Government Academy of the Department of Interior and Local Government and President of the Philippine Society for Public Administration. He obtained his Masters and PhD from the University of Hawaii, and MPA and AB from the University of the Philippines. His areas of expertise are governance, institutions, development administration, local governance and higher education.

John Halligan is Emeritus Professor of Public Administration at the Institute for Governance & Policy Analysis, University of Canberra. Research interests are comparative public management and governance, including public sector reform. He specialises in Anglophone countries: Australia, Canada, New Zealand and United Kingdom, and is currently completing a book on the results of reform in these countries.

Defny Holidin is a Lecturer in Public Administration at Universitas Indonesia. His research areas are public administrative reform, public sector innovation and institutional reengineering. He is currently Co-directing Research and Policy Advocacy of the Universitas Indonesia Center for Study of Governance and Administrative Reform. He has provided policy consultation and advice concerning bureaucracy reform and public service innovation agendas to the Government of Indonesia. He has recently co-authored a policy paper on transformative leadership and competencies of public servants for the 15th Session of the United Nations Committee of Experts on Public Administration (2016) and a book entitled *Bureaucracy Reform Transition in Indonesia* (in Bahasa Indonesia, 2016).

Masahiro Horie is Senior Professor and Director of the Executive Development Center for Global Center of the National Graduate Institute for Policy Studies in Tokyo. Before moving to GRIPS, he worked for the Japanese Government for 35 years. Positions he held in the government includes Vice Minister of the Ministry of Internal Affairs and Communications and Director-General of the Cabinet Secretariat Office for the Promotion of Administrative Reform. Since 2013 he is the Chair of the Programme and Research Advisory Committee of the International Institute of Administrative Sciences. His research concentrates on administrative reform, public management, policy evaluation and comparative public administration.

Shao Jingjun has worked as the Deputy Secretary of Ling County CPC Committee, Shandong Province and has served as the Deputy Discipline Commissioner to the Research Office of Central Commission for Discipline Inspection of CPC and inspector of the Inspection Department. He has served as the Committee Member of Committee of National Philosophy and Social Science Planning Subject, Special Commentator of Central Organization Department of CPC, the Contributing Senior Editor of People's Daily, Adjunct Professor of Chinese Academy of Governance, Hunan University, and Qingdao University, and the Staff Writer of Chinese Public Administration. His main research areas are the social development and governance in current China, and the CPC Building and Anti-Corruption Fight.

David Seth Jones is currently a Consultant in Policy and Management. He previously worked as Associate or Adjunct Professor in the National University of Singapore, Singapore Management University and University of Brunei Darussalam, and as a Course Director in Singapore for a Masters of Public Administration Programme conducted by the Australian National University and the Civil Service College, Singapore. His current research interests are public procurement, public finance, public–private partnerships and land policy and reform. He has published widely in these fields.

Lizan Perante Calina is currently connected with the House of Representatives. She is a University Lecturer at the National College of Public Administration, University of the Philippines. She is actively involved in the discourse of public administration and governance as Executive Director of the Philippine Society for Public Administration and Associate Editor of the Philippine Governance Digest. She obtained her Doctorate and Masters in Public Administration from the same university.

Ha Ngoc Pham is a Lecturer at National Academy of Public Administration in Hanoi, Vietnam. She obtained a Master Degree in Public Administration from University of Leuven, Belgium and is currently doing a PhD in Public Management in Victoria University of Wellington, New Zealand. Her main research areas include public sector leadership, performance management and public administration reform and training. She has published several articles, textbook chapters and conference papers in Vietnamese and English.

Eko Prasojo is Dean of Faculty of Administrative Science, University of Indonesia and the Director of University Centre of Study of Governance and Administrative Reform. He is Professor for Public Administration. From October 2011 until October 2014, he was the Vice Minister of Administrative Reform in the Republic of Indonesia and was involved in several drafts of law on public sector reform and decentralization in Indonesia. He is now president of the Indonesian Association of Public Administration, Vice President of the Asian Association for Public Administration and Member of Committee Expert of Public Administration, the United Nation.

Caroline Rennie has worked in the New Zealand Government for the Ministry of Transport, NZ Treasury and former Ministry of Economic Development. Caroline worked on provided ministerial advice on the management of Crown owned entities and advising on the development of commercial legislation in the transport, electricity and finance sectors. She has for a number of years taken an interest in the changes and reforms to the New Zealand public sector and has qualifications in Law and Economics.

Supachai Yavaprabhas is a Professor in the Department of Public Adminis-tration, Chulalongkorn University, Thailand. His research interests include public policy analysis and public sector reform, especially in the sector of higher education, basic education, police and judicial administration and public health. Recently, he was appointed as a member of the Thailand National Reform Council and later a member of the Constitutional Drafting Committee. He previously served as Secretary to the Minister of University Affairs, and in the last decade, he held positions on the Main Committee, External QA Assessor, Advisor and Senior Administrator in both public and higher education sectors.

Jiang Wu has served as President of the Chinese Academy of Personnel Science and as a member of the 11th and 12th CPPCC National Committee. He served as the Senior Vice President of International Institute of Administrative Sciences from 2009 to 2016. He is currently the President of Asian Group of Public Administration, and also works as the Deputy Director of Research Institute of China's Administrative Reform, the vice chairman of Chinese Public Administration Society and the Deputy Director of Research Institute of China's Public Sectors Management and China Institute for Leadership Science. Prior, he served as Deputy Director of research office of Central Organization Department of CPC in 1993, and Deputy Editor-in-Chief of Party Building Books Publishing House in 1991.

CHAPTER 1

LEADERSHIP AND PUBLIC SECTOR REFORMS IN ASIA: AN OVERVIEW

Evan Berman

ABSTRACT

This introductory chapter explains why public sector reforms matter and why a focus on Asia and leadership is needed. It also provides an overview of highlights, lessons and conclusions in this book. Cases of successful public sector reforms usually show leadership by central agencies, with support of the office of President or Prime Minister. While laws and rules are commonly used to further reform, cases show that more is needed to ensure success and sustainability. A range of strategies include heightened accountability, personnel changes, supporting change leaders in departments, reform through capacity development, and learning from innovations other jurisdictions. Conclusions include suggestions for further research.

This book examines public sector reforms with a focus on Asia and leadership. This introductory chapter explains why public sector reforms matter for meeting many public policy challenges, and why a focus on Asia and

Leadership and Public Sector Reform in Asia
Public Policy and Governance, 1–17
doi:10.1108/S2053-769720180000030001

leadership is needed at this time. This chapter provides an overview of highlights, lessons and conclusions from the chapters that follow and summarises
the highlights and arguments of each. We also offer thoughts for further
research.

WHAT ARE PUBLIC REFORMS?
WHY DO THEY MATTER?

Public sector reforms are changes in government processes or structures that help
to better achieve key public policy challenges. Some processes are directly linked
to citizens, such as when they use new digital processes to obtain government
services quickly and which are free of corruption. Other reforms are less visible
to citizens but are no less salient to those working 'on the inside' of government.
For example, when cross-border pollution is noted as an issue, countries may
increase their cooperation and collaboration by sharing information, sometimes in real-time, and by setting up trans-national working groups to address
specific concerns. In short, public sector reforms are 'deliberate changes to
(the structures and processes of) public sector organizations with the objective of getting them (in some sense) to run better' (Pollitt & Bouckeart, 2011;
United Nations Economic and Social Council, 2006).

The case for public sector reforms is that they provide public managers
with the opportunity to improve processes and produce better public sector
results. The issue in question is not necessarily that the machinery of government is broken and needs fixing, though improvements often are needed.
Rather, public sector reforms usually involve system-wide changes that touch
the many thousands of programs which make up government. Public sector reforms open up new opportunities for thousands of public managers
to improve how their programs work and what targets for performance and
impact can be set, thus providing leverage across manifold programs.

There are many examples of public sector reforms. The following list shows
some of the many ways in which governments have improved how they work
in the last 20 years or so. Jurisdictions vary on how fast and deep they take
to public sector reforms but few may ignore what their neighbours are doing.
Hopefully, some of the following examples readily come to mind for many
readers:

- Decentralization reforms that build up local government and central government programmes in local areas (e.g., improvement in local health care
  services, school, roads and agricultural support services).

- 'Joined up' efforts in decision-making or programme delivery that cut across departments (e.g., coordinated approaches to crime, welfare or business development).
- Reorganization that aligns priorities with efforts and capability (e.g., building new pollution control departments).
- Strengthening anti-corruption oversight and implementation (e.g., new laws and increased independence and capacity in investigations).
- Public–private partnerships (e.g., delivery of welfare service, rocket launches and highways).
- Digital government (e.g., one-stop shopping and integrated/real-time data).
- Transferring functions to new semi-autonomous agencies (including corporatization of higher education).
- New performance management frameworks (e.g., increasing accountability and performance through new reporting standards, also for leadership development).
- New procurement processes (e.g., increased transparency or access by minority vendors).
- New structures or programmes for transnational cooperation (e.g., Association of Southeast Asian Nations, migration and regional pollution).

Public sector reforms are not always at the centre of heated public policy debate but they do matter. Many semi-autonomous agencies work quietly but successfully on health care promotion and infrastructure development, for example. At times, public sector reforms do make headlines, such as on matters of privatization or anti-corruption, or when they are launched by leading elected officials. However, many public sector reforms fly a bit under the radar of public consciousness, and hence the media, certainly beyond any initial launch. They often are driven by senior public leaders and involve specific concerns or opportunities. This not to say that citizens are not grateful for them or that they don't make a difference or lack accountability – many of today's governments work vastly more effectively and efficiently than they ever did.

Yet, even the most casual observer may note very large differences in the use of these reforms across countries and jurisdictions within them. Some agencies and cities are clearly on the cutting edge of adopting reforms, whereas others are locked into the ways of yesteryear. This is not to say that tried and true bureaucratic routine and rules are necessarily bad – predictability and accountability are important values for government – and many public sector reforms are built on well-established processes because they work. However, a need also exists for responding to changing citizen needs, incorporating changing global expectations and taking advantage of increased capability. As the following chapters will show, leadership is needed at many levels to help bring public sector reforms into reality.

WHY THIS BOOK?

This book acknowledges that present day knowledge about public sector reforms in Asia is quite scattered and seldom focusses on the challenges of leadership. Given the current state of global knowledge on public sector reforms, as well as the needs of scholars and public managers working on reforms, more knowledge is needed about reforms in Asia and the leadership that is required.

Asia is a fascinating region for focussing on public leadership, including reforms. Specifically, this book focusses on the Asia-Pacific region, defined as roughly East and Southeast Asia in which about one-third of the world's population, about 2.3 billion people, live. This area is hugely diverse. Governments include democracies (e.g., Australia or Japan), one-party states (e.g., China and Vietnam) and unstable systems (e.g., Thailand). They have a broad range of cultural legacies such as Confucian (Japan and Vietnam), Buddhist (Thailand) and Western (e.g., Australia) and vastly different levels of economic development (e.g., Singapore and Indonesia). The region includes countries with the least corruption (e.g., Singapore) and those with high corruption levels (e.g., Vietnam). The region includes the world's most populous country (China) as well as some of the smallest states (e.g., New Zealand). In the Asia-Pacific states, governments typically play leading roles in social and economic development (e.g., Malaysia and China), yet by measures of expenditures or civil servants per capita, most are among the smaller ones in the world. The country cases, identified above, reflect this great diversity.

Public sector reforms are very relevant to these countries and their leaders. Matters of food supply, housing, education, public health and national security are key priorities. In Asia, strong governments are needed and valued to ensure these; weak governments are associated with public suffering and a lack of governability. The quality of government planning and execution is important to economic development and political stability. Public sector reforms to increase government effectiveness, assist leaders to achieve their policy aims and are often picked up in government agendas and as executive priorities.

Our interest in this book is to explore what is known about these reforms with an eye towards helping leaders responsible for such reforms. Clearly, there is a very large variation; some Asia-Pacific countries are leading in public sector reforms, while others are surely not. This is not only a matter of understanding as to which factors are associated with success and failure, as many scholarly studies are apt to do, but it is also to further our understanding about what leaders might need to do to be successful. If a strong (or at least effective) government is sought, then leaders are needed who know how to realize the effective use of public sector reform, as well.

The global literature on public sector reforms, which is fairly extensive, has not been particularly focussed on this leadership matter, to which this book adds. Generally speaking, studies of public sector reforms often discuss broad paradigms of reforms and their content, such as New Public Management, New Public Governance and Neo-Weberian State, which are reflected in the above examples (e.g., Brinkerhoff & Brinkerhoff, 2015; Laegrid & Christensen, 2013; Wong, 2015). Other reform studies describe specific reforms, such as public–private partnerships, e-government or personnel reforms, focussed on specific countries and programmes or policy settings (e.g., Berman, 2015; Phua, Ling, & Phua, 2014; Wu, Ramesh, & Yu, 2017). Some studies assess reform outcomes, although often qualitatively as quantification is not easy and often limited to narrow measures of specific reforms in specific settings.

Of most relevance to the theme of leadership are past studies that describe how reforms emerge. While some focus on broad trends of, say, technology (e.g., e-government and energy trends) or social change (social media and transparency) as driving factors (e.g., de Vries, Bekkers, & Tummers, 2016; Pollitt & Bouckeart, 2011), almost all studies also note the role of political elites and bureaucratic actors in leading or picking up reforms and realizing them (e.g., Choi, 2010; Sobis, Berg, & Vries, 2012). This book builds on the latter, focussing on the leadership of political executives and bureaucratic actors.

The chapters that follow examine the strategies and contexts of reform leadership. Authors were instructed to focus on the following matters in their chapters; identifying the locus and drivers of reforms, the extent and manner that leadership is seen to further reform efforts, how leaders address resisting actors inside organizations, overcome public distrust, address relations with the authorizing environment; and how leaders build operational capacity to succeed reform implementation and making reform efforts sustainable. Authors were also instructed to provide one or more cases illustrating the above practices of leadership. The chapters are informed by cutting edge interests in theses areas.

The results of these efforts are contained in the following pages. The following section brings together some of the main highlights.

6

EVAN BERMAN

TOWARDS A THEORY OF LEADERSHIP IN PUBLIC SECTOR REFORMS

In what follows, we draw on the book chapters to highlight matters of leadership in public sector reforms. As the range of constitutional practices varies, we use the term 'presidents' to refer to prime ministers (e.g., New Zealand), presidents (e.g., Thailand) and party secretary generals (e.g., China), and the term 'department head' to refer to ministers, vice ministers, director-generals and chief executives who lead departments and agencies. We clarify instances where other meanings are used, such as ministers who are not also department heads (e.g., in Westminster systems).

WHO LEADS IN INITIATING PROPOSALS FOR PUBLIC SECTOR REFORMS?

Public sector reforms, even when not government-wide, typically involve quite fundamental changes in structure and processes that require new policies at the highest levels, sometimes requiring legal or legislative actions as well. In all chapters, these involve the presidents and/or cabinet. Public sector reforms often include parts that are aligned with governance platforms of political parties and their presidents (e.g., privatization in Japan, one-stop shopping in Malaysia and anti-corruption in China), and chapters in this book clearly show that presidents often take a strong interest in leading certain reforms. While public sector reforms seldom arise from voter priorities, in recent years, key policy targets of education, crime, environment, welfare and job creation have led to 'whole-of-government' actions in each area and included direct involvement of the president and cabinet (e.g., Malaysia, New Zealand and Singapore).

However, public sector reform does not always originate from political processes or platforms. Central agencies such as the treasury, national planning, budget, administration and civil service reform offices also lead the development of public sector reforms. Central offices have relevant mandates, led prior reform efforts, and are well-positioned to lead consultation processes with departments across government. Officials in central agencies often have broad relations with other departments and, in some countries, even come from them, too. The cases of Singapore and Japan show senior officials playing important roles, working together with ministers to formulate specific reform plans and initiatives. In such instances, 'teamwork' of high-level officials and ministers is described and is at play.

Thus, the source of initiative of public sector reforms is varied. The case of Thailand also shows societal actors working with bureaucrats over many years dealing with successive ministers (e.g., 'jazz-based' model). A concern is that leadership that builds successful support for reform initiatives does not also always generate pathways for success and address barriers that may need to be overcome. The chapters on Indonesia, Vietnam, Thailand and Australia also show instances where reform leadership did not include strategies or conceptualizations for lower level leaders to be successful – which they were not. While this might be seen as implementation, it is also an issue of decision-making that does not thoroughly identify and provide pathways for success. The cases of Singapore and Japan show the use of fact-based analysis and input from senior public managers that may help identify success factors, which no doubt is furthered by involving those responsible for subsequent implementation of success. The use of rule-, law- or ideology-based analysis as frameworks may lead to blind spots about the realities that reform leaders face.

In short, some chapters in this book raise concern about insufficiently adequate (i.e., low quality) decision-making for reform. Also, the case of Malaysia shows the unwillingness of political leaders to address some core challenges, which no doubt is present in other countries too. We raise these matters as suggestions for further research.

HOW ARE PUBLIC SECTOR REFORMS IMPLEMENTED?

The nature of the public sector involving high-level policy often leads to a high-level of involvement in implementation. Different practices are reported, usually involving presidents, cabinets or core agencies. The underlying logic is that implementation from the highest levels is needed to ensure (i) implementation across the entire government (all departments and quasi-autonomous agencies), (ii) overcome resistance at the very top layer of the departments and provide senior department managers with tools for implementation (e.g., mandates, budgets and interventions) and (iii) provide accountability and oversight so that reforms proceed and are achieved.

The cases report a range of organizational practices. In Japan, the administrative management agency was established in the president's office, but various presidents also created advisory councils reporting to them when they wanted support from business and other societal leaders for reforms.

In Indonesia, the Ministry of Administrative Reform was created, and the Office of the Public Sector Development Commission was created in Thailand. In New Zealand, the State Services Commission (SSC) was created that today leads many reforms. In Australia, the Treasury and Public Service Commission leads reform. While the power of these organizations waxes and wanes, there is little doubt that they have the ears of presidents and are involved or lead in implementing reforms. In China and Vietnam, central party congresses are the source of documents and the framework is enforced from top down.

The chapters discuss various tools of implementation. Laws and rules set up new organizations, requirements, processes and accountability, involving privatization, management, corruption and more. Leaders use appointment and promotion to encourage lower level managers to implement reforms, and they remove and replace resisting actors and use audits to ensure compliance. They provide clear policy announcements and training to increase and further accountability and expectations. In the case of anti-corruption, audits are also used to lead criminal investigations and punishment. The above agencies usually provide reports on monitoring the progress of the reforms and call upon ministers and cabinets when interventions are needed. Together, the chapters help piece together what is a pretty clear framework. The chapters on Japan and China, taken together, provide a clear overview that is reinforced and extended by others as discussed below.

However, new laws and rules are not enough and also contain problems. Many chapters report concerns about lack of conditions, resistance and sustainability over time. In Vietnam, the scope of reform is said to be too broad, the capacity of public agencies and civil servants is limited, and existing monitoring, evaluation and reporting systems are weak. In Thailand, strict and narrow financial rules limit resourcing for reforms. In Indonesia, innovation can cause leaders to tread beyond parameters, resulting in prosecution. Public sector reforms in China too are seen to take many cycles, suggesting many challenges as well. Bureaucratic, rule-based and/or corrupt cultures can be highly resistant to client-focussed and outcome-oriented reforms, and the chapters from Australia and New Zealand raise additional implementation issues for management reforms. Training is mentioned in some chapters, but it needs to be specific and deal with actual situations.

There are other problems as well. There are inherent principal–agent problems; high-level leaders may not get accurate information from subordinate agencies and their leader managers about the implementation of state reforms. Gaming with performance-based reporting is well documented in China. There are also challenges of political turnover in democracies and leadership turnover in one-party systems. The threat of discontinuity of political or party leadership means that implementation needs to be institutionalized before political change occurs. The Australian case shows that a relatively stable political environment allowed implementation to proceed in the mid-term. The same can be said of reforms in Malaysia and Singapore. With so many problems, it is small wonder that reform outcomes are mixed or take a long time to occur.

HORIZONS AND INNOVATIONS IN REFORM LEADERSHIP

The chapters in this book include practices that also extend beyond the above framework. The case of New Zealand is noteworthy in that it establishes a non-political, professional process that increases accountability for department performance. The performance improvement framework (PIF) provides expert assessment of department readiness for meeting prospective mid-term targets, which include organizational capabilities. The PIF stands alongside traditional democratic and political accountability mechanisms and gains its force by being tied to the contract renewal and performance appraisal of department heads. This not only gives an additional locus for driving public sector reforms but also gives a non-political focus to reform and to priorities that can broaden content when issues are beyond the interest of presidents and their cabinet, such as issues of management reforms and long-term changes.

The Indonesian chapter describes efforts to find and support reform 'champions' in departments. The idea is that over time reforms are implemented in cascading sequence and that this process itself creates new leaders who learn to address and overcome obstacles; successive leaders share in lessons. The idea is intellectually well stabled in the organizational development literature. The case shows leaders turning threats into new reform opportunities and engaging in collaboration across departments and jurisdictions in building new coalitions for change and engaging with the authorizing environment. While the success of this strategy is untested, does not address overarching constraints (e.g., corruption), and may initially lead to somewhat scattered progress, it nonetheless aims to build capacity and progress in decentralized systems and one can easily imagine policies and practices in support of these efforts.

Accountability of department managers is taken yet further in cases of Singapore and China. In the case of Singapore, it is reported that managers get frequent feedback at all levels and strict performance standards are held; promotion is merit based and competitive. The idea is to increase innovation and reform in the appraisal and selection of public managers as well as in dialogue and feedback processes that speak to the organizational culture. In China and Singapore, strict accountability audits keep people on their toes when presidents express clear priorities that are followed by persistent audits and harsh consequences. Leaders show that they mean business when there is accountability. (However, chapters also show that this is not always the case. In theory, double accountability in one-party systems to both government and party officials should keep reform implementation high, yet in Vietnam poor capacity and corruption are said to thwart this.)

The chapters on Vietnam and the Philippines also point to the role of local governments as a source of reform innovation. In Vietnam, local governments are given leeway to 'break fences' and inspire new innovation that could be later adopted in other jurisdictions or the national government. The chapter on the Philippines discusses that in spite of the numerous public sector reforms being primary concerns of successive national leaders of the Philippines, massive – and sometimes impressive – reorganization plans have not met their declared objectives. Instead, these authors focus on the role of leaders at all levels of government, including local governments, civil society and universities. Leaders work by developing capacities of themselves and others, by pushing the boundaries of continuous improvement and by focussing on reforms of institutions, structures and procedures that are anchored in behaviour, values and vision. In doing so, these change leaders become the sources of reform.

Finally, it would appear that some path dependency in public sector reforms may exist. It is very hard to succeed in reforms where high corruption and low professional capacity exist. This is supported by the cases in this book, both comparatively and in time. Many current reforms assume transparency and professional orientations in managers' discretionary authority, and countries such as Singapore, New Zealand and Australia have high transparency rankings. While it may be that building anti-corruption procedures and professionalism is a first or necessary public sector reform at some point, the cases of the Philippines show that reform is possible even in the presence of some corruption.

There is still much that we do not know about leadership in public sector reforms research always has a next frontier. The following are the topics for further research: What are the motivations of reform leaders and senior public managers, and what rewards and opportunities might drive them? What rewards and opportunities encourage those at lower levels who are involved in implementation? What skills do reform leaders need to have, and how can these be built up at lower levels? How do top leaders remain involved in reform efforts? How do reform decisions avoid or minimize deficiencies in decision-making that trip up subsequent implementation? How can reforms best be implemented beyond central government agencies? How does corruption negatively affect reform success specifically, and how can anti-corruption efforts be integrated to further public sector reform efforts? How can reporting and performance management practices be strengthened to support implementation? How do financial rules and accountability affect reform success? How can reform success be leveraged into creating cultural change in organizations? How does shaping organizational culture affect the success of reform implementation, and what is the evidence that organizational cultures can be shaped? How do jurisdictions learn from each other and how can that be improved? How can the lessons from smaller, reform-minded jurisdictions, either smaller countries or in local governments, be used to further reform processes in larger jurisdiction and national departments that may be lagging? We hope that these frontier questions aid in thinking about the future research.

In sum, public sector reforms vary in the degree of commitment and success. We hope that the above analysis, and the chapters that follow, can help inform and guide the work of reform leaders.

ABOUT THE CHAPTERS

While authors were asked to follow the above-mentioned 'guiding issues' on reform leadership, authors used their discretion to highlight themes in their countries and bring forth additional cases and evidence as available to them. The chapters of the book thus bring out somewhat different aspects and themes. These are discussed below for the readers' reference.

Japan has had four periods of public sector reforms since World War II. Masahiro Horie discusses leadership for reform during the occupation period, the high economic growth period, the low economic growth period and the search for a 'new' Japan under various present difficulties. Reforms reflect the priorities of the time and interests of prime ministers, whose style also affected how public sector reforms are advanced. During the occupation period, the Administrative Management Agency was established in the Prime Minister's Office and was responsible for the overall management of national government organizations. It was staffed by civil servants who become experts in their areas. Since the 1980s, furthering privatization, deregulation and reorganization, advisory councils for the prime minister were also used involving influential business leaders and scholars.

Horie shows that 'political leadership, especially that of the prime minister and minister in charge of administrative reform, is important in deciding on highly political issues, to persuade or direct politicians and administrators to follow the leadership, to inspire and get support of the general public, and to ensure the support or acceptance of those concerned'. Where prime ministers are not directly involved, leadership is provided by professional administrators under the general support of the prime minister and the minister responsible for administrative reform. He describes detailed analyses and notes that reform sustainability occurs through institutionalization, incentives, management and producing meaningful results.

Leadership for public sector reforms in *Indonesia* involves both national level efforts and leadership from local levels that have been empowered by prior decentralization. Eko Prasojo and Defny Holidin focus on reforms by the national government, which have been guided by values of serving the public, increasing efficiency and becoming corruption-free. Although the National Development Agency and the Ministry for Administrative Reform provide central impetus and coordination, reforms are seen as quite fragmented across ministries, with uneven results. The authors are concerned about reform effectiveness and sustainability. Reform leadership is challenged by human capital and legally mandated but inefficient bureaucratic processes and structures, as well as challenges of public distrust and disobedient civil servants. The latter is sometimes dealt with by using patronage to insert allies for reform, and they note leaders gaining leverage from working across boundaries and jurisdictions and by improving their authorizing environment. Prasojo and Holidin describe a strategy of leaders-led efforts that are cascaded through ministries through institutionalization (e.g., of policies) and obtaining support from successive reform champions at different levels and locations. The authors argue for increasing the number of 'champion leaders' who pragmatically, transactionally and successfully get subordinates to commit to reform efforts.

In his chapter on *China*, Jiang Wu and Shao Jingjuin discusse how China's rapid economic development since the 1970s has involved three different periods of administrative reforms, stretching out over seven successive five-year plans. Wu focusses on leadership style, specifically, the thinking that is expected from leaders in each period of leadership for development, open leadership and innovative leadership. Wu discusses that leadership for these reforms comes from the highest levels, the Communist Party of China (CPC), as articulated by successive secretary generals of the CPC, that the reform purpose is not only to achieve policy goals but also to uphold CPC leadership in China, and that public managers throughout China are assessed by the party as well as the government. Wu also provides an excellent case of reform leadership in anti-corruption that shows how the CPC deals with complex and entrenched issues through education and strict implementation, leading to punishment of 1.2 million people, including senior officials. The case shows senior officials setting the general direction, preserving the role of the CPC and achieving results learned through practice and innovation, trends towards increasing the rule of law and the use of audits.

Thailand has continuously had administrative reforms, in spite of periods of military regime and democratic government. Supachai Yavaprabhas describes leadership of administration reforms coming from issue experts and senior civil service officers described as a 'jazz-banded' leadership model of different actors. Political parties pick up reform packages consistent with their policy platforms, while the military looks for ready-to-deliver-policy packages. Supachai discusses the example of education and health care reforms and the role of the Public Sector Development Commission (OPDC). In Thailand, resistance usually occurs during the implementation stage than at the formulation stage. Supachai discusses OPDC initiatives that were implemented with bonuses of up to 12-month salary for some senior officers and department heads. In health care, success came from concerted efforts of health care experts who promoted their ideas for long periods of time and successfully continued to convince politicians running the Ministry of Public Health. In other instances, however, budget allocations may bump up against financial procedures that are detailed and tight due to anti-corruption practices. In education reforms, teachers were placed at different school districts that the lacked commitment. In decentralization reforms, resistance come from line ministries wanting to secure their authority, although local authorities may be very active. Resistance often requires negotiation of many parties and rarely do politicians step in to overcome and assist.

In her chapter on *Vietnam*, Ha Pham describes how in 1986 public sector reforms became important following the Doi Moi programme. Restructuring of the state-owned sector was regarded as crucial for ensuring the quality of economic growth, and the Vietnamese government placed considerable effort in public sector reforms. The 8th Party Congress (1996) emphasized the urgent need for a more transparent, capable and modern public sector, including efforts to improve law-making process and capacity, reducing burdensome bureaucracy, fighting corruption, increasing leadership by senior officials and improving public service delivery. The government specifies the national Public sector Reform (PSR) master programme, and the Ministry of

Home Affairs coordinates implementation among ministries, central agencies and provincial governments. Local political leaders (party leaders) determine reforms based on the guidelines of the party and the government. Ha Pham writes that in spite of ambitious public service reform programmes and some positive achievements, the quality of the public sector remains poor. The professional capacity of the civil service is low, pay is low, corruption is high and processes and structures seem ill-fitted for the market economy. Reform scope is too broad, the capacity of public agencies and civil servants is limited and existing monitoring, evaluation and reporting systems are weak. In some successes, leaders use appointment and promotion to encourage those at the lower level to implement reforms and provide training to increase understanding. She believes that Vietnamese leadership has become less proactive and vigorous in practicing or embracing bold reform experiments.

In their chapter on *The Philippines*, Alex Brillantes and Lizan Perante-Calina discuss that in spite of public sector reforms being one of the primary concerns of successive national leaders of the Philippines, the 'massive – and sometimes impressive – reorganization plans have not met their declared objectives.' They note that intractable and stubborn problems of Weberian bureaucracy, such as excessive rules and regulations, overlapping structures and procedures, inefficient procedures, lack of coordination, excessive partisan politics and corruption, continue. They examine how the leadership can play a pivotal and key role in addressing these problems. Specifically, they argue that reforms should be multidimensional, going beyond reorganization and shifting organizational boxes, and encompassing changes in behaviour, perspectives and attitudes. Using the concept of 'phronetic leadership', they examined three cases of a national, local and civil society leader, as well as a survey of university leaders. They conclude that leaders can make a difference by developing capacities of themselves and others and pushing the boundaries of continuous improvement. However, to be sustainable, public sector reforms have to be complemented by reforms of institutions, structures and procedures, and anchored in behaviour, values and a common vision that are communicated well and owned by all.

In the chapter on *Singapore*, David Seth Jones discusses reforms to increase customer-centredness, public consultation (including professional, business and community associations), whole-of-government approaches (and a case of trafficking in persons), increased budget, personnel and procurement delegation to departments and increased role of statutory boards (autonomous agencies). He writes that the driving force behind public sector reforms emanates from the inner core of ministers, and most particularly the prime minister and deputy prime minister, working in close conjunction with senior permanent secretaries, directors of boards and Government Linked Companies (GLCs). In Singapore, power is concentrated in the hands of political executives and senior levels of civil service; ministers set the policy agenda and make final policy decisions on important issues. The administrative service is the elite service (of about 250 persons) within the civil service that shapes policy, especially permanent secretaries and deputy secretaries. Objections to reforms are anticipated through inputs to the reform process from key stakeholders and experts in the relevant field from inter-ministerial and inter-agency committees and through public consultations. Singapore has achieved an exceptional level of prosperity, and Jones writes that civil service is guided by practices of meritocracy (e.g., in promotion) and strict accountability through audits and anti-corruption efforts.

Malaysia has experienced a successful economy at different stages since independence, writes Loo-See Beh. The development of the administration and institution-building phase was followed by reform initiatives, and the 22-year long political leadership under Tun Mahathir Mohamed included accelerating ethnic Malays' participation. Master industrial plans, 5-year development plans and other mid-term plans are used, which included governance and performance management reforms. Today, public service reforms continue to evolve with emphasis on better counter services, 3-government, one-stop clearance centres. Under the Government Transformation Programme launched in 2010, seven national key results areas have been identified (e.g., reducing crime, fighting corruption, improving education and raising living standards of low-income households. Within this framework, the political transformation programme, digital transformation programme, community transformation programme and social transformation programme have been created to advance public sector reforms. Beh writes that while states and leaders remain powerful actors, as public confidence declines in their ability, leaders recognize the need to reform and overcome unethical and inefficient bureaucratic dysfunctions or keep them at a minimum. Leaders manage such problems by using transparency to address problems of vested interests, stringent audits and punishing civil servants for criminal breaches of trust, removal of ministerial control over government-linked companies and removing resisting actors. Yet, allegations of massive corruption persist at the highest level of government, and race relations have regressed. Beh calls for increased value-based leadership that is inclusive at the highest levels.

Australia was one of the Anglophone countries that readily adapted to a public management approach, writes John Halligan. Reforms since the 1980s show remarkable breadth, longevity and significance. The reforms acknowledge the failure of the existing approaches and the need to address management deficiencies, fiscal stress and increased complexity. Halligan discusses four cases, reflecting on leadership from core agencies and executives in other departments. Financial management was pursued by the treasury, which later became a broader managing for results overseen by a senior management committee in the Department of Prime Minister and Cabinet (DPMC) that conducted specialized inquiries. However, devolution of responsibilities from central agencies did not appear to make managers more accountable. Halligan analyses that the treasury failed to exercise appropriate leadership and that agencies did not integrate management reforms with internal planning processes. By contrast, a one-stop shopping service for welfare was successful, although it later folded in with the Department of Human Services. The DPMC also launched reform process in the 2010s. Although not a priority of the prime minister, some recommendations were implemented that increased public service capacity, such as leadership development and talent management. The Australian case shows that in spite of variable political support and leadership by central agencies, a relatively stable environment (governments serving multiple terms) allowed implementation to proceed in the mid-term, including incentives, to ensure responsiveness at department levels.

New Zealand is a small country with a rich history of pioneering administrative reforms. Caroline Rennie and Evan M. Berman describe administrative reform processes emanating from the 'core agencies' of the SSC, treasury and the Department of the Prime Minister and Cabinet. They describe the new public management reforms of the late 1980s–2000s led by the treasury that restructured ministries (creating more agencies that are single purpose), rewrote policy rules (e.g., the same laws for public and private sector employees) and created accountability from agency heads to ministers as well as SSCs who evaluate and reappoint agency heads. It should be noted that in this Westminster system, ministers provide policy leadership but not executive leadership of the ministries. They describe in detail two reform processes led or administered by SSC since the mid-2000s to increase accountability for the mid-term policy of the ministry and organizational capability targets (PIF) as well as well cross-ministry goals (better public services). These efforts have been evaluated as being quite effective and are noted for their sustainability and improvement over time.

REFERENCES

Berman, E. M. (2015). HRM in development: Lessons and frontiers. *Public Administration and Development*, 35(2), 113–127.

Brinkerhoff, D. W., & Brinkerhoff, J. M. (2015). Public sector management reform in developing countries: Perspectives beyond NPM orthodoxy. *Public Administration and Development*, 35(4), 222–237.

Choi, H. (2010). E-government in South Korea. In E. Berman, M. J. Moon, & H.-S. Choi. (Eds.), *Public administration in east Asia* (pp. 473–493). Oxfordshire: Taylor & Francis.

de Vries, H., Bekkers, V., & Tummers, L. (2016). Innovation in the public sector: A systematic review and future research agenda. *Public Administration, 94*(1), 146–166.

Laegreid, P., & Christensen, T. (Eds.). (2013). *Transcending new public management: The transformation of public sector reforms*. Farnham: Ashgate.

Phua, K. L., Ling, S. W. H., & Phua, K. H. (2014). Public–private partnerships in health in Malaysia: Lessons for policy implementation. *International Journal of Public Administration, 37*(8), 506–513.

Pollitt, C., & Bouckaert, G. (2011). *Public management reform: A comparative analysis – new public management, governance, and the neo-Weberian state*. Oxford: Oxford University Press.

Sobis, I., Berg, F. V. D., & Vries, M. S. D. (2012). The limits of leadership. *NISPAcee Journal of Public Administration and Policy, 5*(1), 131–154.

United Nations Economic and Social Council. (2006). *Compendium of basic terminology in governance and public administration*. Document E/C.16/2006/4. Retrieved from http://unpan1.un.org/intradoc/groups/public/documents/un/unpan022332.pdf. Accessed on July 31, 2017.

Wong. W. (2015). Public managers must also be leaders: The hollowing-out of leadership and public management reform in Hong Kong. In E. Berman & S. Haque (Eds.), *Asian leadership in policy and governance* (pp. 261–286). Bingley: Emerald.

Wu, X., Ramesh, M., & Yu, J. (2017). Autonomy and performance: Decentralization reforms in Zhejiang Province, China. *Public Administration and Development, 37*(2), 94–109.

CHAPTER 2

LEADERSHIP AND PUBLIC SECTOR REFORM IN JAPAN

Masahiro Horie

ABSTRACT

Japan has had four periods of public sector reform since World War II. This chapter discusses the leadership for reform during the occupation period, the high economic growth period, the low economic growth period and the search for a 'new' Japan under various present difficulties. Reforms reflect the priorities of the time and interests of prime ministers, whose style of functioning also affects how public sector reforms are advanced. During the occupation period, the Administrative Management Agency was established in the Prime Minister's Office and was responsible for the overall management of national government organizations. It was staffed by civil servants who were experts in their areas. Since the 1980s, furthering privatization, deregulation and reorganization, advisory councils for the prime minister were also used, involving influential business leaders and scholars.

This chapter shows that political leadership, especially that of the prime minister and minister in charge of administrative reform, is important in deciding on highly political issues, to persuade or direct politicians and administrators to follow the leadership, to inspire and get the support of the

Leadership and Public Sector Reform in Asia
Public Policy and Governance, 19–52
doi:10.1108/S2053-769720180000030002

general public and to ensure the support or acceptance of those concerned.
Where prime ministers are not directly involved, leadership is provided by
professional administrators under the general support of the prime minister
and the minister responsible for administrative reforms. It is also pointed
out that reform sustainability occurs through institutionalization, incen-
tives, management and producing meaningful results.

Keywords: Economic growth; political leadership; Japan

INTRODUCTION

Public sector reform has always been on the agenda of the government of
any political party in Japan, even though the priority and specific subjects
or issues are not same all the time. Priority and specific contents of administrative reform change because the specific necessity and importance of the
time is different according to the stage of development of the country, social,
economic and fiscal conditions of the time, changes of government parties,
changes in relations between central and local governments and in relations
between the government and the people, people's demands of the government
and for other reasons. Specific interests of political leaders, especially the
prime minister, of the time also influence the priority and specific contents
of administrative reform. While some prime ministers have regarded administrative reform as the top priority issue and exercised strong leadership with
enthusiasm to promote administrative reform, there have been prime ministers who were not much interested in it and did not show leadership in this
area. The personality or character of the prime minister and his style of getting things done also affected the apparatus and process of the administrative
reform and eventually the success or failure of administrative reform efforts.

In this chapter, based on the analysis of administrative reform efforts
after World War II (WW II) in Japan, but mainly in the last three or four
decades, trends or characteristics of administrative reform is briefly discussed in relation to the political, social and economic background and
the context for reform, and then reasons and objectives of reform, specific
target areas and contents of reform, organizations and systems to promote reform and political and administrative leadership for reform are discussed. In the latter part of the chapter, specific cases of reform is discussed
with special emphasis on the role of leadership in promoting administrative reform.

1. HISTORY AND POLITICAL, SOCIAL AND ECONOMIC BACKGROUND OF PUBLIC SECTOR REFORMS

For the analysis and discussion of administrative reforms in Japan, it is useful to see post-WW II Japan during different periods in relation to the political, social and economic background or context: the occupation period, high economic growth period, low economic growth period and period in search for new Japan under various difficulties.

Occupation Period

The occupation period occurred from 1945 to 1952 when the Peace Treaty took effect and Japan became independent in the real sense. It was a period for reconstruction of Japan from the ruins of WW II. Various temporary administrative organizations and public corporations were created to carry out urgent social and economic programmes such as rationing and distributing goods and materials indispensable for people's lives and economic and industrial activities.

This was also the period when Japan was rebuilt under the rule of the Occupation Force, the General Headquarters (GHQ) of Allied Forces. The old constitution of Imperial Japan was replaced with the new constitution of Japan, which is based on the principle of sovereign power of the people. Legal systems, governmental and administrative systems, administrative organization systems, civil service systems and other systems related to government and public administration were changed in accordance with the new constitution. Under the new constitution, which took effect in 1947, the prime minister is to be chosen by the members of the parliament from among the members of the parliament and more than half of ministers of state must be appointed from among the members of the parliament. As to ministries and agencies, instead of Imperial Edicts, the National Government Organization Act was enacted and specific establishment acts were enacted to establish specific ministries and agencies and to stipulate roles, authorities and responsibilities of specific ministries. The Administrative Management Agency was established in the Prime Minister's Office as a responsible organization for overall management of national government organizations.

The National Government Employees Act was enacted to introduce a new civil service system. Civil servants became the servants of the people, not the servants of the Emperor any more. To implement the new civil service system, the National Personnel Authority was established as a commission type organization similar to the Civil Service Commission of the US Federal Government.

During this period, several ministries were reorganized because of the changes in major missions from war time to peace time or divided or even abolished under a strong demand from the GHQ. For example, the Ministry of Interior, which was responsible for wide-range administration such as local government administration, police administration, construction and management of social infrastructures, was abolished by the order of GHQ and was divided into separate organizations. The system of appointing prefectural governors by the Ministry of Interior was also abolished and the new system of electing governors by local residents was adopted. Many big changes during this period were probably impossible without the force of the GHQ. The abolition of the mighty Ministry of Interior was an example of such cases. In fact, after the occupation period was over, the Ministry of Home Affairs (new name for the old Ministry of Interior) was established in 1960 by integrating several organizations (excluding police administration and infrastructure construction and management) and by upgrading the status to ministry.

High Economic Growth Period

The average economic growth rate of Japan from 1956 to 1973 was 9.1%. Owing to this high economic growth rate, the period from the middle of 1950s to the early 1970s is regarded as the high economic growth period in Japan.

During the high economic growth period, many new policies were introduced to promote economic development and to provide social and other conditions conducive to economic and social development necessary for overall development. To implement these policies and programmes, many public corporations were created in almost all substantive policy areas, such as various public financial institutions, social infrastructure construction public corporations, industrial promotion public corporations, social welfare services public corporations and education, and science and research promotion public corporations. A number of government employees in ministries and agencies increased considerably for the implementation of new policies and for the expansion of existing policies and programmes. Although the Provisional Commission for Administrative Reform was created in 1961 (for two-year term, and later extended for one more year), taking the model of the Hoover Commission in the United States, to discuss the necessary administrative reform, it could not stop this trend of expansion of the government.

One of the reasons for the unsuccessful results of the Commission was that it made recommendations for only one time at the end of the extended term of office, that is, when the prime minister who created it and appointed its members was about to retire because of serious illness. Strong political leadership could not be expected to promote the implementation of recommendations of the commission, even if the contents of the recommendations were good.

The government (to be more specific, the Administrative Management Agency of the prime minister's office) felt the necessity to prevent the further increase of public corporations and the expansion of government organizations. Existing public corporations were reviewed and requests for new corporations began to be severely examined by the Administrative Management Agency. The Administrative Management Agency began to strictly apply the so-called 'scrap and build' principle while examining the request for a new organization or new public corporation. Any ministry was required to abolish ('scrap') existing organization(s) when it requested to establish ('build') an organization such as a bureau or department. In 1969, the Ceiling Number Control Act was enacted for the manpower of ministries and agencies. The Administrative Management Agency began to enforce a planned reduction in force involving all the ministries and agencies of the national government.

Low Economic Growth Period

The high economic growth period was over in the early 1970s, with 5.1% growth rate in 1973 and –0.5% in 1974. Economic and fiscal conditions got worse due to many events and factors, including the so-called 'Nixon Shock in 1971' (change in the exchange rate system of Japanese yen from fixed to floating system), 'oil shock (in 1973 and 1979)' resulting from repeated Middle East wars and world-wide economic recession. In spite of the difficult fiscal conditions, Japan was expected to play the role of a locomotive to stimulate world economy, but this worsened the fiscal condition of the Japanese government. The government issued deficit financing bonds for the FY 1975 supplementary budget for the first time since its first case in FY 1965, and continued to depend on it in making the annual budget. The dependence rate on bond issue of the FY 1979 general account budget of the national government soared up to 34.7%.

Reduction in force had been continuously carried out. The necessity of large scale expenditure cut and other reform efforts began to be discussed. The Administrative Management Agency organized a study group within the agency to consider the necessary reform from the viewpoints different from

conventional or ordinary administrative reform, not only from the management aspect of government organizations and operations but also for the
necessity of substantive policies. From around the end of 1970s, the introduction of a new tax, the 'general consumption tax', began to be discussed in
the government. To get the understanding and support for the introduction
of the new tax, it was also necessary to make utmost efforts for expenditure
cut or cut of 'wasteful' policies and programmes.

To address wide-ranging reform issues and subjects, the Provisional
Commission for Administrative Reform was established in 1981 as a high profile advisory council for the prime minister with an office term of two years.
This Commission began to be called 'the Second Provisional Commission
for Administrative Reform' or 'the Second Provisional Commission', since,
as mentioned above, there was a commission with the same name established
20 years ago. This Second Provisional Commission was also called 'Doko
Commission' by the name of its chairman. As will be discussed more in detail
later in this chapter, this Second Provisional Commission dealt with all possible
subjects and targets to be discussed under the name of 'administrative reform' –
not only reform of administrative systems, organizations and operations,
including privatization of big public corporations (such as National Railways)
but also reform of substantive policies with sizable expenditure or subsidies.
Government ministries, organizations, manpower of government and civil service system, budgeting system, deregulation and regulatory reform, decentralization and/or intergovernmental relations and reform of relations between the
government and the people were among those subjects and targets discussed
by this Commission. Recommendations were made in series (five times in two
years), and the commission supervised their implementation by the government. It is quite different from the first provisional commission established
20 years ago. As will be discussed more in detail later in this chapter, the administrative reform by this commission was regarded successful. Prime Minister
Nakasone, minister of state and the director-general of Administrative
Management Agency, exercised strong leadership to establish this commission
and to continuously promote administrative reform.

Period in Search for New Japan under Various Difficulties

The period from the 1980s and 1990s to the present, after the Second Provisional
Commission for Administrative Reform completed its task, successive administrative reform promotion advisory councils for the prime minister were created
to oversee the implementation of reform recommended by the commission and

also to make new recommendations on the subjects which were not fully discussed or which needed further discussion and recommendations to promote reform. Among these subjects were the deregulation and regulatory reform, introduction of administrative procedure law and government information disclosure law (or freedom of information act), decentralization and/or reform of intergovernmental relations and others. In addition to efficiency and economy of government activities, fairness, responsiveness, transparency, integrity and trustworthiness of government were regarded highly and became the centre of discussion for administrative reform.

During this period, two prime ministers played a major role in promoting big-scale administrative reform, challenging the subjects which had been regarded 'taboo' or 'untouchable'. In 1996, Prime Minister Hashimoto established Administrative Reform Council, the advisory council for the prime minister, to discuss the reorganization of the national government as a whole. As will be discussed more in detail later in this chapter, the reshuffle of the national government on the biggest scale in peace time Japan was carried out in January 2001. Prime Minister Koizumi, who came into office in 2001, launched the privatization of postal services. This case will also be discussed more in detail later in this chapter. The privatization was carried out by overcoming various barriers and difficulties. Both Hashimoto and Koizumi were in office for quite a long period, and carried out difficult issues with strong will and leadership. Prime ministers who held office after Koizumi could not survive long enough, just for less than a year to one and half years, to exercise strong leadership.

Current Prime Minister Abe is in office for more than five years, one of the longest surviving prime ministers in the last three decades, and is likely to become the longest one very soon. He must be considering Japan's future from a long-term perspective. However, it is yet to be seen as to what he is going to do in the field of administrative reforms in pursuit of new Japan under the present difficulties.

2. REASONS AND OBJECTIVES OF ADMINISTRATIVE REFORM

From the preceding part, it is clear that there are various reasons and objectives of administrative reform. It is also clear that specific reasons and objectives and the priority among them are different depending on the specific necessity of the reform of the time. Therefore, it must be meaningful to list up the major reasons or objectives of administrative reform with reference to Japan. These are as follows:

1. To examine systems, policies, organizations and operations of public administration to ensure that
   o Changes are in accordance with constitutional and/or governmental changes (this is what happened in Japan soon after WW II and the change of government occurred in 1993, 1994, 2009 and 2012 and may occur any time in the future).
   o Streamlined, efficient and effective government organizations and operations (this is always mentioned in any reform effort, even if it may not be the first in the list).
   o Comprehensive (well integrated) and consistent government policies and operations (this is emphasized in Japan, where every ministry strongly pursues its own policy and course of action, even when coordination with other organizations is necessary).
   o Government adapted (or adaptable) to change and innovative government (this is pointed out as an increasingly important objective in the time of rapid and big changes).
   o Fairness, transparency and trustworthiness of the government (this is regarded as one of the most important objectives in recent administrative reform).
2. To rationalize and reduce government expenditures as follows.
   o Expenditure cut, downsizing, etc. (this is similar to streamlining to increase efficiency but different as reducing expenditures and downsizing is required).

These aspects of government and public administration can also be approached from various viewpoints. Aspects and viewpoints of administrative reform and target areas and direction of the contents of reform observed in the actual administrative reform in the last three or four decades are as follows:

• Government roles, responsibilities and functions
   o Key question to be asked here is: 'What are the appropriate roles of government?'
• Tools, process, procedure and others to play and implement government roles, responsibilities and functions
   o Key question to be asked here is: 'How and by what means does the government exercise its responsibilities?'

- Government organizations and other bodies and public servants and other people working for public administration and related functions
  - Key questions to be asked here are: 'What is an appropriate apparatus to implement public administration?'; 'What kind of people should government organizations be composed of?'; 'What is the appropriate size of workforce?'; 'How are these organizations and people to be managed?', etc.

From the viewpoints mentioned above, systems, policies, government organizations, public corporations and other government-affiliated organizations, civil service system and personnel management, regulatory system and regulations, administrative procedure and relationship between the government and people (and private enterprises) have been reviewed and examined repeatedly and many administrative reform programmes have been made and implemented as follows. As shown below, subjects or the focus of administrative reform have changed over time, while there are several areas which continue to be the target of administrative reform. Important examples are as follows:

A. Reform of Public Policies, Programmes and Projects

  - Specific policies (including substantive policies with sizable government expenditures or subsidies such as foodstuff management policy, health care policies, social infrastructure construction and management policies), programmes and projects have been reformed and streamlined.

B. Reform of Central Government Organizations

  - Organizational adjustment of the central government to changes had been done mainly by a piecemeal approach until government-wide reshuffle of ministries and agencies was implemented in 2001.
  - In this reshuffle, ministries and agencies were abolished or merged with others.
  - Many organizations in ministries were separated from ministries and transformed into independent incorporated organizations, which may be called Japanese type of 'executive agencies'.
  - The number of bureaus and divisions in bureaus in the central government ministries and agencies was reduced.
  - Postal Services Enterprise as a government ministry was transformed into a public corporation in 2003 and then privatized.

C. Reform of Public Corporations

o Public corporations have been privatized or abolished or streamlined.
o Government supervision and the management systems of remaining corporations have been changed to increase the managerial flexibility and responsibility of corporations.
o The biggest public corporations, National Railways and Telephone and Telegraph, were privatized in the 1980s.

D. Manpower Control and Reform of Civil Service System and Management

o Manpower of government ministries and agencies has been strictly controlled by the so-called 'Ceiling Number Control Act', which was enacted almost 50 years ago, and by carrying out a series of planned reduction in force for the same period.
o The National Government Employees Ethics Act was enacted at the end of the 1990s to ensure the ethics and integrity of government employees.
o The recruitment system of civil service was reformed. A new competency and performance evaluation system has been introduced.

E. Deregulation and Regulatory Reform

o A series of government-wide deregulation and regulatory reform programmes have been made and carried out continuously over several decades.

F. Reform to Increase Fairness and Transparency of Government

o The Administrative Procedure Act and the Government Information Disclosure Act (Japanese name for the Freedom of Information Act) were enacted in the 1990s. Legislations to protect information on individual persons stored in the government were also enacted.

G. E-Government

o E-government has been promoted government-wide.

H. Decentralization, Intergovernmental Reform and Reform of Local Government

o Decentralization and reform of intergovernmental relations has been promoted for several decades.
o Reform at the local government level, including merging of municipalities, has also been implemented.

3. ORGANIZATIONS TO PROMOTE ADMINISTRATIVE REFORM IN JAPAN

There are two kinds of administrative organizations which have played central roles to promote administrative or public sector reform in Japan. One is an administrative organization, such as the Administrative Management Agency mentioned above, comprising full-time professionals, permanent civil servants and other employees, and the other is an advisory organ, usually a provisional or ad hoc council comprising well-informed influential members such as scholars, business leaders, trade union leaders, media people appointed from outside the government to advise and make recommendations to the government. The advisory council may be organized to address wide-ranging subjects and areas of administrative reform or organized for specifically limited target areas such as deregulation, decentralization and civil service reform.

Permanent Administrative Organization for Administrative Reform

Compared with other countries, Japan has a long history of a high level administrative office solely responsible for administrative management and reform. By the end of October 1946, during the transitional period from the old Imperial Japan constitution to the new constitution of Japan, which was promulgated in November 1946, the Administrative Research Office was established in the cabinet to survey, research and plan reforms of administrative organizations and the civil service system and the operation of government in accordance with the new systems and principles of the new constitution. After the new constitution took effect in May 1947, the roles and responsibility, except for the civil service system, of the Administrative Research Office of the cabinet were succeeded by the newly created Administrative Management Agency in July 1948. The Administrative Management Agency was established and headed by the minister of state as was the case with the Administrative Research Office of the cabinet.

The roles and responsibilities of the Administrative Management Agency were expanded to cover various government-wide management functions. In relation to administrative reform, the following responsibilities are important.

- Planning administrative systems in general to be applied government-wide.
- Planning and coordinating matters concerning the structure of administrative organs, number of civil servants and operation of administrative organizations.

- Examining requests of creation, change or abolition of administrative organizations.
- Examining requests of increase or decrease of number of civil servants.
- Examining requests of creation, change or abolition of public corporations.
- Conducting administrative inspection and making recommendations on operations and activities of administrative organizations and evaluating public policies and programmes.

All of these functions and responsibilities are conducive to reform or improve good government and administration. For this reason, the Administrative Management Agency became the central organ to promote government-wide administrative reform and improvement activities. Officials of the Administrative Management Agency have been recruited by the agency through a merit-based competitive examination and trained to be professionals on these matters. They work in this agency as civil servants for most of their public life. They become experts in the areas they are in charge of and accumulate experience. They become familiar with organizations, policies and programmes and with how these are made and implemented. They conduct research, surveys, site visits and discussions with experts and others concerned, and analyse and detect problems and matters to be reformed or improved and make necessary recommendations. They are not bound by interests of specific ministries and specific policy areas. They enter the Administrative Management Agency with strong passion to work for general public interest and social justice and keep this passion as long as they work in the government. They are really reform-minded.

Because of these responsibilities and functions and officials with reform-minded expertise and experiences, the Administrative Management Agency has promoted various kinds of government-wide administrative reforms on its own initiatives, including streamlining government organizations, reducing the number of government employees, rationalizing public corporations, deregulation and simplification of regulatory systems, rationalization of subsidies and other expenditure programmes. The Administrative Management Agency has dealt with most of administrative subjects and issues. But on drastic reform matters (such as government-wide reshuffling of ministerial level organizations) or matters of highly political nature (such as privatization of the National Railways and the Postal Services), which cannot be solved or agreed upon through negotiation among the officials concerned, what the Administrative Management Agency could achieve was limited or those matters were not dealt with to the fullest extent. To promote these drastic reforms or reforms of a highly political nature, strong political leadership and influential organizational apparatus is necessary. The Provisional Commission for Administrative Reform under the strong leadership of a minister is an example of this kind, which is discussed in the next section.

Advisory Council for Administrative Reform

Advisory bodies for administrative reform have been established repeatedly in Japan.

As mentioned above, there are two kinds of advisory councils for administrative reform from the viewpoint of width of coverage or term of reference; one is an overarching advisory council with a wide-ranging term of reference, and the other is an advisory council with a limited term of reference. The Provisional Commissions for Administrative Reform, mentioned earlier in this chapter as the first Provisional Commission and the second Provisional Commission, are examples with wide-ranging administrative reform responsibilities. The Decentralization Promotion Committee and the Deregulation and Regulatory Reform Council are examples with limited term of references.

Each kind of advisory council has merits and demerits as follows.

An advisory council with overarching responsibilities deals with wideranging reform subjects under one big umbrella and therefore it is easier to ensure the consistency of discussion, direction and contents of reform of different reform subjects. However, members of this overarching advisory council, usually less than 10 in number in Japan, are not familiar with all the areas and the subjects to be dealt with. Even though they are supported by professional executive staff such as those seconded from the Administrative Management Agency, it is not enough for a small number of members to deal with all the areas and subjects. Therefore, sub-committees for specific limited reform subjects, such as reform of government organization, reform of public corporation and reform of regulatory system and deregulation, are usually organized under the council. These sub-committees comprise expert members such as university professors and others appointed from outside the government. A member of the council may join sub-committees. They are also supported by professional executive staff. Sub-committees make interim reports to the council and get the opinions, direction and guidance from the council. Since the subject matter discussed by different sub-committees are often interrelated, possible differences should be and can be avoided before final reports and recommendations are made by the overarching advisory council. Another strong point or advantage of a big scale overarching advisory council is that it can easily attract the attention of the general public because the council looks like making epoch-making big reform efforts and also because mass media frequently report the activities of the advisory council as there are many subjects to deal with. It is important to get the support of the general public to promote big scale or drastic reforms.

On the other hand, an advisory council with a limited term of reference comprises members who are familiar with subjects to be dealt with. It may be less time-consuming than the case of an overarching council with sub-committees. However, when there are several advisory councils, independent of each other and dealing with interrelated subjects, there is a possibility of confusion, contradiction and inconsistency in their reports and recommendations. Efforts are made informally by the executive staff of councils, and if necessary by core members of councils, to avoid contradiction and inconsistencies. If the differences among different advisory councils cannot be solved, the recommendations may not be implemented or it is likely to take much time to arrive at a conclusion in the form of government policy. As to the interest or attention of the general public, it is usually less in activities of advisory councils with a limited term of reference than in activities with wide-ranging, big scale advisory council for administrative reforms. It is often the case that mass media deal with the activities of advisory councils with limited terms of reference only sporadically. Attention of the general public is likely to be dispersed and not continuous.

4. IMPORTANCE OF LEADERSHIP TO PROMOTE ADMINISTRATIVE REFORM: CASES

Even if the organizational apparatus is well established to promote administrative reform, and even if there are well-trained and experienced professionals to promote administrative reform, there are kinds of reforms for which these conditions are not enough to make those efforts successful. To promote reforms such as drastic change, big scale reforms and reforms of a highly political nature, strong leadership, strategic planning and management of administrative reform efforts and support of the general public are indispensable.

Political leadership, especially that of the prime minister and minister in charge of administrative reform, is important to decide on highly political issues, to persuade or direct politicians as well as administrators to follow the leadership, to inspire and get the support of general public and to ensure the support or acceptance of those concerned. High ranking officials to be engaged in administrative reform need to have good relations with political leaders and are to be trusted by them. Administrative leadership is necessary to organize and manage well-structured professional organizations to promote administrative reform efforts and activities. Administrative leadership is also necessary to make effective strategic plans to manage and promote administrative reform activities. High ranking officials to lead administrative reform activities also need to be able to negotiate well with the highest level officials of the target organizations.

In the following section, specific cases of administrative reform and leadership will be discussed.

Case 1: Administrative Reform by Prime Minister Nakasone and the Provisional Commission for Administrative Reform

Nakasone (Yasuhiro Nakasone) became the minister of state and the director-general of the Administrative Management Agency in 1980, and the Provisional Commission for Administrative Reform, overarching advisory council, was established in 1981 for a period of two years. Nakasone became prime minister in November 1982 and continued to promote administrative reform up to November 1987. This section deals with administrative reform by Nakasone and his leadership.

Nakasone was born in 1918 and entered the Ministry of Interior in 1941 after graduating from the University of Tokyo. But his career in the ministry was very short because of the war. He entered politics and became a member of the House of Representatives in 1947. It is said that since he became a member of the parliament, he longed for the day to become the prime minister and continued to write in his notebook what he wanted to do as the future prime minister. It is said that some 20 or 30 or even more notebooks were piled up before he actually became the prime minister. He worked with various ministries before he was appointed as a minister of state and the director-general of the Administrative Management Agency. He was not satisfied with this appointment as he was pursuing to be prime minister and this position was too light for the would-be prime minister in the near future.

In the Administrative Management Agency, the administrative vice minister, top-most bureaucrat and other executives considered what to propose to the new director-general, especially if the new director-general is a big influential political leader. Soon after Nakasone was appointed, the administrative vice minister proposed Nakasone to establish the new epoch making

Provisional Commission for Administrative Reform and launch a big scale, drastic administrative reforms. It would be a big project worthwhile for the would-be prime minister. Nakasone adopted the proposal.

The new commission was to be established as an authoritative statutory advisory body, and the appointment of its members were to be agreed upon by the parliament. With the consent of Prime Minister Suzuki and the support of executive officials of the Administrative Management Agency, Nakasone chose nine members of the commission. Toshio Doko, former president of the Federation of Economic Organizations, the most influential economic organization in Japan, was requested to become the chairman, and eight persons with different backgrounds were chosen; two from the economic sector, one from mass media, two from trade unions, two ex-government officials (one of the Ministry of Finance and the other of Ministry of Interior) and one from academia (professor of public administration at the University of Tokyo). Since the Provisional Commission was an overarching advisory reform commission to deal with almost all possible areas and subjects of administrative reform, including substantive policy matters, sub-committees were to be created and many expert members were appointed to work as members of sub-committees. A large independent executive office was organized comprising more than 100 research staff and other employees to support the activities of the Advisory Commission and its sub-committees by arranging hearings and meetings, making detailed analyses of reform issues, preparing possible reform measures and alternatives etc. Half of the staff was from the Administrative Management Agency and the rest was from other ministries and agencies, and some from local governments and from private organizations. Almost all ministries and agencies sent their officials as staff of the executive office.

Mr. Doko submitted the following five conditions in accepting the request to become the chairman: (1) to carry out fiscal reconstruction without raising tax, (2) to carry out drastic reform of food management programme, National Railways and Health Insurance Programme to resolve huge deficit in these areas, (3) to carry out reform of public corporations, (4) to carry out reform of the local administration and (5) to implement recommendations of the Provisional Commission exactly as recommended. Minister Nakasone accepted these conditions. Being in his eighties, Doko decided to take this job as the last job of his life to serve the country and the people of Japan. He resigned all other jobs, substantive or honorary jobs of more than hundred, to devote whole of his time and energy to the new task. He had been a respected, charismatic leader of economic community and a person of integrity. When his humble life was televised, people were surprised and the passionate support of the people to his commission's efforts for administrative reform increased dramatically.

The Provisional Commission organized two special sub-committees in March 1981 and submitted urgent recommendations in July 1981 to cut subsidies and other expenditures of substantive policies and also to streamline administrative organizations and carry out medium-term reduction in force. These recommendations were immediately put into implementation by submitting necessary legislations to the newly created parliamentary special committees for administrative reform and making budget according to the recommendations. After this first recommendation, four sub-committees and some small research groups were organized to consider reform of substantive policies, reform of government organizations, reform of regulations and regulatory systems, decentralization and reform of intergovernmental relations and local governments, reform of public corporations and other government-affiliated organizations, reform of budgeting system and others. The Provisional Commission held frequent meetings and hearings, providing those concerned with pros and cons. After the meetings, briefings were provided to press corps. Since the administrative reform was a top priority of the government, what was discussed by the commission became big news.

Based on detailed analysis and intensive discussion of reform issues and reform measures, the Provisional Commission submitted four more big recommendations by the end of its term (March 1983), in which the privatization of three gigantic public corporations (National Railways, Telephone and Telegraph, Tobacco and Salt Monopoly) and reform of other public corporations were included. While the Provisional Commission was working to produce final reports and recommendations, Nakasone became prime minister in November 1982 after Prime Minister Suzuki suddenly stepped down.

Privatization of the National Railways was the biggest and the most difficult reform issue. Both trade unions and management (beginning with the president and vice president) were against the privatization. They moved politically, visiting politicians who might support or help them by opposing or resisting reforms. However, there were also 'reformists' in the National Railways. They had close relations with responsible officials of the executive office and members of the Provisional Commission. They supported the reform from behind the scene. Ruling party members of parliament were divided into pros and cons. Nakasone exercised leadership to overcome difficulties. He could get the support of influential faction leaders and obtained the majority support. To show his strong will and determination, he fired the president of National Railways who was resisting drastic reforms, and replaced him with the former administrative vice minister of the Ministry of Transport whom Nakasone knew and could trust since when he was the Minister of Transport.

In 1987, the National Railways was privatized and divided into six regional passenger railway companies (such as East Japan Railway Company), the Shinkansen (bullet train system), one country-wide freight railway company, the National Railway Settlement Corporation to deal with long-term debt and other matters, including the measures for re-employment of redundant personnel by private companies and governments. 'Reformists' of the former National Railways were appointed as chief executives of the new railway companies. New companies, because of separation of huge long-term debt and redundant personnel, gave enough competition to private railways. As a result of reform, no increase in charges or fare was necessary for several years after privatization. Mind-sets, attitudes and behaviours of employees of new companies changed drastically. New companies were ranked high in customer satisfaction surveys. All stocks of three profitable regional passenger railway companies held by the government were sold out in the stock market and were completely privatized.

Nakasone was the minister of state and the director general of the Administrative Management Agency from 1980 to 1982 and the Prime Minister from November 1982 to November 1987, or for 1806 days, one of the longest tenure after WW II. During this period, administrative reform was the most important task for him. Recommendations of the Provisional Commission and its succeeding advisory councils were carried out under him. These recommendations were the reforms which he committed to himself as the minister of state for administrative reform and as the Prime Minister. He could establish a mutual trust relationship with leading members of advisory bodies and officials of executive office for advisory bodies. Hearing reports and having discussions with trusted core members and officials, he left most of the matters to organizations working under those trusted members and officials. He did not say much on details of the matters but exercised strong leadership when necessary. He was a political leader of orthodox style.

Case 2: Administrative Reform by Prime Minister Hashimoto and Administrative Reform Council

Hashimoto (Ryutaro Hashimoto) became the Prime Minister in January 1996 and stayed in the office until July 1998. The Administrative Reform Council was established in November 1996 to discuss and recommend overall reshuffling of the central government and related reforms. It has been an untouchable issue which no prime minister dared to challenge in peacetime Japan. This section deals with Hashimoto's administrative reform and his leadership.

Hashimoto was born in 1937. After graduating from Keio University, a prestigious private university, he began to work for a private company. After the sudden death of his father in 1962, he was pulled in politics and ran the election successfully for the House of Representatives in 1963. His father was a member of the parliament and also one time minister of state and the director-general of the Administrative Management Agency (1951–1952). Hashimoto was continuously elected successfully, and appointed as a young Minister of Health and Welfare in 1978. When the Provisional Commission for Administrative Reform was established in 1981, he was the chairman of the Administrative and Fiscal Affairs Research Committee of the Liberal Democratic Party, which was in charge of administrative reforms. It means that he was in charge of making and coordinating party policies on administrative and fiscal reform of the government. He was in a position to examine as well as support and promote administrative reform efforts of the government. He supported Nakasone as the chairman of the party's committee, and was appointed- the Minister of Transport when the legislative bills to privatize the National Railways were deliberated in the parliament. He held many ministerial positions, including the Minister of Finance and the Minister of Trade and Industry. As Prime Minister Murayama suddenly stepped down by his own decision in January 1996, Hashimoto succeeded him as the new Prime Minister.

Although Hashimoto held various ministerial positions, he had always shown interest in administrative management and reforms, including management of administrative organizations and public corporations and management of manpower of civil service workforce.

In the first policy speech in January 1996 at the beginning of the regular session of the Diet, Prime Minister Hashimoto emphasized the reconstruction of a resilient Japanese economy, construction of longevity society where people can feel the goodness of longevity, self-reliant diplomacy for peace, prosperity and innovative creation, and administrative and fiscal reform to realize these objectives. In the policy speech made in November 1996, he listed five policy areas as his top priority on the agenda of the Hashimoto Administration: administrative reform, economic structure reform, financial system reform, social security reform, and fiscal structure reform. In the policy speech made in January 1997, he added education reform as the sixth reform area.

As to administrative reform, he made a surprising announcement of his idea of a drastic reshuffle in the central government and reduction in the number of ministries and agencies headed by ministers by halving the number of ministerial organizations. The announcement was made at the press conference in September 1996 before the dissolution and election of the House of Representatives. He could appeal to the general public and his party, Liberal Democratic Party, to win a big victory in the election. People's support rate was as high as around 60%. He began to work on reshuffling and related reforms of the central government.

The Administrative Reform Council was created in November 1996 by a cabinet ordinance to discuss and make recommendations on reshuffling of central government organizations and related reforms. Different from the case of the Provisional Commission for Administrative Reform, which was established by law, this new council was created by cabinet ordinance. It was faster to create and it was not necessary to have the consent of the parliament on the appointment of members of the council. It comprised 15 members, including university professors, mass media people, trade union leader and three chairmen of other advisory councils (Administrative Reform Committee, Economic Council and Decentralization Promotion Committee) with a term of reference related to administrative reforms. Interestingly enough, Prime Minister Hashimoto became the chairman of the council in spite of the fact that the new council was an advisory council to the prime minister. The minister of state for administrative reform, who was also the director-general of the Management and Coordination Agency (which was formerly the Administrative Management Agency), became the vice-chairman of the council. The independent executive office was organized as is often the case with this kind of advisory council for administrative reform. Many officials were seconded from the Management and Coordination Agency and other organizations. A retired politician, and former minister of state and the director-general of the Management and Coordination Agency and chairman of the Administrative and Fiscal Affairs Committee of the Liberal Democratic Party, became a council member as well as the chief of the executive office. This is different from the preceding cases of advisory bodies for administrative reform. This way was adopted as the new Council must deal with the drastic issues of high political nature with the needed support through a veteran politician close to the prime minister.

Prime Minister Hashimoto attended every meeting of the council and led the discussions. Those concerned with drastic reorganizations were invited to express their opinions, pros and cons, and respond to questions. After the meetings of the council, briefings were made to the press corps. What was discussed by the council became big news, which attracted the attention of the general public. Compared with preceding advisory bodies of administrative reform, political leaders played a bigger role from the beginning. Government-wide reshuffling of central government ministries was rarely carried out in peacetime Japan. It was a big challenge against the taboo or untouchable issue. Hashimoto, who was proud of being most familiar with administrative organizations and behaviour of bureaucrats, wanted to challenge this taboo.

After intensive discussion, based on detailed analysis of merits and demerits of several reorganization alternatives, the Administrative Reform Council made an interim report on September 3, 1997, with the plan of a new ministerial structure of the central government which was made open to the public. As predicted, the new plan caused controversies. Politicians, bureaucrats and others who were not happy about the new plan tried to resist or change the plan. Political leaders, such as the minister of state for administrative reform, responsible for promoting reform tried to persuade ranking members and others concerned. Three months later, a final report and recommendations were submitted, making changes including changes of the names of new ministries, to make final recommendations acceptable. The cabinet meeting was held to decide to pay respect to report and recommendations of the Administrative Reform Council to the fullest extent. Prime Minister Hashimoto wished to realize the new central government structure at the beginning of the 21st century. He ordered offices concerned to prepare necessary bills as fast as possible. In a few months, the Basic Bill for the Reform of Central Government Ministries was submitted to the parliament with names of new Ministries attached to the bill.

The Basic Bill for the Reform of Central Government Ministries was deliberated by the special committee on administrative reform, organized in both houses to intensively discuss on this bill. If this special committee was not organized and it was necessary to be debated by an existing standing committee, which had so many bills to deliberate, the reform bill should have waited for long. During the deliberation in the parliament, Prime Minister Hashimoto willingly responded to many questions personally. It is rare that the prime minister personally responds to so many questions, as the prime minister usually asks other ministers in charge of the affairs to respond. The bill was passed in both houses and became law in June 1997.

In the following month, the election for the House of Councillors was held, and the ruling party, Liberal Democratic Party, lost unexpectedly, allegedly because what Prime Minister said changed on certain tax issues. Even though the ruling party still had the safe majority in the House of Representatives, Prime Minister Hashimoto stepped down taking responsibility for the defeat in the election of the House of Councillors. Obuchi, the next prime minister, was also the leader of Liberal Democratic Party. The policy priority of the new government shifted to economic policies. However, fortunately, as the Basic Law for the Reform of Central Government Ministries was enacted and as people continued to support the reform, the reform progressed as stipulated by the law. The executive office responsible for implementing government-wide reshuffling was maintained and continued strenuous work to carry out the big reform. To implement the reform, huge and voluminous bills were submitted to amend existing laws and to introduce new systems and organizations in accordance with the Basic Law for Reform of Central Government Ministries. All these bills being acted upon and preparatory works, including the relocation of ministries and other offices, being completed, the new structure and system of the central government ministries started in January 2001 as expected by Prime Minister Hashimoto.

Major contents of the Reform of the Central Government Ministries are as follows.

Content of the reform of the central government ministries

- Reshuffling of central government ministries and agencies
  Reorganizing the prime minister's office and 22 ministries and agencies headed by ministers
  →Cabinet office and 10 ministries and 1 agency and 1 commission headed by ministers
  New structure from 2001
    Cabinet office (in addition to the main office)
      (Economic Planning Agency and Okinawa Development Agency were abolished and their functions were transferred to the main office of the cabinet office)
      National Safety Commission (as attached to the cabinet office)
      Financial Services Agency (as attached to the cabinet office)
    Ministry of Internal Affairs and Communications
      (Management and Coordination Agency, Ministry of Posts and Telecommunications and Ministry of Home Affairs were merged)
        Fair Trade Commission was attached to this Ministry in 2001 but later (in 2003) moved to the cabinet office as its attached organization
    Ministry of Justice
    Ministry of Foreign Affairs
    Ministry of Finance (Japanese name was changed)

Ministry of Education, Culture, Sports, Science and Technology
  (Ministry of Education and Science and Technology Agency were merged)
Ministry of Health, Labour and Welfare
  (Ministry of Health and Welfare and Ministry of Labour were merged)
Ministry of Agriculture, Forestry and Fisheries
Ministry of Economy, Trade and Industry (name of the ministry was changed with some new additional roles)
Ministry of Land, Infrastructure, Transport and Tourism
  (Ministry of Transport, Ministry of Construction, National Land Agency and Hokkaido Development Agency were merged)
Ministry of the Environment (changed from agency to ministry)
Defence Agency (later in 2007 changed to the Ministry of Defence)
• Strengthening the leadership of the cabinet and the prime minister
• Streamlining of public administration
• Introduction of independent incorporated corporation system (Japanese type of 'executive agency')
• Transformation of government organizations into independent incorporated corporations

The leadership style of Prime Minister Hashimoto was quite different from that of Nakasone and Koizumi. Hashimoto liked to study and discuss or debate on the subjects of his interest and concerns. He seriously and passionately discussed and debated even with officials. He did not like to be beaten in debate. The attitude and behaviour at the meeting of the Administrative Reform Council and his willingness to respond to questions in the parliament shows his personality and character. At the same time, it should be understood that it reflects his strong passion and sense of responsibility for what he was responsible. Without such strong sense of responsibility and leadership, the taboo or untouchable could not be challenged successfully.

Case 3: Administrative Reform by Prime Minister Koizumi
and His Leadership

Koizumi (Junichiro Koizumi) became prime minister in April 2001 after the reshuffling of the central government was implemented, and systems and organizations were introduced to strengthen the leadership of the prime minister. Utilizing these new systems and organizations, when it was necessary or effective, he realized what he wanted to do. He challenged the untouchable issue, the privatization of postal services. Overcoming difficulties, he got the necessary bills passed in the Diet in 2005.

Postal privatization was implemented. This section deals with administrative reforms, especially the privatization of postal services, by Prime Minister Koizumi and his leadership.

Koizumi was born in 1942 in a political family. Both his father and grandfather were members of the parliament and became ministers. After graduating from Keio University, he went to London to study but was called back in 1969 because of the sudden death of his father who was a member of the Parliament then. In 1969, he failed in his first challenge to the parliament. He became secretary to Takeo Fukuda, member of the parliament, before Fukuda became prime minister. In 1972 election, Koizumi successfully won seat in the House of Representatives. He was appointed as the Minister of Posts and Telecommunications and later as Minister of Health and Welfare. While he had not experienced other ministerial positions and was not a head of any faction in Liberal Democratic Party, he ran for the party president's election. Although he was defeated, he could still appeal his long-held idea of postal privatization. When Prime Minister Mori, leader of the faction to which Koizumi belonged, stepped down, Koizumi again ran for the party president's election. Since people were fed up with the conservative, old fashioned style of politics, Koizumi could attract the attention of the people by emphasizing 'change', saying, 'I will destroy the Liberal Democratic Party' and appealing to the freshness of his style during the election. He could win the election, defeating former Prime Minister Hashimoto, and eventually became prime minister in April 2001. Support rate at the beginning of his cabinet was as high as 90%. He was often called a 'lone wolf' and 'stranger' in politics as he did not want to make a group or faction and did not follow the customs and rules in politics. In choosing ministers of his cabinet, he did not consult any faction leader. He picked up three ministers from outside of politics, and five female ministers in 17 ministers of state. He picked up Keio University's economics professor Takenaka as the Minister for Economic and Fiscal Policy, who steered the Economic and Fiscal Policy Council to be chaired by the Prime Minister and comprised the Prime Minister, Chief Cabinet Secretary, Minister of Economic and Fiscal Policy and some other ministers and informed members appointed by the Prime Minister. The Finance Minister, the Minister of Internal Affairs and Communications and the Minister of Economy. Trade and Industry were appointed. The governor of the Bank of Japan, two economists and two influential business leaders were also included. This council became the central place for discussing, coordinating and deciding on almost all major policies of the government. Takenaka became the most trusted minister of the Koizumi government and stayed in the cabinet for 1980 days from the beginning to the end of Koizumi regime.

Since the time he was a young member of the parliament, especially when he was the parliamentary vice minister of finance, Koizumi had been interested in the reform of postal services. It was one of the few policy interests of Koizumi. Postal services are composed of three pillars: mail and parcel services, postal saving and postal insurance. He thought that mail and parcel services might be necessary as a universal service to the people wherever they live but postal savings and postal insurance are not necessary to be provided by the government or public enterprise since there are many private financial institutions and people can get their services from them. He also emphasized that the huge amount of money collected by postal savings and postal insurance was poured into fiscal investment and the loan programme of the government and used for unnecessary or wasteful public projects and other purposes. Still, when he became the minister of posts and telecommunications in 1992, he could not realize his dream. Quite naturally, officials of the ministry did not obediently or seriously listen to what he believed in and it was too big a political issue. Postmasters of post offices, especially those in local areas, had been solid supporters of Liberal Democratic Party and employees unions were against drastic reform or change. Members of parliament elected from local constituencies were supported by these people, called 'Postal Family'. However, Koizumi did not give up.

The year 2001 was the first year of the reshuffled central government ministries and the former Ministry of Posts and Telecommunications was merged into the new Ministry of Internal Affairs and Communications. According to the basic law for reform of central government ministries, organizations for postal services were first to be changed into postal services agency attached to the Ministry of Internal Affairs and Communications and then to be separated from the ministry to become an independent public corporation. As was stipulated by the basic law for the reform of central government ministries the legislative bill to transform the postal services agency to the Japan Post Corporation was submitted in 2002 and implemented in 2003.

Koizumi became the Prime Minister in the end of April 2001 and began his challenge against the taboo. Soon after he became the Prime Minister, he organized a Round Table of scholars and others in the cabinet secretariat in May 2001 in the form of the prime minister's decision, not in a statutory form such as law or cabinet ordinance, to consider how the postal services should be after they were changed into a public corporation, while the Ministry of Internal Affairs and Communications and the Postal Services Agency were still preparing the bill for transformation to a public corporation. He asked the

Round Table to consider postal services specifically including the issue of postal privatization. The Round Table submitted its report in September 2002. Then, after the Japan Post Corporation (public corporation) was established in 2003, official preparatory work for postal privatization became possible. The office to prepare for postal privatization was established in the cabinet secretariat in May 2004. Former administrative vice minister of the ministry of agriculture, forestry and fisheries, who was not obviously familiar with postal services, was appointed as the director of this new office. Koizumi did not trust senior executive officials of postal services. He also tried to prevent the influence of the ministry of internal affairs and communications in charge of postal services. Takenaka, minister for economic and fiscal policy, was appointed as the minister to be in charge of the preparation of postal privatization and to supervise the work of the cabinet secretariat office for postal privatization. As the minister for steering economic and fiscal policy council as well, whose chairman was prime minister, Takenaka used the economic and fiscal policy council as central place to discuss and decide on postal privatization. Even though the minister of internal affairs and communications was also a member of the council, he could not resist when Koizumi supported and took the side of Takenaka. Takenaka had begun his preparatory work with his close aids even before the cabinet secretariat office for postal privatization was established. A paper on the issues of postal privatization was submitted to the economic and fiscal policy council in April 2004 and after a series of discussions by the council, in September 2004, the basic principle of privatization was decided as the cabinet decision. Even though the executive office was created in the cabinet secretariat to prepare for postal privatization, essential and crucial preparatory work was actually done by the small group of aids and advisors close to minister Takenaka. They did all their work behind closed doors until the time came when they went through necessary procedures to submit bills to the Diet. The bills for postal privatization were prepared in 2005.

According to the established rule of the Liberal Democratic Party, if not a written statutory rule, bills must be explained to and accepted by the committee of the party before they are submitted to the parliament. Otherwise, they say that members of the party cannot be held responsible for getting them acted in the parliament. On the bills for postal privatization, the committee of the party could not conclude the deliberation and postponed its decision to accept or reject them. Bills were submitted without the full support of members of the ruling party. Deliberation by the committee of the House of Representatives started and acted on the bills and sent them to the plenary session of the House. The bills were passed in the plenary session with a narrow margin (233 for the bills and 228 against the bills) because there were many (37) among the Liberal Democratic Party members who voted against the bills. Bills were sent to the House of Councillors. They were voted down in the plenary session of the House of Councillors (108 for the bills and 125 against the bills). Here again, there were many (22) among the Liberal Democratic Party members who voted against the bills. Then, on August 8 Prime Minister Koizumi dissolved the House of Representatives, saying, 'I want to ask the opinion of the people, I want to ask people whether they support reform or not'. The reason why the House of Representatives, which passed the bills, was dissolved is that the Constitution allows the dissolution of the House of Representatives only, and there was no provision for dissolution of the House of Councillors. Koizumi also said: 'I do not allow those who did not vote for the bills to be candidates for the coming election by the tickets of the Liberal Democratic Party. In addition, I will select strong competitors against them'. Koizumi even fired one minister who did not sign the cabinet's decision to dissolve the House of Representatives. During the election, Koizumi repeatedly appealed to the voters, saying: 'Whether you support the reform or not'. The election became the one-issue election. Koizumi got landslide victory with two-thirds majority (together with the seats of coalition party Komeito) in this election of 2005. Many who voted against the bills lost their seats. After the election was over in September 2005, the bills for postal privatization were submitted again to the special session of Diet in October 2005. The bills were passed immediately in the House of Representatives. Bills were sent to the House of Councillors and passed immediately with almost no opposition this time from the Liberal Democratic Party. Koizumi got it. On October 31, 2005, Koizumi changed the line-up of his cabinet and appointed Takenaka to two ministerial jobs: the Minister of Internal Affairs and Communications and the minister for postal privatization. Takenaka became the minister to control and manage the ministry of internal affairs and communications and to promote the implementation of postal privatization.

Now that the postal privatization which he wanted most got going on a solid rail and Koizumi had no other important policy matters which he passionately wanted to address, he stepped down as the president of Liberal Democratic Party when the term of this office expired in September 2006 in spite of having exceptionally high support of the people. After serving the remaining days of the term as a member of the House of Representatives, he did not run for election and retired from politics in 2009.

After the world financial crisis or 'the so-called Lehman Shock', the Liberal Democratic Party was severely defeated in the election held in September 2009 in which Koizumi did not run, and lost power. The new government of the Democratic Party of Japan tried to change the content and course of postal privatization but could not stop it. The Liberal Democratic Party came back to power in December 2012. The postal privatization went on as shown below, and in 2015, stocks of Japan Post Holding, Japan Post Bank and Japan Post Insurance were put on the market.

Transition of postal services in Japan

2001 The Ministry of Posts and Telecommunications was merged with the Ministry of Home Affairs and the Management and Coordination Agency of the Prime Minister's Office to become the Ministry of Internal Affairs and Communications. The Postal Services Agency was attached to the new ministry as the organization to carry out postal services.

↓

2003 Japan Post Corporation was established, separating the postal services agency as a public corporation.

↓

2007 Japan Post Holding Inc. → 2012 Japan Post Holding Inc.*
    Japan Post Office Inc
    Japan Postal Services Inc.   Japan Post Inc.

(Post office and postal services were merged)

    Japan Post Bank Inc.   Japan Post Bank Inc.*
    Japan Post Insurance Inc.   Japan Post Insurance Inc.*

Note: In 2015, stock of the companies with asterisk mark (*) were put in the market.

Leadership of Koizumi was very unique, quite different from that of Nakasone and Hashimoto. Although he was the Prime Minister, he did not make any big group or faction of his own. He identified persons whom he could trust and not trust.

Prime Minister Koizumi assigned the most important job to the person who would wisely, faithfully and tactically carry out his mission. As long as the basic principles of postal privatization were kept or protected he did not stick to the details. When he was asked questions in the Diet, he referred the matter to minister Takenaka. When he was asked the same question again, he responded, 'Minister responsible for the matter is here to respond to your question'. He was stubborn and did not give in. He went straightforward to achieve what he wanted. He was a man of strategy and tactics, yet appeared to be a man of intuition. His strength was his ability to choose the right person for the right position to do what he wanted and the strong will and determination to overcome difficulties to challenge the taboo, using every possible means, even the dissolution of the House of Representatives which voted for the reform bills.

5. LESSONS FROM THE JAPANESE EXPERIENCES

Based on the analysis of Japanese cases of drastic reforms and reforms of highly political nature, the following lessons could be learned as key factors for the success.

First, the strong will and leadership of the Prime Minister is important. Drastic reforms and reforms of a highly political nature involve serious loss of vested interests of influential organizations and people, including politicians, in the society. It is difficult even for professional experienced reformers to overcome the strong resistance without the strong leadership of the Prime Minister or influential political leaders favourable to reform. The exercise of leadership and direct involvement of the Prime Minister attracts people's attention through frequent mass media coverage. People remember big reforms by the prime minister's name, such as 'Nakasone Administrative Reform', 'Hashimoto Administrative Reform' and 'Koizumi Administrative Reform'. Even though other politicians such as ministers for administrative reform and professional officials engaged in reforms have done a lot successfully, their names would not be remembered. In addition to strong will and leadership, the length of the prime minister's term also affects the success of drastic and big scale reforms or reforms of a highly political nature, as it may need many years to deliberate, decide and carry out those reforms. The term of the office of the Prime Minister of Japan is not fixed by law. If the Prime Minister changes and the new leader is not interested in the on-going reform, then that reform may not continue. Three prime ministers, of the 18 prime ministers in 30 years from 1982 to 2012, who promoted the above-analysed big reforms stayed in the office for the longest period; Nakasone for 1,806 days, Hashimoto for 932 days and Koizumi for 1,980 days. Analysis of the cases of administrative reforms by these prime ministers shows three different successful styles of leadership. They had their way to address the issues of their interest and used apparatus suitable to their style of leadership.

Second, detailed analysis, discussion or deliberation on problems to be addressed and their possible solutions are important. Even if the Prime Minister has a strong will and tells what he wants to do, usually he is not familiar with the details of the problems and related systems and has no concrete and specific ideas of possible solutions. His reform ideas need to be discussed from various viewpoints, elaborated and detailed into feasible reform plans and programmes. He depends on administrative reform organizations (comprising professional and experienced reform-minded officials) and advisory bodies or other organizations and advisors of any status or type. For drastic or big scale reforms and reforms of highly political nature, a special organization is often created to infuse various opinions and ideas from outside the government and certain consensus is built up to promote those reforms. The Provisional Commission for Administrative Reform for Prime Minister Nakasone, the Administrative Reform Council for Prime Minister Hashimoto and the Economic and Fiscal Policy Council for Prime Minister Koizumi are examples of such advisory bodies. Establishing a new authoritative advisory council for reform could symbolically show the strong will of the Prime Minister. As was the case of chairman Doko of the Provisional Commission for Administrative Reform, he could also be the symbol of reform efforts of the government and contribute to attract the attention and support of the people. However, members of these advisory organizations also need to depend on the intensive work by executive staff organizations to support their activities. Here again, the effective leadership of senior executive staff is indispensable to manage a big executive office and carry out well-organized supporting activities. It is said that the Provisional Commission for Administrative Reform was the most desirable office as a strong mutual trust was built up between the Prime Minister and members of the commission and professional reform-minded officials of the executive office. The case of postal privatization by Prime Minister Koizumi was different from other cases in that the essential crucial staff work was done by a small group of aids and advisors close to minister Takenaka, and he personally managed this staff work.

Third, support of the general public is important, especially in the case of drastic reform, government-wide big reforms and reforms of a highly political nature, as there are a large number of vested interest groups, influential organizations and people, including politicians. To overcome the resistance or reluctant attitudes of these forces, strong support of general public is important, even for any strong Prime Minister to go forward with his reform ideas. The cases of privatization of the National Railways and the Postal Services are good examples. However, the interest of the general public changes as time passes by, and even mass media coverage decreases if the reform is still in the process of implementation. Therefore, effort by the government to ensure continuous public support is important by disseminating the product and benefits of reform.

Fourth, people in target organizations or those directly concerned with reform need to be involved in the process of discussion and implementation of reform. Those directly concerned with reform need to understand the necessity and content of reform, either actively willing to do reform or passively being persuaded. Without their involvement and commitment, the reform process may be sabotaged or derailed from its intended course. In fact, quite often, these people are more familiar with problems of existing systems, organizations and practices. Yet, ironically, they may be resistant to changes from the state they are accustomed to. Even though there is usually objection or reluctance at the beginning, attitudes and mindsets of those directly concerned begin to change once they understand that reform is inevitable. In the final analysis, it is their job and workplace. They may wish reform at their job and organization, and wish to commit themselves with the reform and feel 'ownership' of successful reforms.

Fifth, sustainability of reform is important. Involvement and commitment of those directly concerned in the target organizations mentioned above is one way to ensure the sustainability of reforms. A typical example is the appointment of 'reformists' with the National Railways as chief executives of new, privatized railway companies carrying out the reform. The following are important for the sustainability of reform, and also seen in the reformed cases discussed:

- Clarification and sharing of objectives of reform.
- Institutionalization or legislation of basic components of reform.
- Clarification (by designating or establishing) of organization responsible for the promotion (implementation) of reform.
- Scheduling of the implementation of reform: steps and speed of implementation should be set forth, such as in the form of action plan.
- Providing incentives and/or disincentives for those concerned; encouraging and rewarding those contributing the implementation of reform.
- Management, supervision and dissemination of the progress of reform.
- Producing positive and meaningful results of reform.

6. CONCLUDING REMARKS – PROSPECTS OF REFORM IN THE NEAR FUTURE

A wide range of administrative and public sector reforms has been carried out for many decades in Japan. In this chapter, drastic or government-wide big scale reforms and reforms of highly political nature were mainly dealt with to discuss the importance of leadership, especially the leadership of prime ministers. But it is important to note here that there are other, less political wide-ranging administrative reform efforts which have been carried out or being discussed and carried out continuously by professional administrators with the help of advisory councils, when necessary. Deregulation and regulatory reforms, decentralization and reform of local governments, reform of systems and practices concerning the relationship between the government and people are examples of such reform areas. In these cases, the Prime Minister may not be directly involved to exercise the leadership, and as a result people's interest and attention may be dispersed. However, gradual and step-by-step reforms were carried out and are still going on in these areas. These are promoted by professional administrators responsible for government-wide reforms under the general support of prime minister and the minister responsible for administrative reform. It is important to know these activities and to have a whole picture and full understanding of these administrative reform efforts in Japan.

Thirty-six years have passed since the Provisional Commission for Administrative Reform was started by Nakasone for wide-range administrative reforms, and almost 20 years have passed since Hashimoto started the Administrative Reform Council for government-wide reshuffling of Central Government Ministries, and almost 15 years have passed since Koizumi started his challenge against the taboo, the privatization of postal services. In view of social, economic and other changes (including relationship changes between politicians and administrators) in Japanese government and the society with low fertility rate and ultra-aged population, and stringent fiscal conditions with huge amounts of accumulated outstanding bond issue, it is necessary to launch new round of long-term reform efforts.

Current Prime Minister Abe has been in the office for more than 2,000 days, much longer than Prime Minister Hashimoto, at the end of the year 2017. He is understood now as the Prime Minister strong enough to do whatever he wants to do in substantive domestic policy issues, he is devoting much time and energy to the issue of decreasing population with low fertility rate and disparity between urban metropolitan areas and countrysides. Revitalization or restoration of local areas and change in the life style of Japanese people, such as the policy called 'promoting dynamic engaging for all citizens' (or 'one hundred million total active society policy' is the literal translation of the original Japanese policy title), are some policies he set with high priority. However, it is not clear what he is interested in and what he wants to do in the field of administrative reforms. He may not be interested in administrative reform very much. Or, what he thinks as necessary administrative reform for the future of Japan may be quite different from the conventional types of administrative reforms. It is necessary to keep watching what he will do for the future of Japan and, what type of leadership he is going to exercise as Prime Minister.

REFERENCES

Eda, K., & Nishino, T. (2002). *Kaikakuseiken ga kowarerutoki (When the reform government collapses)*. Tokyo: Nikkei BP Sya.

Gotou, K. (2014). *Heisei seijishi 1,2,3 (Political history of Heisei period 1,2,3)*. Tokyo: Iwanami Syoten.

Gyousei Kaikaku Kaigi Jimukyoku, OB Kai. (1998). *21 seiki no nihon no gyouseikaikaku (Administrative reform in Japan of the 21st century)*. Tokyo: Institute of Administrative Management.

Horie, M. (2000a). Shouchou saihensei no igi to kadai (Significance of restructuring ministries and agencies by the hashimoto reform and the future challenge). *Public Administration Review Quarterly, 92*, 15–23.

Horie, M. (2000b). Administrative reform in Japan – Reflection and future perspective. Paper presented at the symposium at Fudan University in Shanghai, China.

Horie, M. (2011a). Administrative reform in Japan: Subjects, methods and results. Paper presented at the annual conference of the Asian Association of Public Administration at Jakarta, Indonesia.

Horie, M. (2011b). Changing roles and responsibilities of government in Japan. Paper presented at the annual conference of the International Institute of Administrative Sciences at Bali, Indonesia.

Horie, M. (2012). Evolving state-market relations in Japan. In M. S. de Vries & J. Nemec (Eds.), *Global trends in public sector reform* (pp. 185–199). Bruxelles.

Horie, M. (2014). Change of government and challenge of reform – What is happening in Japan? In *Public management in the 21st century: Opportunities and challenges* (Selected papers from the fifth international conference at Sun Yat-Sun University, Macao), Sun Yat-Sun University Center for Public Administration Research and Others (Eds.), pp. 303–324.

Horie, M. (2014). Change of government and challenge of reform – What is happening in Japan? In *Public management in the 21st century: Opportunities and challenges* (Selected papers from the fifth international conference at Sun Yat-Sun University, Macao).

Japan Society for Public Administration. (1985). *Rincho to gyouseikaikaku (Provisional commission for administrative reform and administrative reform)*. Tokyo: Gyousei.

Japan Society for Public Administration. (2006). *Hashimoto gyoukaku no kensyou (Review of Hashimoto administrative reform)*. Tokyo: Gyousei.

Kasai, T. (2007). *Kokutetsu kaikaku no shinjitsu (Truth of the reform of the national railways)*. Tokyo: Chuoukouron Shinsya.

Kato, H., & Takenaka, H. (2008). *Philosophy and strategy of reform*. Tokyo: Nikkei Publishing Co.

Masujima, T. (2004). *Gyouseikaikaku no shiten to tenkai (Viewpoints and development of administrative reform)*. Tokyo: Gyousei.

Masujima, T. (2009). *Administrative reform in Japan*. Tokyo: The Institute of Administrative Management.

Masujima, T., & Kobayashi, H. (2001). *Syogen: Daikaikaku wa Ikani nasaretaka* (*How was big reform done?*). Tokyo: Gyousei.
Masujima, T., & Kobayashi, H. (2004). *Shogen: Daikaikaku wo sasaeru mekanizumu* (*Testimony: Mechanism to support reform*). Tokyo: Gyousei.
Rincho Gyoukakushin, OB kai. (1991). *Nihon wo kaeta 10 nen: Rincho to gyoukakushin* (Ten years which changed Japan: Provisional commission for administrative reform and provisional council to promote administrative reform). Tokyo: Gyousei.
Tanaka, K. (2006). *Gyousei kaikaku* (*Administrative reform*). Tokyo: Gyousei.
Tanaka, K., & Horie, M. (1995). Privatization of the big three. In M. Tishiyuki & O. Minoru (Eds.), *The management and reform of the Japanese government* (pp. 214–229) (2nd ed.). Tokyo: The Institute of Administrative Management.
Tanaka, K., & Okada, A. (2000). *Chuou shocho kaikaku* (*Reform of central government ministries and agencies*). Tokyo: Nihon Hyoron Sya.
Yamamoto, S. (2003). *Seikimatsu 20 nen no gyouzaiseikaikaku to 21 seiki no kadai* (*Administrative and fiscal reform in twenty years in the end of the 20th century and challenges of the 21st century*). Tokyo: Jihyou Sya.
Yamawaki, T. (2005). *Yusei – Koubou* (*Offense and defense on postal services reform*). Tokyo: Aasahi Shinbun Sya.

CHAPTER 3

LEADERSHIP AND PUBLIC SECTOR REFORM IN INDONESIA

Eko Prasojo and Defny Holidin

ABSTRACT

Leadership for public sector reforms in Indonesia involves both national level efforts and leadership from local levels that have been empowered by prior decentralization. This chapter focuses on reforms made by the national government, which has been guided by the values of serving public, increasing efficiency and becoming corruption-free. Although the National Development Agency and the Ministry for Administrative Reform provided central impetus and coordination, reforms were seen as quite fragmented across ministries with uneven results. The authors are concerned about reform effectiveness and sustainability. Reform leadership is challenged by human capital and legally mandated but inefficient bureaucratic processes and structures as well as challenges of public distrust and disobedient civil servants. The latter is sometimes dealt with by using patronage to insert allies for reform, and they take note of leaders gaining leverage from working across boundaries and jurisdictions, and by improving their authorizing environment. The chapter describes a strategy of leaders-led efforts that are cascaded through ministries through institutionalization (e.g., of policies) and obtaining support from successive reform champions at different levels

Leadership and Public Sector Reform in Asia
Public Policy and Governance, 53–83
Copyright © 2018 by Emerald Publishing Limited
All rights of reproduction in any form reserved
doi:10.1108/S2053-769720180000030003

and locations. The authors argue for increasing the number of 'champion leaders' who pragmatically, transactionally and successfully get subordinates to commit to reform efforts.

Keywords: Decentralization; institutionalization; champion leaders; reform effectiveness; Indonesia

PUBLIC SECTOR REFORM IN THE CONTEXT OF THE INDONESIAN CHANGING STATE

Indonesia is one of the Southeast Asian countries affected by the 1997 Asian Financial Crisis (AFC), which in 1998 led to the dismantling of 32 years of Soeharto's New Order authoritarian regime (Crawford & Hermawan, 2002). To date the country has successfully managed its economic recovery and development; it has even kept being resilient, albeit at a slower pace, in coping with the effects of the 2008 global financial crisis (Hill, 2014; Pepinsky, 2009). Nevertheless, the country has not yet been able to escalate beyond development level of middle economies in the region. Although Indonesia has successfully maintained its economic resilience throughout the crises, the annual gross domestic product of Indonesia has slightly decreased from 6.2% in 2011 to 4.8% in 2015 (World Bank, 2016). It in 2015–2016 was ranked 37th of 140 countries on the global competitiveness scale, which dropped from the previous 34th rank (World Economic Forum, 2015). All those achievements have fluctuated through the 1997 AFC and the 2008 global financial crisis to present conditions.

In spite of sluggish improvement in recent economic development, the 1997 AFC brought a momentum for the general public to ask the Government of Indonesia (GoI) to carry out public sector reform compensating the destructive effects of rampant corruption within the Indonesian politico-administrative system. Successor of the Soeharto regime, the Habibie administration, attempted to respond to this public demand through a number of constitutional and administrative reform practices along with mainstreaming procedural democracy (Ashshiddiqie, 2003; Bertelsmann Stiftung, 2014; Dwiyanto, 2004; Prasojo, 2009; Prasojo, Kurniawan, & Holidin, 2007a). They shifted the balance of power from executive to legislative – along with rearranging state institutions – i.e., the President (*Presiden*), the House of Representatives (Dewan Perwakilan Rakyat), the Senate (Dewan Perwakilan Daerah), the Supreme Court (Mahkamah Agung), and the Constitutional Court (Mahkamah Konstitusi, MK) and State Examination Body (Badan Pemeriksa Keuangan) – to be at equal level through the balance of distinguished power and proportionally shared authority. Besides strengthening law enforcement and reaffirming the free press, governance reform has been completed by empowering various state auxiliary bodies. In terms of vertical balance of authority, Indonesia has also implemented devolutionary-liberal decentralization, which has been followed up by central–local fiscal balance (Aspinal & Fealy, 2003; Kersting, Caulfield, Nickson, Olowu, & Wollman, 2009; Prasojo, Maksum, & Kurniawan, 2006; Rohdewold, 2003). Public financial reform has taken into effect after stipulation of law No. 17/2003, including privatization of state-owned enterprises (SOEs), which has taken the lead of major aspects of subsequent public sector reforms in Indonesia (Hill, 2014).

As for law enforcement to guard the reform process, new state bodies established following matured legal–formal framework for reform. A number of efforts were also intended to strengthen this sector, for instance, the Commission for Corruption Eradication established in 2003. Empowering of authority and strengthening roles of administrative court and national ombudsman were further steps. Traditional bureaucracy was also challenged by the introduction of state-of-the-art private counterparts along with legal reconciliation of sectors and different levels of government.

As a matter of fact, Indonesia has suffered from the lack of proper institutional arrangement to cope with the side effects of previous economic policies (Basri, 2013). Although public sector reform has taken place since 1998 along with the democratization process, an impediment to grasping economic growth has come from state regulations that created a high barrier to market entry (Touchton, 2015), and any significant efforts to ensure that the regulations were effectively enforced were missing. Overlapping regulations were widely known, but the consolidation process was very slow. Nevertheless, a number of institutional loopholes have remained due to ambiguity, leading to underperformance, maladministration as well as corruption (Holidin, Layuk Allo, Pramusinto, Rahardjo, & Litaay, 2014). These politico-economic problems persist, for they are entrenched in the political stagnancy of Indonesian state institutions (Mietzner, 2015).

HISTORY AND CHARACTER OF INDONESIAN PUBLIC SECTOR REFORMS

Mainstreaming political and economic reform has caused the administrative reform agenda to be left behind in previous period; both the elites and the people were not aware of and have not paid enough attention to the problems of internal working mechanisms for producing and delivering public services (Prasojo, Kurniawan, & Holidin, 2007b; Weiser, 2008).

After experiencing sporadic, undesignated and pragmatic changes for more than a decade, administrative reform in Indonesia has recently entered a new phase through more designated and institutionalized implementation with the launching of national grand design of bureaucratic reforms in 2010 (Holidin, 2016). It is acknowledged that to reach such institutionalized administrative reforms was not an easy step.

Pragmatic reform was taken without any strong ideological basis for reform efforts. The GoI had to obey instructions written in the Letter of Intent (LoI) of the International Monetary Fund, e.g., reducing allocations for subsidized public goods and services, implementing decentralization through local autonomy policy, implementing privatization over a number of targeted SOEs etc. Moreover, the new regime after reform movement of 1998 needed to strengthen their legitimacy by fulfilling wide-range aspirations of pressure groups; which were similar to essentials of obligatory agendas written on the LoI. *Reactionary reform* policies had inevitably become a reason for undesignated reform efforts to appear, since they departed from different rationale. While the GoI had practiced pragmatic reform policies, civil society organizations, established as one of the results of democratization in Indonesia, have seen directions and objectives of reform from various donors' concerns combined with actual problems in grass roots societies, and the private sectors had stayed in their role of government counterpart in privatization and procurement, although they have suffered excesses of bribery by the bureaucracy. Sub-national governments, both at province and municipality levels, have been at the crossroads to execute local development under local autonomy policy and the dilemma of the so-called 'decentralized corruption'. Reactionary reform efforts have led to both vertically and horizontally uncoordinated development. Bertelsmann Stiftung (2012, p. 17) points out that lack of policy coherence at national and local levels, as well as poor network development among innovation actors, hampers Indonesian economy to become more competitive. Wide-range of changes in policy areas would be acknowledged as true initiatives of reform efforts. Nevertheless, these might also be an indication that reform had run *sporadically* since their initiatives were fragmented in different sectors and levels of government.

Institutionalization of reform means strengthened consensus reached for more sustainable steps forward. It is also sought for systematic and measurable reform progress achieved by all the involved parties. The content of administrative reform policy has nevertheless substantially fragmented in that it is more accommodating to bureaucratic interests than what people perceived to be the real problem suffered in bureaucracy, whereas the implementation of bureaucracy reform is trapped in bureaucratic programmatic ways without any room left for a breakthrough for those regulated by the Ministry of Administrative Reform (MAR, n.d.) and Holidin et al. (2014). Bureaucracy has remained the executive's instrument for mere policy implementation with poor professional autonomy. What is to be blamed is the absence of a solid grand design as well as a strategic roadmap in the early stages of reform. This condition reaffirms the thesis of Andrews, Pritchett, and Woolcock (2012) that there are tendencies in countries to prevent any positive deviances in practicing bureaucracy reform. Since the state was in the process of transformation, it might have been better to conduct a kind of iterative adaptation than merely replicating international best practices of reform. While administrative reform is expected to improve government effectiveness and efficiency in performing its functions, experiences in Indonesia show that sustaining innovations of administrative reform has become an agenda that is not easy to be carried out.

LEADERS DETERMINING REFORM PROGRESS

Locus of Reformist Leadership

Leadership for reform in Indonesia seems to take role at national, subnational and local levels, in different patterns with different levels of outcome. In spite of the institutionalizing reform led by the vice president and the national committee, it is worth to take decentralization into account. Nevertheless, Indonesia is a unitary republic; an asymmetric implementation of local autonomy policy has led to various circumstances among different levels of government, even among municipalities (Prasojo et al., 2007a).

Administrative reform at local levels in Indonesia was featured by widespread practices of a variety of public sector innovation. These reform-oriented innovations have been pioneered from the very early reform decades since 1998 by head of local governments of, for instance, Yogyakarta, Sragen, Surakarta, Solok, Jembrana, Tarakan, Tanah Datar and Surabaya (Bulan, 2014; Chalid, Mursitama, Hariyati, & Prianto, 2012; Eko, 2008; Hamudy, 2010; Muslim, Miftahul Jannah, Sakapurnama, & Hariyati, 2012; Prasojo, 2009; Prasojo, Kurniawan, & Holidin, 2008; Prasojo et al., 2006, 2007b; Triwibowo, Muhajir, & Mutasya, 2010; Widianingsih, 2005; World Bank, 2006a, 2006b; Yunairi, 2011; Zuhriyanti, Darumurti, & Rahmawati, 2012). Innovations by these pioneering local governments include, but are not limited to, integrated permit and investment services, cost-effectiveness-oriented local budget, performance-based remuneration, tuition-free education, public insurance for health services, e-office as well as bureaucracy right sizing by introducing the ad hoc-type agency units. Leadership at these levels is not the only indicator to mark the occurrence of reform but also sustainability in implementation, synchronization in arrangement and engagement with stakeholders. The number of such reform-oriented local governments is less than 5% of the total of about 500 municipalities and 33 – currently 34 – provinces, but there is potential replication in other (local) governments, which explains why these numbers are still growing (Holidin, 2007). These variations in reforms initiated by leaders of local governments show the urgency of programmes delivered by local governments as subsidiaries to public services which provide daily needs to the people.

Benefitting from obtaining higher authority to make policies and to administer acquired resources after decentralization came into effect in 2001, all innovative reforms have been featured by modernizing the way of bureaucracy performs its functions, increasing capabilities, enforcing efficiency of local budget under a higher authority to get better results with less resources as well as re-engineering frontline services in basic social services, e.g., education, health, permits and investment. These patterns are the antithesis of decentralization of corruption in the implementation of local autonomy policy, which led to imprisonment of quite a number of mayors/regents and governors (Isra, 2008; Kurniawan, 2011; Rinaldi, Purnomo, & Damayanti, 2007).

At national level, reformist leaders have appeared as champions in sectors that were suffering most from bureau-pathology, especially in terms of misuse of public resources, for instance, procurement, fiscal policy and budget management, personnel administration, etc. Procurement has been acknowledged to be the most corrupted sector (Hukumonline.com, 2011; Transparency International, 2013), and a strong leader is indispensable in fighting corruption. In the past, the National Development Planning Agency (*Badan Perencanaan Pembangunan Nasional*, Bappenas) established a division under its jurisdiction but since it focused its work on fighting corruption, the division was then turned into a government agency directly accountable to the president, namely the Government Agency of Procurement Policy (*Lembaga Kebijakan Pengadaan Pemerintah*, LKPP) but still under the coordination of Bappenas Layanan Pengadaan secara Elektronik (LPSE), 2010). This sort of institutional independence makes easier for LKPP leaders to issue procurement reform policies, including the development of an e-procurement system and selection of their own employees based on their criteria. Former finance minister Sri Mulyani, who has recently taken the office under the Joko Widodo administration, had remarkably led the ministry to succeed in public finance reform under Law No. 17/2003 on Public Finance as well as institutional rearrangement for bureaucracy reform during her first period as minister. The MAR (n.d.; Kementerian Pendayagunaan Aparatur Negara dan Reformasi Birokrasi/Kemen-PANRB) has been mandated to coordinate bureaucracy reform policy implementation across ministries and agencies in cooperation with the Personnel Administration Agency (Badan Kepegawaian Negara, BKN) to strengthen personnel administration reform even before the Law of State Civil Apparatus (Law No. 9/2014) was implemented. To make it succeed, President Soesilo Bambang Yudhoyono reshuffled MAR by appointing Eko Prasojo, a public administration expert, as a deputy minister to lead this process under minister Azwar Abu Bakar, a businessman with experience in government reform in the province of Aceh.

Public Values Upheld by Leaders

Governments in previous regimes have left a legacy of insufficient public services to fulfill people's needs. It is the leaders who are supposed to commit reform and manage resources accordantly. However, it is extremely hard to conduct reform agenda under less capable bureaucracy and in an atmosphere of public distrust. The creation of public values to be upheld by leaders is inevitable in these complex and uncertain circumstances, as suggested by Benington and Moore (2010), by creating authorizing environment and enhancing operational capacity. This truly occurred in recent Indonesian governance which left leaders with all kinds of problematic situations. At a subsidiary level employing higher authority to serve the people, the local government has no other objective than serving them all. It is also the case for those at national level. Leaders at national and local levels have initiated enhanced public service delivery with more value-added services, opening more opportunities to regain rights to earn basic social needs and repositioning citizens as not only stakeholders but also as strategic partners in governance (Prasojo & Holidin, 2018).

One significant value upheld by Indonesian leaders in reforming their governments is 'serving the public' (Dwiyanto, 2004; Holidin et al., 2014). The aforementioned pioneering local governments show many evidences of this. Making education and health services free is publicly accepted, but it is not the case. Increasing procedural easiness and certainty in many sectors – citizenship and various permits – is the main and also the common way of how Indonesian leaders have guaranteed people to regain their rights, and investors to have more confidence to set up business in certain areas. To make this come true, mayors/regents in pioneering municipalities have established integrated service procedures and merged overlapped agencies towards a one-stop services mode. It was reasonable for the mayors/regents in the first place to handle main authority approval for the permits and to delegate gradually authority to the agency head when experiments in capability enhancement and deregulated procedures were making some progress. Similarly, reform-oriented government agencies at national level have followed this way of local government to reform.

Another value is 'efficiency', which is perceived by Indonesian leaders as a constraint to gain further success in accomplishment of development programmes (Holidin, 2007; Prasojo, 2009; Prasojo et al., 2006). For local governments, higher authority under local autonomy policy means higher needs of resources to achieve objectives, and thus every local government is obliged to raise revenues by tapping inner local resources as well as inter-municipalities trade. This was a sort of dilemma faced by local governments. It is true that national governments provide a revenue-sharing mechanism and various schemes (block, specific and mutual) of grants for local governments. However, the problem is more 'how' to manage the resources than 'how much' they could gain and spend. Most of the governors and mayors/regents reverted business as usual. However, innovative local leaders knew how to transform these constraints into opportunities. One of the reform pioneers at local level, former regent of Jembrana, I Gede Winase (Prasojo, Kurniawan, & Hasan, 2004) during his period used to manifest this value by evaluating big spenders – any expenditure item that overwhelmed the budget – due to potential marked up and misallocation. He also used to lease official vehicles from private corporations instead of buying new cars which previously left questionable and illegal asset transfers from the office to individuals; in addition, the leasing gave another benefit of lower costs. Former regent of Sragen, Untung Wiyono (Prasojo et al., 2007b) formed an owner-estimate team with the task of evaluating price rates of every single budget item, especially for infrastructure and social services, these two being big spenders. He also right sized the structure of bureaucracy by merging agencies with overlapping functions, as well as introduced ad hoc unit to perform better tasks without making new structures. Regent of Tanah Datar (World Bank, 2006b) in 2006 drastically right-sized the number of local agencies from 22 to only eight, thus saving at least IDR 10 billion, which was then reallocated to education sector. Lessons learned from these pioneers have been implemented by former mayor of Surakarta, Joko Widodo (Majeed, 2012; Prihantika & Hardjosoekarto, 2011) and current mayor of Surabaya, Tri Rismaharini.

All these value manifestations are supported by people observing the manner and the amount of budget the government spends. However, at national level, efficiency did not seem to attract interest of most officials till the National Grand Design of Bureaucracy Reform laid out more opportunities for employees to receive higher remuneration as compensation for institutional success in reducing ministerial expenditures. The focus of many national agencies still is on earning more revenues than reducing spending.

Along with 'serve the people' and 'efficiency', there is another value which is more popular than these two: 'corruption-free' value. It gained popularity as a trademark of reform, since corruption was associated with the former 'New Order' under Soeharto's regime. This value was commonly seen as one of the main goals of reform, but Indonesian leaders perceived it as a spirit to conduct good and even better governance. Indonesian governance is highly concerned about the fact that corruption is the main problem that made Indonesia suffers low-development results (Prasojo, 2009). There are at least two levels of corruption captured by public attention: street-level corruption committed by frontline daily services, and higher level corruption in the procurement of activities. Local governments, such as Sragen, Surakarta and Yogyakarta, introduced integrated one-stop services and deregulated local regulations as the two methods for leaders to prevent street-level corruption, and also to open the way for mayors/regents to control bureaucrats' behaviour (Prasojo et al., 2006). For Jembrana, Surabaya and Sragen, rationalizing budget value and giving dissenting estimation are two of methods for reducing corruption. Former mayor of Surakarta, Joko Widodo, started anti-bribe public campaigns for bureaucrats and private individuals/business entities (Majeed, 2012). Leaders at national level have been seen paying higher attention to and giving a broader picture to this phenomenon, showing that the major area of corruption is procurement, which has slowed down development considerably (LPSE, 2010; Transparency International, 2013). No wonder that ministries dealing with state apparatus behaviour and performance (MAR), state financing (MoF) and development (Bappenas), especially procurement (LKPP), have given attention to prevailing corruption, and have campaigned for this issue.

Cascading Ideas of Reform from Leaders to Constituents

A certain type of leadership style and a kind of personal mastery influence the working of organization. This is also the case in Indonesian ministries/agencies and local governments. As a matter of fact, most reformist leaders have different backgrounds from those of tenured bureaucrats and have antithesis of bureaucratic style in carrying out the government duties. Facing the facts that red tape bureaucracy is against the values, it is natural for them to be eager to make changes according to their own ideals of reform. Cascading ideas of reform become inevitable to be carried out when they want the bureaucracy to suit their ideals.

Beyond hero leaders – or the so-called 'champions' – in a government institution, there must be others who have similar ideals or have attempted reform based on their capabilities. It is also the task of a leader to find similar companions, otherwise it would be difficult to develop. Cascading ideas should be attempted by any leader to influence people to have the same ideals, and then employ them to achieve goals. This is based on the cases from the pioneers of reform in different municipalities. Indonesian reformist leaders in local governments mainly used interpersonal ways to cascade their ideals through two-way dialogues in special meetings to articulate ideas and to turn tacit knowledge into explicit knowledge, or doing after-work activities together.

Ministries and government agencies apparently experience difficulties in carrying out this method of cascading reform ideas due to their wide scope of tasks and national level authority. Under such conditions, institutionalization of this cascading process has become inevitable, and interpersonal relations between reformist leaders and their subordinates should be implemented in micro-level administration in any office following borders of authority and hierarchy.

The MoF is one of the best examples of institutionalized cascading ideas of reform. Former minister Sri Mulyani acted as a champion in this case. She highlighted performance enhancement as one of her objectives under one package of bureaucracy reform in the ministry since 2007 (Ministry of Finance, 2010; Scharff, Majeed, & Iyer, 2012). It did not take more than a year; in early 2008, a balanced scorecard (BSC) was introduced for this purpose and implemented gradually following the hierarchy starting from first level (directorate general) in 2009 to third level (sub-directorates) in 2010. This gradual implementation was due to the issuance of related regulations, which mentioned that detailed implementation of balanced scorecard started with the lowest rank of employees in 2011. Institutionalized cascading ideas of reform have been conducted through general meetings in early 2008 between former minister Sri Mulyani and director generals to translate the vision and mission within the strategic plan of the ministry into a detailed roadmap for further measurable change indicators with multiple perspectives: 'stakeholders', 'finance', 'internal process' and 'learning and growth'. The minister took this opportunity through fostered debates to strengthen her subordinates' understanding of the urgency and know-how of reform implementation and its impacts to not only on the people's prosperity but also the ministry employees. This is not merely a managerial communication but linking the balanced scorecard with team and personal goals, persuading the apparatus to perceive institution goals of reform as their personal goals. The same method was gradually applied to the next hierarchy. The minister employed strategic management officers to make sure that all cascading processes go well, and she simultaneously secured her subordinates' commitment in every single hierarchy by having them sign a performance pact.

Both the interpersonal approach used by local governments and the institutional approach used by MoF and MAR have supported the vice president as the national bureaucracy reform coordinator to institutionalize those approaches in the national grand design of bureaucracy reform issued in 2010. As the executing coordinator of bureaucracy reform, MAR ensures that all ministries implement the grand design. The cascading process could advance well through the assignment of selected employees to become change agents within every single division at each hierarchy level of ministry/government agency. The change agents have similar roles as that of strategic management officers at MoF. More than just a formal institutionalized cascading process, this method has raised wider opportunities to establish more cadres to secure the success of reform. To support the top-down cascading process, MAR in early 2014 established the 'reformist leader forum', comprising top officials of both ministries/agencies and local governments, which had regular meetings to discuss current issues of reform and their ideas.

The idea behind MAR establishing change agents is somewhat similar to the method the reformist local government leaders have used to cascade their ideas and to stimulate the enthusiasm of other officials to conduct reform programmes. The local champions infiltrated local government bureaus and agencies with people who support reform ideals, and caught the interest of leaders to reform before and during the government period. Current regent of South-Halmahera, Muhammad Kasuba, used mentoring/coaching method to change the mindset and culture of his apparatus on religious-moral basis (Holidin & Hariyati, 2012; Malut Post, 2012), established as *Pembinaan Aparatur Berbasis Nilai* (PABN, i.e., value-based personnel reform). But, prior to the establishment of PABN, he had actually found that only a limited number of employees supported his ideals. To be successful, regent Kasuba infiltrated bureaucracy with ad hoc team with a non-civil service formation to support his performance as a regent as well as cascading process through PABN. The same method was also used by former regent of Sragen, Untung Wiyono, by the establishment of an ad hoc marketing team to support him in cascading his ideas of local economic and bureaucracy reform (Prasojo et al., 2007b). Former mayor of Tarakan, J. S. Kasim, employed tenured employees to support him in cascading reform. He appointed a fresh Australian PhD holder, who was also a tenured bureaucrat, to head the Local Board of Development Planning (Bappeda), whose assigned tasks were aligning reform strategies with development planning as well as establishing teams to cascade reform ideas from top officials to local agency officers (Prasojo et al., 2008). These local champions assumed that this type of patronage would have positive implications on the success of reform which is completely different from the perspective of institutionalization by MAR and MoF.

Leaders eventually need outsiders to help them influence their subordinates, making cascading reform succeed, especially those in local governments. As it is common for Indonesian officials to be sent abroad for further education, local governments sought skillful and professional people to have experience from other places. That is why many reformist leaders sent their local apparatus to have short training courses from other successful local governments. Former regent of Jembrana, I Gede Winase, sent his apparatus to Gianyar regency for three to four months to learn integrated one-stop service. In turn, the former regent of Sragen, Untung Wiyono, did the same. They assumed that formal education, even from abroad, doesn't give employees the opportunity to learn new skills along with reform-oriented minds and better attitudes; reform needs to take root in them to make it succeed. This way of cascading reform is recorded as one of the successful methods, and other reformist leaders such as the former mayor of Surakarta, Joko Widodo, replicated it. To enrich the knowledge of 'how' and 'why' reform, these champions later invited other heads of local governments and experts to give in-house lectures attended by officials from various levels.

Operational Capacity Building to Make Reform Implementation successful

Ideals of leaders without sufficient institutional capability would make all reform efforts useless if not a failure. Different from local governments, human capital building at ministries and government agencies treated their employees by sending them abroad for further studies. Besides common in-house training, there were bigger opportunities for scholarship for civil servants offered by foreign scholarship schemes, such as Australian Awards, the Chevening Award etc, as well as domestic funding sourced by national budget carried out by a number of ministries such as the MoF, the Ministry of Communication and Information, and Bappenas. However, as mentioned above, at intuition level there is a bigger need to change mindsets and their culture rather than merely increasing their act.

Training of civil servants to improve their expertise, skills and attitude is possible, although this apparently does not happen over a short time. In spite of the availability of funds, ministries/agencies and local governments in time need new and fresh employees not only to fill some vacant positions but also to support reform (Effendi, 2011). Almost all reformist leaders sought to use new recruitment to speed up reforms. Former heads of local governments of Yogyakarta, Sragen, Jembrana, Solok, Surakarta and Tarakan realized their plans by creating new vacancies to run the newly established one-stop service agency (*Badan Pelayanan Terpadu*, BPT; names used by different local authorities vary) in collaboration with existing employees. They also employed them to strengthen the management information system operated under Information and Communication Technology (ICT) bureaus. The regents of Sragen and South-Halmahera also needed more temporary untenured employees to run ad hoc teams to support reform. MAR and the former governor of Jakarta, Joko Widodo began in 2013 merit-based open and competitive selection for the recruitment of top officials; more deputies in MAR as well as head of sub-districts (*camat*) and villages (*lurah*) were appointed through the reform-oriented process. This was in advance, since at that time the Bill of State Apparatus was not yet issued – it was finally issued as Law No. 5/2014 in January 2014. Prior to this practice, since 2011, the head of National Personnel Agency (BKN) had initiated the assessment centre as well as computer-assisted test for merit-based recruitment. Thanks to the lessons learned from MoF under former minister Sri Mulyani and former regent of Sragen, Untung Wiyono who had initiated such practice in advance.

In spite of the advantages in human capital development, one of the biggest challenges that every leader faced was rationalization of bureaucracy structure. No matter how the apparatus capabilities improved, structure matters. Unfortunately, from the early stages of reform, this issue remained the same. Ever since local autonomy policy had been implemented, local governments took this opportunity to broaden their scope of tasks to carry out decentralization of higher authority. As a matter of fact, broader scope and bigger size nevertheless did not improve the functions performed. This led to an increase in the size of bureaucratic structure. Decentralization did not make ministries' and government agencies' bureaucracy structure of right size, although most functions were decentralized to governments at sub-national and local levels (Prasojo, 2009; Prasojo et al., 2007a). At national level, all presidents have paid attention to this issue (Holidin et al., 2014). Former president Abdurrahman Wahid had once dissolved the Ministry of Social Affairs and Ministry of Information and rotated the staff of both ministries to other ministries.

His successor, former president Megawati Soekarnoputri re-established those ministries but got a significant number of SOEs privatized in terms of ownership and management to decrease burden on state budget to finance tertiary/additional state functions. Both former presidents Megawati Soekarnoputri and Soesilo Bambang Yudhoyono have issued government regulations (*peraturan pemerintah*, PP) on local government organization structure, i.e., PP No. 8/2003 and later revised to PP No. 41/2007.

The situation could not be helped since the two PPs at the time have provided justification for local governments to prevent their bureaucratic structure from being right-sized. However, in spite of those regulations, reformist leaders put their rationalization agenda as 'first things first'. Former regent of Sragen, Untung Wiyono, started the evaluation of standard operating procedures to identify parts of ineffective and redundant procedures and implications of inefficient service costs; one of these measures resulted in the establishment of one-stop service agencies. The same pattern had also applied by former mayor of Surakarta, Joko Widodo, and former mayor of Yogyakarta, Herry Zudianto. The regent of Tanah Datar until 2006 found over-specialization in his agencies and thus drastically downsized the number of local agencies from 22 to only 8 by means of merger, reducing structure but enhancing functions. Right sizing and mergers left another problem of excessive employees but with low productivity. One single administrative task that could be handled by three employees was handled by 20 in most of the bureaucracies (Katharina, 2013). Governor of West Java, Ahmad Heryawan, was also concerned of this complexity (Jabarprov.go.id, 2012). Along with MAR's plan to put an early-retirement policy into effect, he implemented in advance one package of structure rationalization. Through his persuasive communicative role, he asked the province government to gradually implement early-retirement policy in 2010, and by 2012, 209 employees took this opportunity of voluntary retirement (province government of West Java, 11/06/2012). Under the Joko Widodo administration the PP was once again revised to become PP No. 18/2016 in accordance with the new local government act, Law No. 23/2014, which stressed upon a preventive approach of requiring central government approval prior to setting up local government organization structure.

Besides rationalization of bureaucracy's structure, reformist leaders also prioritized performance improvement. One intermediate path between rationalization of structure and improvement in performance is a legally binding performance. Local governments had once again applied this in advance. Former mayor of Sragen, Untung Wiyono, highlighted the importance of an employee to be productive. He realized the plan through establishing a legally binding performance by which each agency should reassess their job descriptions and identify their feasible performance targets to the level of every single employee to accomplish in a period of time. This remarkably improved bureaucracy output, especially those in the one-stop service agency. A similar method was also applied by former governor of Gorontalo, Fadel Muhammad (Holidin, 2007; Pranadji, 2008). He also initiated to publish the accomplishments of performance targets of each agency in local mass media. Having achieved their targets, the employees had their payment from province's budget. This in turn introduced performance-based budgets which were re-applied at the MoF since the early stages of reform under former minister Sri Mulyani's leadership in 2008 along with the operationalization of BSC.

What was practiced in Sragen regency and the province of Gorontalo was not easy to be replicated by other ministries/agencies and local governments. Such partial reform in managing performance did not obtain further sustainable success even in Sragen and Gorontalo after their leadership periods were over. MAR and MoF took their lessons from such practices and found that the crucial thing behind these ideas was how organizations could translate their workload and job variants into accountability mapping. Realizing the crucial point made MAR, BKN and Ministry of Home Affairs (MoHA) established three versions of regulations on workload mapping – these are currently being reconciled. However, former governor of Jakarta, Joko Widodo, thanks to his strategic top position as governor, brought this practice from his period as a mayor in Surakarta to be replicated in Jakarta before mechanism of merit-based open selection of top official positions came into effect (Kurtz & van Zorge, 2013). However, to apply the same mechanism, a middle-level manager such as Teuku Roni Yuliadi, the head of Prosperity and Legal Standing Division of BKPP (personnel education & training body), province of Aceh, had to convince his superiors and colleagues and cope with multiple resistance when initiating drafts of job and workload analyses in 2013 before the Bill of State Apparatus was issued in 2014. After this, personnel positioning was more accountable than before.

LEADERSHIP IN MANAGING RISKS OF REFORM INITIATIVES

Leaders Coping with Public Distrust

After former regime was toppled by the people who demanded reform, the incoming government faced high expectations of Indonesian people to gain better life and a bright future of prosperity. This was indicated by wide-spread civil society organizations that carried out society's agenda to the government as well as the high number of electoral participation of since the beginning of change of the regime. Nevertheless, at the same time, the trauma of being governed by the authoritarian regime under the Soeharto leadership has led the Indonesian people to be skeptic towards politicians due to the high occurrences of corruption. This has become worse since economic recovery policy produced high performance at macro-level but not necessarily strengthened the economic real sector, such as agriculture and manufacturing.

Reformist leaders know this situation best and those at local governments are the best example to show how reform initiatives can be carried out smoothly under risks. Although their numbers are too small in comparison to all the provinces, cities, and regencies, the local autonomy policy that went into effect in 2001 has given them very big opportunity to use their authority to bring more benefits for the people. Distrust is one threat all reformist leaders have to face, a risk of being seen as useless –and consequently lose support from the society – whatever reformist policies they conduct. For these leaders, regaining public trust became the prime priority to obtain legitimacy to carry out further development programmes.

There has been virtually no strategy implemented effectively by local reformist leaders to regain public trust. However, they managed to set up effective informal communication as a bridge directly reaching the grass-roots of the general public and a commitment to improve government performance. Engaging societies have also become a trending pattern through more frequent direct informal meetings up with communities, and going directly to a number of communities and their neighbourhoods and then having on-site dialogues and inspection, which is popularly known as 'turba' (*turun ke bawah* or going-down to grass roots) or 'blusukan' in the Javanese language. Former mayors of Surakarta, Joko Widodo, and Surabaya, Tri Rismaharani, are popularly known for this. Former Governor of North Sumatera Gatot Pujo Nugroho even disguised himself and regularly stayed overnight in targeted or random citizens' houses for close intensive discussions. Former regent of Sragen, Untung Wiyono, used to conduct a traditional Javanese puppet (the 'Wayang') show to communicate his proposed policy to the people; he also acted as a 'dalang' (puppet master) instead of deploying professional ones. He took this opportunity to obtain suggestions from the people concerning the real situations that they had experienced. Since he brought in almost all heads of local agencies to such events, he moderated two-way dialogues between his subordinates and audiences.

This method of direct communication with grass roots did not solve bureaucratic problems, especially those related to delivering more productive public services. While mobilizing his subordinates to change their views on how the government–society relation ought to be, the 'turba' or 'blusukan' seemed to be a matter of a leader paying attention to the people to gain a higher degree of trust, especially for those leaders who had to face cultural and patrimonial sentiments based on ethnic and/or religiosity biases, such as Joko Widodo from Surakarta coming to an original Betawinese Jakarta, and Gatot Pujo Nugroho, a moslem coming to North-Sumatera, a Christian/Catholic majority. For these leaders, showing the right attitude in governing people is more powerful than instructions and revising the procedures. Getting in touch directly with grass roots could not be replaced by hierarchy-heavy bureaucracies.

Realizing that the method of getting in touch or 'turba' alone with grass roots would not necessarily be effective to maintain public trust continuously, the aforementioned leaders attempted to generate concrete programmes from simple ideas that came from root problems that might lead to what people perceive as 'high-wide' impact. Their choices have been laid down to public services reform of basic social needs, such as simplifying residency administration procedures, tuition-free education and health services, and ease of business permit administration through integrated one-stop services (Prasojo, Permana, & Hiqmah, 2006). Their programmes where derived from general public services reform policies. Although the reform programmes had wide coverage in terms of budget allocation, number of beneficiaries and expected outcomes, limited resources, especially in the early local autonomy implementation, made these leaders focus on what they assumed to be the most affordable policy objectives in each sector and easy to prove to people that the local government was seriously doing best for them.

Dealing with Resisting Actors Inside the Organization

Threats to reform also came from internal of organizations. One might note that lacking knowledge of high benefits of reform could be one factor. However, enjoying too much and too long a comfort zone probably contributes to more threats. Roadblocks from internal bureaucracy are apparently a bad news for reformist leaders. In spite of strong reform orientation and political legitimacy, a reformist leader would depend on civil servants who have long-tenured career in bureaucracy with some particular knowledge and expertise. Coping with resistance is also a leadership skill, and some reformist leaders in Indonesia have displayed this.

There are at least two main strategies undertaken by pioneers of administrative reforms at local level. They maintain personal relations with their subordinates, change their work environment and announce threats of firing disobedient employees.

The first strategy of maintaining personal relations with subordinates has been a benefit for communal life of Indonesian people in general. This type of atmosphere is especially found in village-like municipalities where people enjoy greeting everyone they meet and inquire about family conditions. Regent Wiyono even started a unit to perform assessment, the first of its kind in Indonesian personnel administration, and dealt with human resources management functions; it also assessed civil servants with problematic performances due to office issues or family's well-being. Meeting people every working day in the early morning helped reformist leaders, especially in Yogyakarta, Surakarta, Sragen, Jembrana, Tanah Datar and Solok, to foster discussions, which not only increased awareness but also led to a common understanding and sense of ownership of reform issues.

The second strategy assumes that the Indonesian experience also affirms that the higher skills of trained civil servants do not necessarily lead to higher support for reform. Change in working environment is needed to change attitude and transform the mindsets of civil servants. Reformist leaders realize this importance. Sending civil servants to other local governments with a reformist environment for internship was also used for developing reformist attitudes and exchange of knowledge while learning improved skills. Examples of this are what former mayor of Surakarta Widodo did when sending his employees to the City Government of Yogyakarta, or former Mayor of Sragen Wiyono in cooperation with regency government of Jembrana.

Announcement of threat to dismiss disobedient civil servants was the last but not the least strategy used by reformist leaders. Research that we had carried out from 2006 to 2013 did not succeed in gathering the data of the number of civil servants dismissed or rotated under this policy since local officials seemed to be reluctant to disclose it. Nevertheless, through a series of in-depth interviews and observations conducted in separate field studies, we learned that such policy was merely an initial warning to civil servants, which is perceived effective to anticipate growing tendencies to resist reform initiatives. While it is apparent that resistant civil servants would have manifested their disagreement with reform initiatives in many implicit ways, we have learned that being dismissed and downgraded was typically fearful for them.

Initiating Reconciliation Strategies that Turn Threats into Opportunities

Dealing with resistant actors inside the organization did not necessarily involve the aforementioned strategies, especially when internal and external threats are combined. Reformist leaders realized this critical point at a very early stage of reform when external challenges, threats and opportunities came together. In that problematic situation reconciliation strategies were perceived as an answer to address the combined internal and external challenges. The fact was that reforms could not be favoured voluntarily by many people, in both organization and external environment. In many ways reformist leaders had to make decisions in difficult situations, especially when reform initiatives had to be moderated with tactics perceived as 'bad' or 'corrupt'. Compensating corrupt tactics with potential gains increased the feasibility of achieving certain reform goals undertaken by certain reformist leaders. This can be called a transactional approach or style of leadership.

The transactional approach has at least two main strategies. First, implementing remuneration policy to compensate potential 'income' loss due to bureaucracy reform policy, and second, using approaches which were usually considered as public sector pathology, especially patronage, and giving political concession.

The MoF under Sri Mulyani's leadership had run bureaucracy reform since 2007 with remuneration policy as a starting point, with a higher target of performance to be achieved. The policy was intended to change the way of working, work behaviour and work ethics to increase organizational productivity. Regardless of highly qualified civil servants in MoF in terms of education and achieving complex targets, it was found that civil servants were not satisfied with the imbalance between their workload and salaries. The bureaucracy reform policy has taken this into consideration when the government launched the National Grand Design of Bureaucracy Reform in 2010, which was technically managed under the coordination of MAR. This performance-used compensation was a type of stick and carrot policy: higher remuneration was given to those having better performance, while sanctions were given to those lacking performance. It also meant that as a matter of fact, many people have seen reform in the precise calculation of costs and benefits in accordance with personal gains.

Other reformist leaders took steps beyond boundaries of bureaucracy. When they faced difficulties in employing (local) government staff through the usual bureaucratic procedures, they used their own cadres or definite reform supporters. This kind of patronage opened an opportunity to identify subordinates willing to support reform initiatives and promote them without open and competitive selection mechanisms for job promotion. Another way was by offering a political concession to top officials in exchange of approval to partial reform proposals. Either way could lead to strengthening the existing spoil system within the bureaucracy, but these ways were perceived to be the fastest and the easiest path to get a higher chance of support for reform.

The Sragen Regency under the Wiyono Administration is a very good example of this (Savirani, 2013). While persuading his subordinates to follow his idea of business-like bureaucracy, he realized great difficulties in changing human behaviour of people who are enjoying their comfort zone, especially when he wanted to redistribute some authority to integrated services agency from its counterpart-related function agencies. Almost all heads of local agencies under his administration resisted. Regent Untung, considering the high interest of his subordinates for future higher position, especially beyond the bureaucracy, offered them possibilities to take political positions in his party as well as in the council for next elections, and fortunately this strategy responded very well. Regardless of the fact that patronage is somewhat an antithesis of reform spirit, regent Wiyono had successfully got rid of sectoral egoism suffered by his administration, and that's how local bureaucracy reform occurred with reconciliation paradox. The current regent of Bojonegoro, Suyoto, does not use political concession as done by regent Wiyono. When he first acquired the office, some civil servants were worried that they would be demoted or mutated under new regent, a common phenomenon occurring in other municipalities. However, this did not happen. Having close dialogues and negotiation, regent Suyoto promised that they would remain at their positions unless their productivity decreased. This raised optimism and turned resistance into support for new administration.

SUSTAINING REFORM THROUGH LEADERSHIP

Finding Other Potential Leaders and Allies for Reform

The experiences of reform in Indonesia have definitely reaffirmed Klitgaard's thesis (1991) on existence of potential leaders and allies to be found within corrupted institutions. This is true when we look at some reform initiatives taken by the leaders in particular cases discussed in this chapter. Existing state institutions after the Soeharto's New Order was dismantled became complicated and solidified by networks of corrupt officials, while those against bureau-pathologies seemed to have no choice except to perceive the existing situation. The idea behind finding potential leaders and allies is the need for coping with this complication of corrupted institutions and for sustaining reform even though the institutional constellation changed in time. Another idea was to achieve wider support from internal bureaucracy and to allow the reform to flow smoothly. Combined with implementing the aforementioned reconciliation strategies, finding out potential leaders and allies, even from their subordinates, in addition to 'champions', became indispensable in this matter.

Developing new leaders is closely related to the call for personnel administration reform, especially during recruitment, positioning and performance management. This is true according to several cases in Indonesia. As for recruitment, bottom-up formation openings to be fulfilled through new recruitment proposed by each ministry/government agency and local governments to the MAR and National Personnel Administration Agency (BKN) had undermined appropriate workload analyses and job descriptions. These have contributed to misplaced personnel positioning within the bureaucracy, and in turn have led to structural enlargement. However, there has been no significant progress in performing organizational functions in achieving development goals. To cope with this problem, since 2006, both MAR and BKN together with MoHA have separately developed and imposed their own version of workload analyses and job descriptions to other ministries/government agencies and local governments prior to open recruitment formations.

While increasing competitiveness of more qualified intake seems to be effective, there is a greater need to recruit high caliber candidates to fill top positions of officials through different mechanisms. Prepared in 2012, MAR since 2013 has conducted open competitive selection of public officials for senior executive positions in advance even before the promulgation of Bill of State Apparatus (Aparatur Sipil Negara, ASN) – currently Undang-Undang (UU) No. 5/2014. Both minister and deputy minister of Administration Reform were benefitted from a wider opportunity in the former Law (No. 43/1999 concerning personnel administration) to take discretionary decision to launch such recruitment mechanism to take effect within internal administration of MAR.

The mechanism of open competitive selection consists of a testing process for the candidates passing administrative selection in which they take a written test, and further defend their paper before a panel comprising senior civil servants, prominent academics and renowned practitioners from private sector. Strong coordination has been carried out by the minister and deputy minister of administrative reform and the head of BKN to support this mechanism. The assessment centre – initially used by MoF and the regency government of Sragen for their personnel management – is intensively used to identify the best potentials of candidates: knowing their personality, integrity and expertise, as well as factors coming from their personal lives and families which could potentially influence their performance. This merit-based mechanism has obviously attracted high caliber candidates from both public and private sectors. The MAR has currently considered designing integrated state apparatus management within the preparation of a set of regulations derived from UU ASN to make sure the merit-principle is not only applied at the recruitment phase but also in all human resource management functions within the ministry. Such 360° performance evaluation is being carried out within the MAR to measure the outcome of open-competitive selection towards ministry performance as a whole.

Rising up More Cadres Supporting the Reform

So far, education and training have become the frontier of improving cadres supporting the reform. As a knowledge-based support for institutional reform, the National Institute of Public Administration (*Lembaga Administrasi Negara*, LAN), whose responsibilities include conducting studies for policy recommendation and educating civil servants, has consistently found that the use of training is the best way to reconstruct their mind-set and attitude/culture. In 2013, the leadership of Agus Dwiyanto – a tenured professor of public administration at Universitas Gadjah Mada – developed a new executive training curriculum and method replacing the conventional in-class heavy lecture training carried out for decades. Dwiyanto and his core team realized that the conventional training mode was neither effective to enhance civil servants' administrative skills nor significant to give more value addition to bureaucracy reform in spite of high caliber lecturers being in charge. The conventional curricula were therefore designed without strong relevance to participants' home agency needs.

Based on this evaluation, a new mode of training, the first of its kind, featured participant-centred learning, professionally tailored to their agency's needs, and dealing with multiple supervision by experts from various backgrounds. This reform-oriented executive training does not merely conduct four-week in-class lectures in combination with case-based interactive discussion but also imposes tasks to be accomplished by participants in groups to actively design their own change management project by conducting research to generate practical solutions to real problems suffered in their home agencies. That's why the task accomplishment is carried out over approximately six months as on-the-go training from the time the participants resume their work. The output is, of course, a policy recommendation to be integrated with their problematic conditions in their respective ministry/agency/local government. To assure that the learning process is guided by high quality standards, LAN makes use of multiple experts to work in collaboration to supervise each project. The supervisors come from various ministries/government agencies, employers of respective participant's home agency, and academics.

This is a very good example of a training mode that not only transfers knowledge but also raises the awareness of civil servants. At the same time it also generates various practical solutions to be applied at other agencies.

Improving knowledge, raising awareness of bad governance within agencies and developing skills to solve real problems are somewhat a breakthrough to develop new cadres for public sector reforms.

Creating Authorizing Environment that Leads to Continuing Legitimacy to Reform

Conducting public sector reform does not necessarily mean higher legitimacy to the leaders' policies. Yet, some internal parties would resist reform initiatives, since they would lose something beneficial to corrupted bureaucracy. External parties, such as parliament and council members, sometimes take ambiguous positions in facing the reform agenda: they need the reform agenda for their political campaign for their constituents, but there might also be a high chance that they take advantage of corrupted bureaucracy. Ensuring positive legislation enablers, especially in this context, become an indispensable leadership skill. As for the society as a whole, minimum engagement and socialization deficit would probably lead to a lack of legitimacy, leading to high resistance from external environment. Thus, creating an authorizing environment becomes indispensable for leaders to succeed in public sector reforms.

In undertaking political management to enable legislation, prominent reformist leaders in Indonesia have used authorities within their own boundaries to prove great success in performance. Prior to initiating one-stop service for business permits in Yogyakarta, Sragen and Surakarta, for instance, the mayors and regents at the time committed to issue a series of decrees for experimenting the implementation of bureaucracy reform strategies, gradually enhancing the quality of the newly established institutional arrangements, which showed evidences of successful progress in hand with the councils. The same was also undertaken by former finance minister Mulyani for a series of advanced public finance reform packages as well as internal bureaucracy reform of MoF. The results are remarkable government regulations (PP) and local regulations (*peraturan daerah/perda*) that have even been adopted by the national government within the national grand design of bureaucracy reform, which support the operation of one-stop services and public finance reform package for long-term implementation.

Leaders need more than a mass publication to gain extensive support from external environment. Evidences of high standards of performance would convince public. This was a concern of former mayor of Sragen, Untung Wiyono, who used performance evaluation based on user satisfaction surveys of services delivered by local agencies. Such surveys are apparently not sufficient to know the realities of public service reforms. However, the idea behind this type of evaluation is quite simple. Service users are vulnerable to bureaucracy treatment and they know best how appropriate local agencies perform their functions. Moreover, being surveyed could mean intensified engagement of people representing the whole population in running local governments. The case of Sragen has also shown a high commitment of leadership when dealing with constituents' expectations of reform.

Working in Collaboration Beyond Bureaucracy

Working alone is apparently not typically successful for reformist leaders. Cases of leadership discussed in this chapter are profiles of those who are eager to work beyond boundaries of bureaucracy, engaging broader governance actors, i.e., private sectors, civil society organizations and personal voluntary entities. Cases from Yogyakarta, Sragen, Jembrana, Tanah Datar and Surakarta provide many evidences of this, so do cases from a number of reforming ministries, which are as follows:

- Current regent of Bantaeng and former regent of Jembrana have made collaboration with a Japan-based multinational corporation to implement local development.
- Before many of today's local governments extensively being certified in quality management, former regent Wiyono from Sragen, for instance, used to have close cooperation with Sucofindo International Certification Services to enhance its public service quality until it was certified as ISO 9001:2008.
- MAR (n.d.) has had close collaboration for reform strategies with various development partners such as the German Gesellschaft für Internationale Zusammenarbeit, Korea International Cooperation Agency, Japan International Cooperation Agency, United States Agency for International Development, Australian Department for Foreign Affairs and Trade (formerly managed by Australian Agency for International Development) and national leading civil society organizations (CSOs) such as Kemitraan, a former trustee of United Nations Development Programme (UNDP), and Yappika, a former trustee of Canadian International Development Agency. In 2008, the ministry was supported by alliance with a number of CSOs to draft and propose the Bill of Public Service (UU Pelayanan Publik), namely Masyarakat Peduli Pelayanan Publik (MP3, Society Supporting Public Service), thanks to good faith and openness of the deputy minister for public service of MAR to get along with CSOs. The MP3 also helped the ministry to lobby some of potential reformist legislators to give political support in the parliamentary legislation process.

- Since the beginning of driving the second wave of bureaucracy reform within the MoF, former minister Sri Mulyani asked at least the following three faculties at Universitas Indonesia to conduct research in different topics: the faculty of psychology to conduct research concerning human resource development and work behavior; the faculty of economics to conduct research concerning customer perception and service management and the faculty of social and political sciences to conduct research concerning re-engineering public service delivery in the areas of tax and custom and public expenditure management.
- Since 2011, the MoHA has initiated the aforementioned Indonesian Transformation Forum in collaboration with Rajawali Foundation and Harvard Kennedy School of Government, established under a programme 'Harvard Executive Education', in which selected mayors and regents are invited to participate in this rigorous programme to consolidate reformist leaders in knowledge exchange and mutual cooperation for further bureaucracy reforms and innovation.
- In 2001, the Ministry of Justice and Human Rights (MJHR) established an information technology-based 'Sisminbakum' – later developed as Administration System for Legal Entities to encourage an easier way for corporations to obtain legal status. Since there was sufficient funding to build such system, MJHR developed the system in collaboration with its counterpart, the Sarana Rekatama Dinamika Inc. under public private partnership with scheme of build-operate-transfer. It was mentioned in the memorandum of agreement that all profits earned from registration through the new system would be shared between the two parties until 2010, for after 2010 the system would belong to MJHR.

CONCLUSION

The complicated, uncertain and ambiguous system, and practical experiences of public sector reform in changing the Indonesian state have shown that reform progress is very much determined by leadership and institutional capacity. It is true that public demands of public sector reform are quite high, but these are spread over fragmented issues, from modest service delivery re-engineering to preventing corruption. This has to some extent caused confusion in the public sector reform priorities, and support for reform was going to be weaker than when the actual problem occurred. Besides, attempting examination of state reforms under central–local relations, rising local leadership and institutional capacity building to consolidate reform efforts over various elements in society, including empowering civil society organizations, are also crucial to be considered.

A key take-away from the Indonesian case is that along with institutional rearrangement that drives successful sustainable reform, no matter the locus of reform taking place at different levels of government, champion leaders are those who are managing knowledge and cascading strategic reform ideas to be internalized at their subordinate levels and constituents amidst the changing politico-administrative system. Leaders, especially at executive levels, are about to become central so that people put their hopes on them to cope with their problems. It is true that both national and political transformation during democratization has led Indonesia to implement new check and balance mechanisms that tend to weigh legislative heavier than executives as an antithesis to the former authoritarian regime. However, rather than merely attempting examination of the state reform under executive–legislative frictions or central–local relations, the rising local leadership and institutional capacity building to consolidate reform efforts over various elements in society, including empowering civil society organizations, are more crucial to take into consideration. Thus, with strengthened legitimacy for the executives to take greater roles in the government, along with its precondition established since the early stage of reform, leadership has a crucial role to determine progress of reform.

In order to cope with the complicated, uncertain and ambiguous changing Indonesian state, political management is actually undertaken by reformist leaders to reconcile with pros and counterparties through moderation between achieving normative bureaucracy reform goals and ensuring gain of personal benefits. The transactional approach between leaders and their subordinates/constituents will be inevitable. It is not a matter of how a leadership style is carried out but to what extent is the importance of reform perceived by their subordinates/constituents, as well as democratization process and reform atmosphere. Cases in local governments have also affirmed this pragmatic leadership style differentiation based on contextual situations, since even patronages were committed by reformist leaders to cascade reform ideas as well as cope with inner and external challenging environments.

REFERENCES

Andrew, M., Pritchett, L., & Woolcock, M. (2012). *Escaping capability traps through problem driven iterative adaptation (PDIA)*. CID Working Paper No. 240 (June), Harvard University, Massachusetts.

Ashshiddiqie, J. (2003). Struktur ketatanegaraan Indonesia setelah perubahan keempat uud tahun 1945 (Constitutional structure of Republic of Indonesia after the fourth amendment of constitution 1945). Paper presented at seminar of Indonesian Law Development, Badan Pembinaan Hukum Nasional RI, Denpasar.

Aspinal, E., & Fealy, G. (Eds.). (2003). *Local power in politics in Indonesia: Decentralization and democratization*. Singapore: Institute of Southeast Asian Studies.

Basri, M. C. (2013). *The second east Asian miracle?: Political economy of Asian responses to the 1997/98 and 2008/09 crises (A tale of two crises): Indonesia's political economy*. JICA-RI Working Paper 57 (March), JICA Research Institute, Shinjuku-ku. Retrieved from http://jicari.jica.go.jp/publication/assets/JICA-RI_WP_No.57_2013. Accessed on February 3, 2015.

Benington, J., & Moore, M. H. (2010). *Public value: Theory & practice*. Basingstoke: Palgrave Macmillan.

Bertelsmann Stiftung. (2012). *Bertelsmann transformation index 2012: Indonesia country report*. Gütersloh.

Bertelsmann Stiftung. (2014). *Transformation index BTI 2014*. Retrieved from http://www.bti-project.de/reports/buch-bti-report/. Accessed on June 22.

Bulan, W. R. (2014). Local *reform in Solo city on Jokowi's era (2005–2012)*: Action reform of agent to face structural challenge in case of arrangement street vendor and resetlement banks of the Bengawan solo. *Makalah disampaikan pada Asia Pacific Sociological Association (APSA) conference "Transforming societies: Contestations and convergences in Asia and the Pacific"*, Chiang Mai, Thailand, February, 15–16. Retrieved from http://rcsd.soc.cmu.ac.th/web/apsa2014/download.php?filename=paper-Wahidah%20R% 20Bulan. Accessed on July 11, 2014.

Chalid, H., Mursitama, T., Hariyati, D., & Prianto, S. I. (2012). *Inovasi pelayanan publik di era otonomi daerah: cerita sukses di Purbalingga, Makassar, dan Banjar Baru (Public service innovation in local autonomy era: Success Stories from Purbalinga, Makassar, and Banjar Baru)*. Jakarta: Indonesian Society for Transparency (MTI).

Crawford, G. & Hermawan, Y. P. (2002). Whose agenda? 'Partnership' and international assistance to democratization and governance reform in Indonesia. *Contemporary South East Asia*, 24(2), 203–229.

Dwiyanto, A. (2004). Administrative reforms: What should be done? How?: The case of Indonesia. Paper presented to international seminar entitled "Indonesia: Challenges in the 21st century civil society, administrative culture, and governance issues", Jakarta, September 28.

Effendi, S. (2011). *The pressing need for reform: The provincial civil service*. PGSP Policy Issues, Paper No. 2 (May), UNDP, Jakarta. Retrieved from http://www-wds.worldbank.org/external/default/WDSContentServer/WDSP/IB/2012/03/26/000356161_20120326010532/Rendered/INDEX/676530WP0P11960sing0need0for0reform.txt. Accessed on August 23, 2014.

Eko, S. (2008). *Daerah budiman: Prakarsa and inovasi lokal membangun kesejahteraan (Good municipalities: Local initiatives and innovation to build prosperity)*. IRE's Insight, Working Paper, Eko III, February 2008, Institute for Research and Empowerment (IRE), Yogyakarta. Retrieved from http://web.iaincirebon.ac.id/ebook/moon/Social-Welfare/wp_sutoro3. Accessed on August 21, 2014.

Hamudy, I. A. (2010). Negosiasi dalam reformasi pemerintahan daerah. *Bisnis & Birokrasi: Journal Ilmu Administrasi dan Organisasi, 17*(2, January–April), 52–60. ISSN 0854-3844. Retrieved from http://journal.ui.ac.id/index.php/jbb/article/viewFile/626/611. Accessed on July 8, 2013.

Hill, H. (2014). *Is there a Southeast Asian development model?* In G. G. Schulze (Ed.), Discussion *Series Paper*, 26 (January), Freiburg: Department of International Economic Policy, University of Freiburg.

Holidin, D. (2007). Reformasi dan inovasi pemerintahan daerah dalam pembangunan regional di Indonesia (Local government reform and innovation in regional development in Indonesia). *ALIANSI, 37*(41, August–September), 2–4 (YAPPIKA, Jakarta and USC, Canada).

Holidin, D. (2016). Perkembangan Aktual reformasi birokrasi (Actual progress of bureaucracy reform). In D. Holidin, D. Hariyati, & E. S. Sunarti (Eds.), *Reformasi birokrasi dalam transisi (Bureaucracy reform in transition)* (pp. 13–28). Jakarta: Prenada Media Group.

Holidin, D., & Hariyati, D. (2012). *Dilema partisipasi lokal di daerah hasil pemekaran: Studi di daerah kepulauan (Dilemma of local participation in post-proliferated new municipalities: Studies in archipelagic municipalities)*. Jakarta: Universitas Indonesia Press.

Holidin, D., Layuk Allo, E. D., Pramusinto, A., Rahardjo, B., & Litaay, T. (2014). *Position paper on bureaucracy reform continuation* (in Bahasa Indonesia). Jakarta: Partnership for Governance Reform and Reform the Reformers – Continuation.

Hukumonline.com. (2011). *E-procurement, cara pengadaan bersih dari korupsi (E-procurement, a corruption-free method for procurement)*. Retrieved from http://www.hukumonline.com/berita/baca/lt4d528527af17c/ieprocurementi-cara-pengadaan-bersih-dari-korupsi. Accessed on August 22, 2014.

Isra, S. (2008). Korupsi and desentralisasi korupsi (Corruption and decentralizing corruption). Paper presented at the public discourse on "Decentralizing corruption: A complicated local autonomy?" (in Bahasa), PuKAT (Anti-corruption studies), Universitas Gadjah Mada and House of Regional Representatives (DPD) Republic of Indonesia, Yoyakarta, November 26. Retrieved from http://lib.ugm.ac.id/digitasi/upload/785_MU0906018.pdf. Accessed on August 18, 2014.

Jabarprov.go.id. (2012). Heryawan serahkan 73 SK program rasionalisasi PNS (Heryawan conveyed 73 decisions of civil servant rationalization). Retrieved from http://jabarprov.go.id/index.php/news/4618/Heryawan_Serahkan_73_SK_Program_Rasionalisasi_PNS. Accessed on August 21, 2014.

Katharina, R. (2013). Reformasi administrasi melalui perampingan organisasi birokrasi. In *Info Singkat: Pemerintahan Dalam Negeri* (Vol. V, No. 05/I/P3DI/Maret/2013). Jakarta: Secretariat General of House of Representative (DPR) Republic of Indonesia. Retrieved from http://berkas.dpr.go.id/pengkajian/files/info_singkat/Info%20Singkat-V-5-I-P3DI-Maret-2013-13.pdf. Accessed on August 21, 2014.

Kersting, N., Caulfield, J., Nickson, R. A., Olowu, D., & Wollman, H. (2009). *Local governance reform in global perspective*. Wiesbaden: VS Verlag für Sozialwissenschaften.

Klitgaard, R. (1991). *Controlling Corruption*. Oakland, CA: University of California Press.

Kurniawan, T. (2011). Democratic decentralization and corruption in Indonesia: Why decentralization has caused head of regions affected by corruption cases. Paper presented at the 2011 conference on "Decentralization and democratization in Southeast Asia", held by the Freiburg Southeast Asia Study Group, University of Freiburg, Freiburg, Germany, June 15–17. Retrieved from http://www.researchgate.net/profile/Teguh_Kurniawan/publication/216899479_DEMOCRATIC_DECENTRALIZATION_AND_CORRUPTION_IN_INDONESIA_Why_Decentralization_has_Caused_Head_of_Regions_Affected_by_Corruption_Cases/links/049498630dd33b11b40df204.

Kurtz, J., & van Zorge, J. (2013). Waiting for Indonesian leadership. *The Wall Street Journal*, April 6, 2013. Retrieved from http://www.atkearney.com/documents/10192/1178190/3162240280369(1).pdf/bd2edda3-cde8-45a3-8c1f-8c864c115fb5#!. Accessed on August 11, 2014.

Layanan Pengadaan secara Elektronik (LPSE). (2010). *Sejarah: Beberapa sistem e-procurement pemerintah (History: Some of government e-procurement system in Indonesia)*. Retrieved from http://lpse.blogdetik.com/sejarah/. Accessed on August 23, 2014.

Majeed, R. (2012). *Defusing a volatile city, igniting reforms: Joko widodo and surakarta, Indonesia, 2005–2011. Innovation for successful society*. Princeton, NJ: Princeton University.

Retrieved from http://www.princeton.edu/successfulsocieties/content/data/policy_note/ PN_id199/Policy_Note_ID199. Accessed on April 14, 2013.

Malut Post. (2012). *PABN membentuk aparatur bermoral agamis (PABN created religious moralist apparatus)*. *Malut Post*, December 21, pp. 19. Retrieved from http://issuu.com/malutpost/ docs/malut_post__21_desember_2012/19. Accessed on August 20, 2014.

Mietzner, M. (2015). Indonesia: Democratic consolidation and stagnation under yudhoyono, 2004–2014. In W. Case (Ed.), *Routledge handbook of Southeast Asian democratization* (pp. 370–383). New York, NY: Routledge.

Ministry of Administrative Reform. (n.d.). *Dasar hukum pelaksanaan reformasi birokrasi (Legal basis for bureaucracy reform implementation)*. Retrieved from http://www.menpan.go. id/kedeputian-reformasi-birokrasi/529-dasar-hukum. Accessed on August 23, 2014.

Ministry of Finance. (2010). *Gebrakan dari Lapangan Banteng (A breakthrough from Lapangan Banteng)*. Retrieved from http://www.reform.depkeu.go.id/mainmenu.php?module=news& id=25. Accessed on August 22, 2013.

Muslim, M. A., Miftahul Jannah, L., Sakapurnama, E., & Hariyati, D. (2012). *Peran kepemimpinan dalam reformasi birokrasi di Kota Yogyakarta (Roles of leadership in bureaucracy reform in Yogyakarta City)*. Depok: Universitas Indonesia Press.

Pepinsky, T. B. (2009). *Economic crisis and the breakdown of authoritarian regimes: Indonesian and Malaysia in comparative perspective*. New York, NY: Cambridge University Press.

Pranadji, T. (2008). Membedah Gorontalo sebagai calon 'bintang timur' pertanian Indonesia di Abad 21 (Revealing Gorontalo as a 'rising star' prospectus in Indonesian agriculture in 21st century. *Analisis Kebijakan Pertanian, 6*(3, September), 222–238. Retrieved from http://pse.litbang.deptan.go.id/ind/pdffiles/ART6-3b. Accessed on August 10, 2014.

Prasojo, E. (2009). *Reformasi kedua: Melanjutkan estafet reformasi (The second reform: Continuing reform wave)*. Jakarta: Penerbit Salemba.

Prasojo, E., & Holidin, D. (2013). *Making reform happen (MRH) in Southeast Asia: Comparative analysis between Southeast Asia and Korea: Public administration since 1997 Asian financial crisis*. Paper presented in the MRH policy workshop, Korea Research Institute, the University of New South Wales, Siem Reap, September 4–7.

Prasojo, E., & Holidin, D. (2018). Leadership and management development: The Indonesian experience. A. Hirose Nishihara, M. Matsunaga, I. Nonaka, K. Yokomichi (Eds.). *Knowledge Creation in Public Administrations* (pp. 237–256). Palgrave Macmillan: Cham. DOI https://doi.org/10.1007/978-3-319-57478-3_11.

Prasojo, E, Kurniawan, T., & Hasan, A. (2004). *Reformasi birokrasi dalam praktek: Kasus di jembrana*. Jakarta: TIFA Foundation.

Prasojo, E., Kurniawan, T., & Holidin, D. (2007a). *State reform in Indonesia*. Depok: Administrative Sciences Department, Universitas Indonesia.

Prasojo, E, Kurniawan, T., & Holidin, D. (2007b). *Reformasi dan Inovasi birokrasi: Studi di kabupaten sragen*. Jakarta: Yappika and Administrative Sciences Department, Universitas Indonesia.

Prasojo, E, Kurniawan, T., & Holidin, D. (2008). *Memetakan inovasi pemerintahan daerah di kota tarakan*. Unpublished research report, Yappika, Jakarta.

Prasojo, E., Perdana, A., & Hiqmah, N. (2006). *Kinerja pelayanan publik (Public Service Performance)*. Jakarta: YAPPIKA.

Prihantika, I., & Hardjosukarto, S. (2011). The causal map of the mayor's policies on regional competitiveness. *Bisnis & Birokrasi: Journal of Administrative Sciences & Organization, 18*(1, January–April), 74–87.

Rinaldi, T., Purnomo, M., & Damayanti, D. (2007). *Fighting corruption in decentralized Indonesia: Case studies on handling local government corruption*. The Local Government Corruption Study (LGSC). Retrieved from http://www-wds.worldbank.org/external/default/WDSContentServer/WDSP/IB/2008/05/14/000333037_20080514022211/Rendered/PDF/436410WP0Box321uption0LGCS01PUBLIC1.pdf. Accessed on August 18, 2014.

Rohdewold, R. (2003). Decentralization and the Indonesian bureaucracy: Major changes, minor impact? In E. Aspinal & G. Fealy (Eds.), *Local power and politics in Indonesia: Decentralization and democratization* (pp. 259–274). Singapore: ISEAS.

Savirani, A. (2013). Paradoks praktik inovasi pemerintahan yang baik di kabupaten Sragen (Innovative governance paradox in practice in Sragen municipality). *Analisis CSIS, 42* (1, March), 86–108.

Scharff, M., Majeed, R., & Iyer, D. (2012). *Menerapkan aturan dan akuntabilitas: Standar operasional prosedur di kementerian keuangan Republik Indonesia, 2006–2007* (*Enforcing law and accountability: Standard Operational Procedure in Ministry of Finance – Republic of Indonesia 2006–2007*). Retrieved from http://www.princeton.edu/successfulsocieties/research/translated-cases/Indonesia_RM_SOP.txt. Accessed on August 23, 2014.

Touchton, M. (2015). Trapping the tigers: Regulation of market entry and the rule of law in SE Asia. *The Social Science Journal, 52*, 8–21.

Transparency International. (2013). *Korupsi PBJ, Kasus Terbesar di Indonesia (Corruption in procurement, the biggest case in Indonesia)*. Retrieved from http://ti.or.id/index.php/news/2013/07/18/korupsi-pbj-kasus-terbesar-di-indonesia. Accessed on August 22, 2014.

Triwibowo, D., Muhajir, M., & Mutasya, T. (2010). *Perluasan inovasi kebijakan sosial di tingkat lokal: Studi kasus kebijakan kesehatan (Widening innovation of social policy at local level: A case of health policy)*. Policy Paper. Jakarta: Perkumpulan Prakarsa. Retrieved from http://kellogg.nd.edu/publications/workingpapers/WPS/150. Accessed on December 5, 2012.

Weiser, S. E. T. (2008). *A review of select policies of the Indonesian Ministry of Industry*. Working Paper of Senada – Indonesia Competitiveness Program, USAID, March.

Widianingsih, I. (2005). *Local governance, decentralization, and participatory planning in Indonesia: Seeking a new path to a harmonious society*. Paper presented in network of Asia-Pacific Schools and Institutes of Public Administration and Governance (NAPSIPAG) annual conference on "The role of public administration in building a harmonious society", Beijing, China, December 5–7. Retrieved from http://www.ehs.unu.edu/file/get/9998. Accessed on August 11, 2014.

World Bank. (2006a). *Inovasi di daerah: Prakarsa baru bagi Kota Solok (Innovation in municipalities: New initiatives for Solok City)*. Jakarta: World Bank and the Partnership for Governance Reform in Indonesia. Retrieved from http://www.kemitraan.or.id/sites/default/files/Inovasi. Accessed on August 11, 2014.

World Bank. (2006b). *Inovasi pelayanan pro-miskin: Sembilan studi Kasus di Indonesia*. Jakarta: World Bank Jakarta Office.

World Bank. (2016). Data: Indonesia. Retrieved from http://data.worldbank.org/country/indonesia. Accessed on March 8, 2016.

World Economic Forum. (2015). *The global competitiveness report 2015–2016*. Geneva: The World Economic Forum.

Yunairi, R. (2011). People-oriented approach in rearranging traditional market and street vendor towards a livable city, Solo, Indonesia. In European Union. Best Practices: *Non-state actors and local authorities in development: actions in partner countries (multi-country) for non-state actors.* DELGOSEA (the Partnership for Democratic Local Governance in Southeast Asia), (Volume 4, June, pp. 17–50). http://delgosea.eu/cms/Best-Practices/ Thematic-Area-4-Fiscal-Management-and-Investment-Planning/14-Humane-Relocation-and-Empowerment-of-Street-Vendors, accessed October 15, 2014.

Zuhriyanti, E., Darumurti, A., & Rahmawati, D. E. (2012). *Kepemimpinan transformatif dalam inovasi pemerintah di pemerintahan Kota Yogyakarta di era herry zudianto (Transformational leadership in local government innovation in Yogyakarta City).* Working Paper No. 001/JKSG/2012, JK School of Government,Yogyakarta. Retrieved from http://mip.umy.ac.id/phocadownload/Working_Paper/kepemimpinan%20transformatif% 20dalam%20inovasi%20pemerintah%20di%20pemerintahan%20kota%20yogya-karta%20era%20kepemimpinan%20herry%20zudianto. Accessed on August 11, 2014.

CHAPTER 4

LEADERSHIP AND PUBLIC SECTOR REFORM IN CHINA

Jiang Wu and Shao Jingjun

ABSTRACT

This chapter discusses how China's rapid economic development since the 1970s has involved three different periods of administrative reform, stretching out over seven successive five-year plans. The author focusses on leadership style, specifically, the thinking that is expected from leaders in each period of leadership for development, open leadership and innovative leadership. The author discusses that leadership for these reforms comes from the highest levels, the Communist Party of China (CPC), as articulated by successive secretary generals of the CPC, that the purpose of reform is not only to achieve policy goals but also to uphold CPC leadership in China, and that public managers throughout China are assessed by the party as well as the government. The author also provides an excellent case of reform anti-corruption leadership that shows how the CPC deals with complex and entrenched issues through education and strict implementation, leading to punishment of 1.2 million people, including senior officials. The case shows well senior officials setting the general direction, preserving the role of the CPC, achieving results, learning through

Leadership and Public Sector Reform in Asia
Public Policy and Governance, 85–102
Copyright © 2018 by Emerald Publishing Limited
All rights of reproduction in any form reserved
doi:10.1108/S2053-769720180000030004

practice and innovation, trends towards increasing the rule of law, and the use of audits.

Keywords: Economic development; administrative reform; Communist Party of China; China

Chinese leadership emphasizes the leadership of the party and the country, especially the governing ability of the Communist Party of China (CPC) and the ability of all levels of government to further the development and construction of society. Throughout recent history, China has experienced many changes and challenges that include opening up and transitioning to a market economy, achieving unprecedented economic growth and experiencing strains on society and natural resources. Historical changes always challenges leaders' abilities, and these challenges have often triggered a crisis in leaders' abilities, requiring new comprehensive theoretical thinking and practical exploration, leading to new policies and leaders' increased abilities, and providing a stage to produce new talented leaders. This chapter discusses the seven periods of administrative reforms since 1982, changes in Chinese leadership in public sector reform (from leadership for development to open leadership and now innovative leadership), the case of anti-corruption leadership and concluding thoughts on the development of Chinese leadership.

The main feature of China's political system and the state governance system is to uphold the CPC's leadership. Chinese governmental organs comprise the Central State Council and local people's governments at various levels. The leading group of China's state governance system is composed of the leading members of Party committees, discipline inspection commissions, people's congresses, governments, political consultative conferences, courts, procuratorates and public service sectors at central and local levels and those of the functional departments or organizations of party committees, governments, people's congresses as well as those of various democratic parties. Leading cadres report on their work to party committees at various levels and their organizational departments. In China, most officials are the members of the CPC, which supervises the performance of officials, including their promotion and inspection.

In a general and fundamental sense, Marxist philosophy is the outlook and method that is the ideological theory foundation of leadership construction in China. Philosophical thinking is the essence and core of a leader's comprehensive quality. Higher-level leaders articulate the overall direction, and to improve leadership is to improve the ability to learn and apply Marxist philosophy. To lead any group is to also help its group members improve the application of philosophy, for example, by improving thinking of unity and opposite, dialectical universal principle, dynamic perspective of development and think problems from different angles, they can strengthen effective communication and cooperation with each other. The next section is built on this understanding.

1. SEVEN REFORMS OF THE CHINESE ADMINISTRATIVE SYSTEM AND ITS DEVELOPMENT

Since the 1970s or the 1980s, administrative reforms have been a strong and irresistible world trend, showing at times unprecedented force, range and depth. Such reforms have also occurred in China, and the Chinese government carried out seven centralized reforms of the administrative system in 1982, 1988, 1993, 1998, 2003, 2008 and 2013 – basically, reforms that are carried out every five years.

The main aim of the administrative reform of 1982 was to improve the work efficiency of the government and recruit more young people. The key points of the reform were as follows: First, to abolish lifelong tenure of the leaders; second, laying off the leading teams at all levels and third, recruiting more young people to work in the government. The aim of the administrative reform in 1988, focussing on the transformation of government function, was to weaken the functions of the specialized economic departments, including their roles in distributing money and materials and directly intervening in companies' operation. The focus shifted on strengthening macroeconomic control of the government and increasing industrial (sectoral) management. The historical contribution of this reform was putting forward the idea that changing the government's functions (roles) was the key objective of administrative reform.

The administrative reform in 1993 first put forward that its aim was to adapt to the establishment of a socialist-based market economic system. The key point of this reform was to adapt to the demands of the market economic system, changing government functions (roles), separating government functions from enterprise management, straightening out issues in the relationship between government and enterprises, simplifying administrative structures and improving their efficiency. However, the most important contribution was the change in government functions.

The aim of the administrative reform in 1998 was to change government functions. However, the focus was to optimize the structure of governmental organizations, including strengthening the functions of macroeconomic departments, adjusting and reducing the functions of specialized economic departments, properly adjusting the functions of social service departments, strengthening the functions of law enforcement departments and developing social intermediary organizations. The administrative reform of 1988 was far-reaching, involving many aspects and depth, and the historic achievement was that it achieved great progress in changing government functions. Almost all specialized economic departments were revoked (abolished), and those that did not separate government from enterprises were weakened to a great extent.

The goal of government institutional restructuring 2003 was to deepen the reform of the administrative management system and further transform government functions. This restructuring campaign was launched in the context of China's accession to the World Trade Organization (WTO), and it made clear that government functions should focus on economic regulation, market supervision, social management and public services, aiming to build a just and transparent, hardworking and efficient, honest, upright and clean government that would follow a well-defined code of conduct. A major breakthrough in the institutional restructuring of 2003 was the identifying and linking of prominent problems of the then social and economic development stage with the transformation of government functions.

The aim of the administrative reform of 2008 was to deepen the reforms of the administrative management system and improve the governmental functioning of public services. The key points of this reform were as follows: First, to strengthen and improve macroeconomic control and promote scientific development; second, to focus on protecting and improving people's livelihoods, and strengthening social management and public service; third, to integrate departments whose functions were nearly the same, to set up comprehensive organizations and to figure out the relationship of functions among departments according to the requirements of unifying the functions. The aim of this administrative reform was not to reduce staff or organizations but to relate governmental management ability to corresponding responsibilities and emphasizing service functions. Compared with prior administrative reforms, this reform made great progress in public administration systems.

The goal of the 2013 government institutional restructuring was to collaboratively advance streamlining of administration and delegating powers while strengthening regulation and optimizing services to encourage and promote public entrepreneurship and innovation. Specifically, it included improving and strengthening government administration, boosting the effectiveness of the government, enhancing the legally compliant and comprehensive performance of governmental duties so as to have the market and society activated, and developing in a normal way and promoting sustain-able sound economic development and social justice; further straightening up the relationship between the government and the market, giving priority to the construction of law-based, duties- and services-oriented government, and upholding the principle of delegating authority and power by laws and speeding up the establishment of 'three lists' so as to make clear the authority and responsibility between the government and the market, enterprises and society. Among the 'three lists', the list of powers defines what the govern-ment can do (i.e., 'not performing any duties beyond legal authorization'), the list of responsibilities clarifies how the government can regulate the market (including 'statutory duties that must be done' by the government), and the negative list shows constraints on enterprises, including that 'enterprises can do anything as long as not being prohibited by laws'. Finally, it is held that a government with modern ability can be achieved by defining the 'three lists', controlling legally the 'visible hand', making good use of 'invisible hand' and blocking the 'rent-seeking hand behind the scenes'.

In sum, the content of reforms during the past 30 years reflects the domi-nant policy of the party at different times and the requirements of economic reforms. These reforms can also be roughly divided into three different periods of institutional restructuring: First, streamlining administration, focussing on the number of departments and the size of their staff. Second, chang-ing governmental functions (roles), specifically to adjust the relationships of the government with the society, the market and enterprises and between the central government and the local authorities. Third, enhancing governing capacity to rationalize the relationship between the economic functions and public service functions of the government, between different governmental departments, and strengthening the government's own ability to respond to globalization and deepened government restructuring. The specific reforms show both breakthroughs in these aspects and successive deepening and broadening. It can be said that administrative reforms almost kept up pace with deepening reforms of the economic system and with developments in the economy and the society. The following sections discuss leadership that roughly reflects these three periods.

2. LEADERSHIP OF REFORM I: ADVANCING THE DEVELOPMENT

At the early stage of the reform and opening up, the Chinese government faced the first crisis of leadership. Owing to long-standing problems over overlap between the functions of the party and the government, and between the functions of the government and enterprises, the leadership of the government was seriously weakened. Administrative reform at the time was required to establish evidence-based sound teams and professional leading groups, making the leading teams younger, more professional and more intelligent for tackling the structural crises, dealing with problems in the reform to instruct and lead in economic and social development.

Therefore, at the beginning of the reform, the Chinese government emphasized that the leading groups at all levels must act according to 'scientific laws', finding out and solving new reform problems in a timely way and grasping opportunities to promote the development and the ability to control the market economy. The leadership emphasized on the following three factors: the ability to lead development, the ability to adapt to the market economy, and the ability of making scientific (objective and fact-based) and democratic decisions (in China, the phrase 'democratic decision' means decisions that are made, reviewed and supervised by representatives selected by people in a democratic way).

First, the most important ability to lead development is to lead economic as well as political, social and cultural development. Such leadership requires adopting a scientific outlook on development and setting forth a correct view of its achievement, in a comprehensive way, putting the idea and practice of economic construction at the centre while also establishing a people-oriented concept, coordinating all aspects of sustainable development, and trying to build a well-off and harmonious society in all aspects (i.e., economic, political, social and cultural aspects). Leading groups of the party committee at all levels grasp the direction, plan the overall situation, put forward strategies, promote legislation and create a good environment for efforts. Leading groups of the government at all levels have had to adapt and transform their functions, improving their ability of combining market-based means with administrative means, increasing legal administration, increasing scientific development and showing their ability to build a harmonious society.

Second, leadership in adapting to the market economy is based on the respect for the rule of the market economic development, according to the internal requirements of the market economic development and utilizing more market-based means for adjusting (regulating and guiding) the economy. Thus, leaders had to study the fundamental theory of a market economy and learn how to utilize market-based means to adjust the economy, finding the motivation of proper interest in a smart way and use economic and legal means to instruct people's behaviours. Their efforts had to reflect all this.

Third, leadership in making scientific and democratic decisions involves leaders making decisions according to scientific, democratic and legal principles and rules and ensuring that these decisions meet scientific, democratic and legal standards. To this end, leaders first needed to adopt a 'correct' view of using their power, that is, furthering the interest of the people, enhancing leaders' sense of responsibility of using power to serve people, caring about people and doing something good for the people. Second, leaders needed to follow regulations and procedures for making decisions truly based on science and democracy, ensuring that they collect public opinions through various methods, making the best of think tanks, and using scientific theories and thinking modes in making decisions. Third, leaders were required to make sure that decisions are legitimate, including public policies that had to be made in accordance with law. All these aspects are emphasized in the China's leadership of development.

3. THE LEADERSHIP OF REFORM II: 'OPEN LEADERSHIP' TO ADVANCE WITH THE TIMES

Since the 1990s, economic globalization has swept the world inevitably, and it has changed the administrative environment of the government a lot. The Chinese government faced the second crisis of leadership; with the deep development of reform and opening up, the government had to not only grasp complicated internal changes but also positively deal with international changes. The government needed to broaden its horizon and build an open and intelligent leadership. While governmental systems of leading had improved, the government also faced constantly new challenges, contradictions and crises. Therefore, the Chinese government required the leaders to 'change with the times' when they faced changes and challenges, requiring them to adopt a view of the world with a broad horizon, grasp the correct requirements of the times, think in theoretical and strategic angles, study a lot and liberate thoughts, and practice and innovate more. In China, open leadership focusses on the following several factors: open international horizon, sense of times, systematic theoretical thinking and strategic thinking that can grasp the overall situation.

The first factor is to have and adapt to an open international horizon. It requires leaders, in a globalization regulation system and political environment, to introspect their own leadership comprehensively, find out the differences, figure out the cause and effect and put forward measures, broaden international horizon, centralize international wisdom and learn from international experiences. Since the reform and opening up, Deng Xiaoping emphasized for many times that leaders should look at the world, look at the future and look at all aspects. What he said over and over again was that as China couldn't develop in isolation from the rest of the world, the most important thing was that the horizon should be broadened, the bosom should be opened and that the biggest experiences could never come from isolating ourselves from the rest of the world. It requires leaders to grasp the international economic and political trend, judge the situation in scientific ways, consider the current situation and overcome various risks and difficulties.

The second factor is to have the sense of time. This requires leaders to quickly grasp changes in the world and the time, which, in turn, involves combining the world with China, and combining history with reality when making judgements. Adapting to the times requires leaders to change, to liberate their thoughts, forging ahead with determination, break the routine and keep on exploring and innovating to deal with the problems and contradictions in developing with new ways and thoughts.

The third factor is systematic theoretical thinking. It requires leaders to emphasize theoretical learning, gaining and updating thoughts by systematic and theoretical learning while using instincts and empirical thinking patterns. It also requires leaders to use theories to know the world, analyse problems and instruct practices, grasp the development laws of the world and times, see the essence of problems rather than the surface and utilize dialectical thinking to analyse and solve practical problems comprehensively.

The fourth factor is strategic thinking that can grasp the overall situation, the core ability of leaders to grasp the overall situation scientifically, and to make strategic decisions. Mao Zedong pointed out that directors at all levels should focus their attention on the most important and decisive problems to the overall situation that they command. He wanted leaders of all levels to see things from a wide and strategic perspective rather than a narrow view. He emphasized that any problem should also be considered in the long run and from the overall perspective. For many times, Jiang Zemin had emphasized that leaders should have strategic thinking, think about the overall situation and solve big problems. Xi Jinping also pointed out that the leaders at all the levels should see things from the strategic perspective, judging situations and dealing with problems from a political perspective, strengthening leaders' ability to grasp the overall situation and develop an area from the overall horizon and do great things according to the situation.

4. LEADERSHIP OF REFORM III: 'INNOVATIVE LEADERSHIP'

Against the backdrop of becoming the second largest economy in the world, with per capita gross domestic product substantially increasing to around $7,800, China's development entered a new phase, and people from both home and abroad casted their eyes over China's prospects, strategies and measures for development. The 17th National Congress of the CPC came up with the scientific outlook on development, and the report to the 18th National Congress of the CPC put forward that China's development has entered a new phase, and its reforms have entered a period of overcoming major difficulties. Relatively prominent problems also cropped up in the course of development, including structural imbalance, stagnant social development, imbalanced regional and urban–rural development, expanded income differences, environmental pollution and ecological degradation.

Based on all these, Xi Jinping put forward the concept of innovative, coordinated, green, open and shared development; he further clarified the questions of whom to rely on for development, for whom to develop, how to carry out development, how to straighten up developmental approaches, how to chart the course of development and also noted the major issues of development. The overall objective of deepening all-round reform is to promote the state governance system and modernization of governing capacity. China should focus on more systematic and overall coordinated reforms, and speed up the developing socialist market economy, democratic politics, advanced culture, harmonious society and ecological civilization, so as to give dynamic play to all labour, knowledge, technology, management and capital, allowing the source of social wealth creation to flow fully and ensure that development will bear more fruits and benefits to all people in a more just way.

Against this background, the construction of innovative leadership has become important. In China, innovative leadership includes the following three factors: the ability to face complicated situation and risks, the ability of making overall plans and the ability of innovation. Reform and innovative leadership requires leaders to have the courage and verve of innovation, while also having a sense of progress, opportunity and responsibility, and putting themselves into practice. The current period also sees further strengthening of the rule of law and consultation, which is also discussed here. Innovative leadership needs to be consistent, and follow these too.

The first is the leadership ability of facing complicated situations and risks, requiring leaders who are good at making scientific advanced judgements, preparing for various possible risks, while strengthening abilities for dealing with problems without preparations, and having abilities to change risks into opportunities, and changing a negative position into a positive one. When dealing with such type of contradictions and problems, leaders should also be good at coordinating the interest relations of all classes and communicating with public, and having the ability of solving problems according to the law, policy and reality.

The second leadership ability is the making of overall plans, requiring leaders who are good at concentrating on major issues, discussing major issues, grasping the overall situation, solve the overall, strategic and forward-looking problems, dealing with the relationship between the present and the future, the parts and the overall in a right way, correctly dealing with the relations of reform, development and stability, integrating the force of the reform, the speed of development and the durability of the society, promoting reform and development in the social stability and enhancing social stability through reform and development.

The third is the ability of innovation. This requires leaders who are good at learning, often think, have the courage to face contradictions, tackle difficulties and have an adventurous and innovative spirit. It requires leaders to have the courage and verve of innovation, have adventurous spirit, transcend theory and authority, experience and habits, ego and reality. On the other hand, leaders should have the sense of progress, opportunity and responsibility, put themselves into practice, promote thinking innovation, method innovation, practice innovation and system innovation according to the objective laws of development of things and work innovatively. It requires the leaders to use knowledge and experience to analyse and solve the contradictions and problems existing in work and collect wisdom from all aspects to put forward new thoughts, take new measures and open up a new prospect.

Leadership of reform is never possible in isolation, and the current period also emphasizes strengthening of leadership in ruling by law and increased consultation. General Secretary Xi Jinping emphasized that major reforms must have legal bases and be carried out under law. After 30 years of reform and opening up, public consciousness has increased with respect to democracy and law, as has political involvement and public pursuits of social equality and justice. Decisions made in the Third Plenary Session of the 18th Central Committee of the CPC state that it is essential to simultaneously promote governing the country by law, ruling by law and administration by law, and an integrated construction of the country ruled by law, the government ruled by law and the society ruled by law. Such ruling by law also affects leadership. Leading cadres need to increase their thinking of ruling by law and their ways of ruling by law. It is essential to firmly establish conscious-ness of constitutional supremacy, resolutely safeguard the authority of the constitution and laws, such as thinking of handling problems according to laws, and developing modes of solving problems according to laws. All this is to create a good legal environment of dealing with matters, problems and contradictions according to laws.

Another aspect is leadership by increased consultation. Modern govern-ance emphasizes playing the leading role of leadership by the CPC and exert-ing the effect of several governing subjects (such as government, market and society) in national governance. The modernization of national governance requires leading cadres at all levels to improve governance through consulta-tion. Under the leadership of the CPC, consultation is carried out widely throughout the society before decision-making and during the implementa-tion of any decision. The essence of governance through consultation empha-sizes the utilization of a flexible leading style. In the past, national governance emphasized one-way governance from a high level to a low level as well as control and order, showing a rigid leading style that causes the legality of administration to be doubted and which was often ineffective. With the con-tinuous improvement of a socialist market economy system, current national governance puts increased emphasis on benign interaction, cooperation and mutual benefits and all-embracing among governing subjects. This requires leading cadres to adopt flexible leadership, from comprehensive regulation to governance through consultation, and from emphasizing regulation to emphasizing services, paying more attention to communication, consultation, recognition, guidance and service and improve their own flexible leadership.

Of course, leadership is also present in furthering these aspects. Finally, while the above emphasizes many new and difficult tasks of leadership, there is also emphasis on traditional 'simple leadership' and 'simple ruling'. In the new era of comprehensively deepening reform, the ruling and leading work of the government should be as simple as possible instead of as much as pos-sible. Reform requires the government to streamline administration, delegate power to lower levels, society, market and grassroots and further narrow the range governed by the government. The essence of 'simple ruling' is enabling the leadership of the CPC and the government to take root in general public and grassroots and scatter in society and enterprises through senior leaders who ensure that society and masses are full of energy and power. Simple rul-ing is consistent with the strengthening and improvement of CPC leadership. If organizations have good leadership, the country would automatically have good leadership, and hence state governance system and capacity could be modernized.

5. CASE: ANTI-CORRUPTION LEADERSHIP

Since the birth of state power, corruption has been a haunting reality. In the late 1980s and early 1990s, corruption spiked to unprecedented levels as the Chinese economy gradually shifted from a planned economy to a socialist market economy. Since then, anti-corruption has been a concern for successive leaders. Deng Xiaoping warned the party: 'It is an ill wind and a strong one. Indeed, unless we take it seriously and firmly stop it, the question of whether our Party will change its nature may arise'.[1] Jiang Zemin, general secretary of the CPC, pointed out the following:

> We cannot underestimate the seriousness and harm of corruption, which is like a virus invading the body of the party and state. It will bury our party, our people's regime, and our great cause of socialist modernization if we do not attack it seriously and allow it to spread unchecked.

He further stated: 'We must thoroughly investigate violations of the law and discipline with facts as the basis and the law as the yardstick. Dismissal, sentences and heavy sentences must be imposed if warranted'. In 2012, Xi Jinping stated: 'If corruption becomes increasingly serious, it will inevitably doom the Party and the state!', and

> to fight against corruption, a person's life and death, personal praise or blame, do not matter ... improving the Party's style of work, upholding integrity and combating corruption is a fight we cannot afford to lose and we must fight with determination and win.[2]

Statements and reports draw a broad picture of complex and increased corruption with many examples. Xi Jinping points out as follows:

> Fields such as the management of mineral resources, land transfer, real estate development, construction projects, benefit-the-people funds and scientific research funds are prone to corruption. The problem of leading cadres meddling in construction projects or their relatives or children engaging in business has come to the fore. In some places, cadres even dare to embezzle funds for poverty alleviation, agriculture, health care and minimum living allowance and use the money to pay bribes and buy official positions, turning people's 'life-saving money' into their 'official position buying money'. In developed areas, power is traded for money through construction projects; in poverty-stricken areas, money for poverty alleviation is embezzled.[3]

Region-specific corruption is interwoven with field-specific corruption; corruption in appointing officials and corruption in exercising power go hand in hand. People within the system hook up with people outside the system; power-for-money deals, power-for-sex deals and power-for-power deals coexist and different interests are intricately intertwined to form a 'co-corruption circle'. Violations are found at all levels, from serious violations of the law and discipline committed by 'national-level' officials, such as Zhou Yongkang and Xu Caihou, to widespread violations of law and discipline committed by grassroots cadres. For example, a central leading group for inspection work found that in Heilongjiang province, the buying and selling of official positions was extensive and serious, with farming, forest industry, coal systems, construction and real estate development experiencing frequent violations; some leading cadres were found colluding with businessmen in the cheap selling of state-owned assets, thus providing conveniences for their mistresses, allowing relatives and children to do business within their jurisdictions and taking advantage of weddings and sick relatives to accept gifts and accumulate wealth. In Shanghai, some units in culture, radio and film and TV organizations sold or rented out public properties cheaply; state-owned enterprises, such as land transfer, construction and science and technology, had a high incidence of corruption and leading cadres were seeking personal gains through housing. Such examples are numerous.

In response to such problems, the CPC has successively established rules and increased its efforts. In January 1979, the newly established Central Commission for Discipline Inspection in its first plenary session stressed upon the need for 'strengthening disciplinary education and education on the fine tradition of the Party'. From 1982 to 1987 (12th to 13th National Congress of the CPC), moral cultivation mainly targeted at the unhealthy tendency of some party officials who 'put money above everything else' and those who intended to make fortunes through illegal ways. From 1992 to 1997 (14th to 15th National Congress of the CPC), organizations for discipline inspection organized party cadres at different levels to study socialist theory with Chinese characteristics. After the 16th National Congress of the CPC held in 2002, along with education campaigns on keeping CPC members progressive, innovative and forward-thinking, anti-corruption education and upholding integrity was further strengthened, with the main focus on forming a firm belief, developing correct views on power and abiding by laws and rules.

In 2005, the Central Committee of the CPC launched the Implementation Outline for Establishing and Improving Corruption Prevention and Punishment System with emphasis on education, system building and supervision. Later on, the 2008–2012 work plan on establishing and improving corruption prevention and punishment system was developed. Since the 18th National Congress of CPC, the education on integrity has been strengthened nationwide along with the fight against corruption. Xi Jinping put forward the idea of 'fighting against corruption by legal thoughts and legal methods', in which current efforts are set. The 2013–2017 work plan on establishing and improving the corruption prevention and punishment system was launched, thus establishing and improving the corruption prevention and punishment system as a national strategy and top-down design, stressing systematic advancement in combating corruption and upholding integrity while addressing prominent issues. Many rules and laws have been amended and adopted to improve the party's style of work and to uphold integrity and anti-corruption leadership, thus stressing the importance of severe punishment in corrupt cases, fighting every corrupt phenomenon and punishing every corrupt official. Preventing corruption is also highlighted with the aim to 'dare not to engage in corruption, unable to engage in corruption, and unwilling to engage in corruption'.

Two key aspects of the implementation of anti-corruption leadership are education and inspection. As to education, during the four-year period from 2004 to 2007, over 3,900 special columns on anti-corruption and upholding integrity could be found in newspapers and televisions and radio channels; more than 100,000 relevant articles were published on national or provincial media. In January 2006, the Central Committee of the CPC released regulations on the education and training of cadres, where education on party work style and discipline were the focus. A nationwide campaign on composing and singing songs with anti-corruption and integrity themes was launched, leading to 67,000 new songs and 24,000 singing galas, in which 37 million people participated. Over 20,000 rounds of 'contests' on supervision and disciplinary inspection were held within the party, in which more than 20 million party cadres took part. A number of educational films, such as *Wang Huaizhong* (the dual life of a corrupt official who died in the end), attracted over 20 million audience. The Central Commission for Discipline Inspection of the Central Committee of the CPC opened its website to the public, where officials answered questions from the public. Commissions and organization of discipline inspection at all levels put more emphasis on their websites, adding sections on supervision and tip-off to let the public play a role.

The main approaches of inspecting and dealing with the cases of corruption included finding clues based on people's reports; stressing important and complex cases; strengthening organization and coordination in examining and dealing with cases; and punishing harshly who indulged in corruption, while educating those who made minor mistakes to help correct and avoid future mistakes. From 1979 to 1992, 2.177 million corruption-related cases were registered by organizations for discipline inspection at different levels, and 1.804 million people were punished due to violations. From 1993 to 2007, 2.376 million corruption-related cases were registered, in which 2.333 million people were punished, among which 385,000 were expelled from the party and 181,000 officials were prosecuted for criminal liability (7.8% of the total). The total number of corrupt officials punished has increased since the 18th National Congress of CPC held in 2012. From December 2012 to the end of 2016, 1.162 million cases were registered and 1.199 million people were punished, almost doubling the annual rate, including 223 provincial and ministerial level senior civil servants.

The nature of inspection has changed over time. In the 1980s, the main focus was on cracking down severe economic crimes and correcting the negative trend of bribery and 'harbouring' among officials. In the 1990s, the main target was violation of law and discipline in party and government departments, law enforcement departments, legislation departments, economic management departments and officials above county (division chiefs) level. Inspection focussed on corruption, bribery, embezzlement, smuggling, dereliction of duty, taking bribes, breaking the law and degeneration. Punishment was intensified in the areas of finance, security, real estate, land leasing and building contracting. Since 2000, the main focus was on the abuse of power, bribery and corruption, degeneration and dereliction of duty, seeking personal gains by abusing control over personnel arrangements, judicial power, administrative approval power and administrative enforcement power, cases of collusion between government officials and businessmen and protecting underground gangsters, thus severely harming people's rights. Since 2013, after the 18th National Congress of CPC, anti-corruption leadership has mainly focussed on resolutely dealing with those who continue to be corrupt, those with many complaints of corruption and corrupt officials who have acquired new posts or promotions.

In recent years, China has strengthened international cooperation in the area of anti-corruption leadership. Based on its realities and drawing on positive foreign experiences, China is planning to implement the United Nations protocol on anti-corruption. China has also established and improved work mechanisms on international joint operations, judicial mutual assistance and warning against possible fleeing, repatriation, extradition and retrieval of illegal assets. In January 2014, President Xi Jinping pointed out that

> more efforts should be made in international manhunt, and all departments shall work more actively. We shall not let foreign countries be the safe haven for corrupt officials. No matter where they go, we shall hunt them down for jurisdiction, even if it might take 5 years, 10 years, or even 20 years.

China has also established an anti-corruption law enforcement cooperation mechanism with countries such as the United States, Canada and Australia. The Chinese public security organs have initiated project 'Fox Hunting' to put more emphasis on the inspection of every individual case. From 2014 to 2016, a total of 2,566 corrupt officials at large were arrested, 37 out of China's top 100 fugitives were captured and illegal assets worth 8.64 billion yuan were retrieved.

Inspecting cases of corruption and punishing corrupt officials seek to restore party discipline, educate party cadres and enhance their awareness towards working with integrity. It seeks to build up the prestige of the party and the government, and strengthen people's confidence in anti-corruption leadership. For more than three decades since the reform and opening up, China has been constantly improving its leadership in fighting corruption. A set of code of conduct and ethics, regulating cadres towards clean and honest administration, was initially set up. However, compared with the ever increasing and complicated corrupt atmosphere, leadership in fighting corruption needs continuous improvement, thus requiring strong leadership in both the CCP and the government. The above-mentioned details show many features of Chinese leadership in public administration reforms, such as leadership of senior officials that set general direction, preserving and leading role of the CCP, responding to new or increasing problems in scientific ways, preferences for simple rules and increased trends towards rule of law.

6. DISCUSSION AND CONCLUSION

In the case of China, values are to be placed at the core position of leadership construction. In the leadership construction of our party and government, equal instructions and the core values of service must be dominant. It includes being loyal to the country and people, stick to people-oriented principles, serve people, having firm political faith and strong sense of political responsibility, having the right view of power, position and interest, setting up democratic sense and equal ideas, promoting public interest and welfare etc. China also thinks, in new times, that the party and the government should have the ability of leading and integrating all kinds of thoughts and values, using a socialist core value system to educate and influence all classes, groups and people so as to establish common ideology, wish and dream to become a strong spiritual motivation for whole society.

In China, the core of leadership construction is to improve the leadership of the top leader and the leading group. The top leader, as the monitor of the leading group, is the leading core of the development of a region, department or company. So, the key to the leadership construction is to improve the leadership of the top leading group. In the leadership construction, we should not only pay attention to individual leadership but also emphasize the group's leadership to make one plus one more than two. Therefore, much importance is attached to establishing and improving leaders' educational training system. President Xi pointed out that theory accomplishment is the core of cadres' comprehensive quality, and maturity in theory is the base of maturity in politics. China has built leaders' educational training framework system in which party school, administrative college and cadre academy are the main institutes, and university bases and overseas training organizations are supplementary institutes. Every five years, the Chinese government works out the plan of educating and training national cadres, and conducts educational training for cadres in a large scale at all levels through all channels according to the requirements of development.

In addition, China attaches much importance to establishing and improving leaders' practice system. Practice is seen as an effective way to improve leaders' qualities and ability. Leaders' qualities and ability improvement cannot ignore practice. Cadres should not only strengthen theoretical study, improve party spirit and adhere to the ideals and beliefs but also increase their experiences and practice. Hardships, basic exercises and personal practice are very important for the growth of leaders. Central ministries and provincial, municipal and county organizations organize designed activities especially for young cadres to work at grassroots who have not worked before. At some places, young people are intentionally chosen to work in the areas where the environment is complex and the conditions are difficult. Some people are designated to work as leaders in towns or administrative villages and others are designated to indulge in poverty alleviation work in remote and poor areas.

China attaches much importance to enhancing leadership through innovation. China thinks it must improve a competitive and selective mechanism to establish a system that leaders can be promoted and demoted, employed and fired, so as to motivate leaders to keep improving their quality and ability to adapt to the constant changes of the world that would put forward new requirements to leaders' activity. Much importance is given to reforming a selective system of cadres, improving the evaluation system of leaders, establishing a public supervision system and improving the democratic decision-making system to enhance leadership construction.

NOTES

1. Selected Works of Deng Xiaoping (Vol. 2, 1st ed., October 1998, p. 403). People's Publishing House, China.

2. Xi Jinping's speech at the 5th plenary session of the 18th Central Commission for Discipline Inspection.

3. Excerpts from Xi Jinping's discourse on improving the party's style of work, upholding integrity and combating corruption, p. 99.

CHAPTER 5

LEADERSHIP AND PUBLIC SECTOR REFORM IN THAILAND

Supachai Yavaprabhas

ABSTRACT

Thailand continuously has had administrative reforms in spite of periods of military regime and democratic government. This chapter describes the leadership of administration reforms coming from issue experts and senior civil service officers described as a 'jazz-banded' leadership model of different actors. Political parties pick up reform packages consistent with their policy platforms, while the military looks for ready-to-deliver policy packages. The author discusses the example of education and health care reforms and the role of the Office of Public Sector Development Commission (OPDC). In Thailand, resistance usually occurred during the implantation stage rather than at the formulation stage. The chapter discusses that OPDC initiatives were implemented with bonuses of up to 12-month salary for some senior officers and department heads. In health care, success came from concerted efforts of health care experts who transcend their ideas from one generation to another and who kept convincing politicians running the Ministry of Public Health. However, in other instances, budget allocations may bump up against financial procedures that are detailed and tight due to anti-corruption practices. In education

Leadership and Public Sector Reform in Asia
Public Policy and Governance, 103–126
doi:10.1108/S2053-769720180000030005

reforms, teachers were placed at different school districts that lacked com-
mitment. In the decentralization of reforms, resistance comes from line
ministries wanting to secure their authority, although local authorities are
very active. Resistance often requires negotiation of many parties; rarely
do politicians step in to overcome and assist.

Keywords: Education reform; health care reform;
public sector development Commission; resistance; Thailand

This chapter discusses public sector reforms in Thailand since the 1992
'Black May Day'[1] to the present. It is undeniable that leadership plays a
key role in making public sector reform happen, guaranteeing its further
sustainability and continuity. This chapter, however, argues that, unlike
in Singapore and Malaysia, Thailand's public sector reform for the last
25 years has not been an attempt of any single leader. On the contrary, different players and leaders have been playing their roles in initiating and driving
the reform movements. Cases of decentralization, education reform, reform
of the public health system and reform of the system-wide public administration system are discussed. At the backdrop of the public sector reform is
Thailand's political landscape, which has been steadily changing and is peri-
odically unstable since the country became constitutional democracy in 1932,
and significantly influenced public sector reforms. Politics and public administration in Thailand have been intertwined and one cannot truly understand
Thailand's public sector reform without taking into consideration the background of Thai politics.

PUBLIC SECTOR IN THAILAND

Thailand is at the centre of the inland Southeast Asia, bordered by Myanmar
and Laos in the north, Cambodia in the east, Malaysia in the south, the Gulf
of Thailand in the south and east, and the Andaman Sea in the west. It is the
only country in Southeast Asia to have escaped colonial rule. Its population is
68.1 million as of 2016.[2] The majority of the population are ethnic Thais (96%),
and 95% of the population is Theravada Buddhist.[3] Thailand is a constitutional
monarchy. The military has, however, a history of intervening in politics and has
seized power 12 times since the end of absolute monarchy in 1932. Buddhism,
the monarchy and the military have all been shaping Thai society and politics.

The latest coup happened on 22 May 2014. The interim government first announced a road map leading to elections in 2017. This roadmap has been shifted to the last quarter of 2018 after the promulgation of a new 2017 Constitution on 6 April 2017. In terms of social and economic dimensions, Thailand has become an upper-income economy since 2011 and is likely to meet most of the Millennium Development Goals on an aggregate basis.[4]

On the backdrop of political, economic and social scenes, there is a public sector which has been serving the country for a long time. At present, the public sector comprises 2.19 million public employees with an annual expenditure of around 2.7 trillion baht or US$77,715 million in fiscal year 2016 (see Appendices A and B). These figures are almost four times the figures of 1992, in spite of several efforts to constrain the size of public sector. Public administration in Thailand comprises (1) national or central administration and (2) provincial administration and (3) local administration. At present, there are 20 ministries and 161 departments at the national level. At the provincial level, there are 77 provinces. Within each province, the next tier is *amphoe* (district) and under *amphoe* is *tambon* (sub-district). Currently, there are 878 *amphoe* and 7,255 *tambon* (as on March 2016).[5] Administration at the provincial level and those under it are called provincial administration, which is a part of central or national administration. The head of the provincial administration is a governor appointed by the cabinet and reported to the minister of interior. At the provincial and *tambon* levels, there is a local administration as well. Local administration in Thailand is a two-tier system; one is a provincial administration organization and another is either a municipality or *tambon* administrative organization (TAO). At present (23 March 2017), there are 5,334 TAOs and 2,441 municipalities. There are also two special local administration units: Bangkok Metropolitan Authority and Pattaya City.[6,7] On the one hand, alignment of functions and responsibilities of the provincial administration and local administration, and on the other hand, functions and responsibilities within the local administration level are still relatively unclear. Therefore, proposals for reforming had been discussed and are in process to be considered by the National Reform Steering Assembly.[8]

In addition to ministries and departments, there are also four other types of public sector organizations: public enterprise (PE) or state-owned enterprise, autonomous public organization (APO), special delivery units (SDUs) and office of public funds (OPF). While the Public Enterprise Act has been enacted in 1953, other forms were established in the last 20 years. There are now 67 public enterprises. For APO, it is divided into two categories: those established by their own Acts and others established under the Autonomous Public Organization Act (1999). These are public organizations which are

granted more autonomy compared to regular public agencies. These APOs
are expected to be more efficient in delivering public services. There are now
39 APOs established under the Autonomous Public Organization Act (1999).
SDUs are quasi-autonomous divisions under regular public agencies. At
present, there are only two SDUs and none of them has legislative status.
These SDUs are the Cabinet and Royal Gazette Publishing House, which is
under the purview of the secretariat of the cabinet, and the Institute for Good
Governance Promotion, which is under the purview of the Office of Public
Sector Development Commission (OPDC). The objectives of these units are
to deliver services to their parent organizations. If there are any surplus pro-
ductions, units can deliver the same to other agencies. They have autonomy
in improving their organizational, manpower and salary structure. However,
SDUs need authority delegated from the permanent secretary or the director
general to perform any activities (Lorsuwannarat, 2007). For those under the
category of public funds, they are public organizations which receive annual
budget from the government as stipulated by their own acts. They have their
own autonomy to manage their own organization.[9]

This brief picture of Thailand's public sector has evolved steadily since
the modernization process around a hundred years ago during King Rama V.
(For those who are interested in reading the evolution of the public sector
reform in Thailand, see Bowornwathana, 2011). While big changes in the
Thai public sector did not happen until 1997, it is worth emphasizing that the
political landscape of Thailand has been interrupted with military coups for
12 times since 1932. Every coup was usually followed by the establishment of
a national legislature, which turned state power from the hands of politicians
to public bureaucrats. Major changes in the public sector were initiated during these non-elected governments. It is thus worth exploring the Thai political landscape, which is the backdrop of the Thai public sector reform. Before
delving down to certain changes in the Thai public sector, political landscape,
which is another side of the same coin, will be presented.

THE POLITICAL LANDSCAPE FROM 1992

The 1991 military coup, led by General Sunthorn Kongsompong and
General Suchinda Kraprayoon, appointed Anand Panyarachun, a former permanent secretary and a veteran diplomat as prime minister.
Anand's anti-corruption and straightforward measures, together with
his persuasive leadership, proved popular among the middle class.

During Anand's government, a new constitution was drafted, which was followed by general elections in March 1992. The winning coalition appointed ex-coup leader Suchinda Kraprayoon as the new prime minister, which prompted millions of people to come out in the largest demonstrations ever seen in Bangkok. This finally led to the 'Black May' massacre and riots in Bangkok, in which hundreds died. After intervention by the King, Suchinda resigned, which was followed by an interim government. After the appointment of the interim government, the country was brought back to normal. Meanwhile, key politicians and academic leaders started a rally for political reforms and a more democratic constitution. The campaigns resulted in the 1997 Constitution, which is called the people's constitution.[10] The year 1997 marked at least two significant milestones for Thailand. The first milestone was that it was the year of great financial crisis, which later spread throughout Asia. These crises forced the country to submit a request to the World Bank for loan and also to admit conditions of the loan, one of which was to transform the public sector, including the higher education sector, in a more efficient and effective fashion. The second milestone was related to the political reform movement, which finally led to the 16th Constitution, called the 'People's Constitution'. This 16th Constitution was drafted by the Constitution Drafting Assembly, which comprises 99 members: 76 of them were directly elected from each of the provinces and the rest 23 were qualified persons being shortlisted mainly from academia and other sectors. The draft constitution was later approved by the National Assembly.

The new constitution was drafted in a highly participatory manner. It contains several initiatives, including a reform of the legislative system, an election reform, a mechanism to strengthen executive branch, separation between the executive and legislation branches, an increased check and balance system, an explicit recognition of human rights, a clear separation of the judicial system from the executive branch, establishment of accountability institutions as constitution-independent organizations such as the Administrative Court, the Office of the Ombudsman, the National Counter Corruption Commission, the National Election Commission and the National Audit General Commission. It also provides methods for increasing citizen participation and enhancing transparency and accountability as well as decentralization. It promulgates new standards for transparency and guidelines for decentralizing authority and resources to local administrations. This 1997 Constitution was also drafted with the underlying concept of making an executive branch a strong one. The first general national elections conducted under the 1997 Constitution took place in January 2001. The 'Thai Rak Thai' party, co-founded and led by Thaksin Shinawatra, won the elections and Thaksin became the prime minister of Thailand from 2001–2006. The Thaksin government was recognized as a very strong government as designed by the constitution. He was alleged as dominating both the legislative branch and the constitution independent organizations. His leadership was shining and made him the first prime minister of Thailand to serve a full term of four years. Thaksin's populist policies were very attractive to grassroots level. With populist policies came allegations of corruption, especially at the national policy level. These later became public outcries and political turmoil, which resulted in the November 2006 incident, whereby the armed forces ousted Prime Minister Thaksin's government while he and several other ministers were in New York for attending the UN General Assembly. The military revoked the constitution, dismissed Thaksin and promised political reforms.

After the 2006 coup, the Constitution Drafting Council was created. Members were existing and retired high ranking officers and university professors. This constitution was drafted with the concept of giving powers to constitutionally independent organizations and the Constitutional Court so as to prevent too strong government. The draft constitution was later approved by public referendum in 2007. The 2007 Constitution was in function. General elections were held. The party that won the national election formed the government. Movement from the Thaksin party to amend the constitution had been initiated since 2007. Street protests and riots took place here and there from time to time. In 2014, the situation was getting worse and Bangkok was almost paralysed by the protests. Millions of people were on the streets in Bangkok and nearby areas for political demonstrations. The country was practically paralysed for months, and then another coup took place in May 2014. After the coup, the Constitution Drafting Committee was appointed and a new constitution was drafted. In the meantime, in addition to the political structure and system, issues such as roles of government, decentralization and relationships between politicians and public officers were also raised and discussed for inclusion in the new constitution. The 2016 Draft Constitution was scheduled for public referendum in August 2016.

Against the backdrop of political instability and violence since 1992, major reforms in the public sector had taken place at both national and sector system levels. Among others, Critical reforms were the decentralization of power from the national government to localities, the creation of new forms of public organization, the reform of education and health sectors and the system-wide reform of the public administration system. All these major reforms had their own leaders; most of them were public officers who manoeuvre reforms through key politicians in both government and parliament.

DECENTRALIZATION REFORM

As mentioned previously, public administration in Thailand is composed of national or central administration, provincial administration and local administration (Kokpol, 2012). Power given to localities was quite limited until 1997. After the political crisis of the 1992 Black May, decentralization was put forward, mostly by university professors and key local administration leaders, to be the integral part of political reform agenda. The issue was also tabled to the constitution drafting council to be entered in the constitution. The decentralization reform successfully appeared in the 1997 Constitution, which mandated the state to '*decentralize powers to localities for the purpose of independence and self-determination of local affairs* (Section 78)'. This mandate brought about the decentralization reform that was extensive and comprehensive. From 1992 onwards, the current local administration system has evolved gradually. In 1994, the TAO system was created by the tambon council through TAOs Act of 1994; TAOs became the newest and the smallest type of local administrations. In 1997, the Provincial Administration Organizations (PAOs) Act of 1997 was promulgated, resulting in changing the tier of local administration from one to two-tier system, in which PAOs, as the upper tier of local administration, covered the whole provincial area, while municipalities and TAOs, located within the provincial area, formed the lower tier of local administration. The 1997 Constitution also granted more autonomy to localities in both budget and human resources. Even though the 1997 Constitution was revoked due to 2006 military intervention, the 2007 Constitution still retained the decentralization process.

The road to decentralization reform, which took place long before 1997 and was successfully implemented with the mandate of the 1997 Constitution, was not smooth. It took those advocating for decentralization reform years to gain support from both politicians and public. This was made mostly through higher education. With the rise of massification of higher education in Thailand, one of the most popular programmes among public officers and politicians was public administration. Within the public administration programme, the subject of local administration was taught and researched. When the public administration students became mid-level and high-level officers, they carried with them the concept of decentralization and local administration. Some became members of the parliament. Some were elected as members of parliament. A few became ministers. They recognized what local administration is and how it is good for the country. Streams of decentralization reforms thus became waves and when different waves were woven together, local administration was guaranteed in the 1997 Constitution and the 2017 Constitution.

From the beginning until present, decentralization reform has been facing resistance. Resistance mainly came from national ministries. The Ministry of interior was afraid of losing power if provincial governors were elected.[11] The Ministry of Education resisted the transfer of schools to local authorities by creating various conditions for transfer, which finally made school transfer very difficult. Other line ministries had their own ways of resistance. On another end, local authorities were slow to get ready for new responsibilities such as tax collection. The decentralization reform was, however, moving forward by those who championed the concept and transferred it from one generation to another and from one group to others. With the creation of social media, concepts spread widely and rapidly. Supporters were getting stronger and finally outlasted those who opposed the concept.

If asked who championed the decentralization reform movement, credits should be given to different personalities, including key political leaders, local administration leaders, and academicians. They together had their share of success in the reform process.

NEW FORMS OF PUBLIC ORGANIZATIONS

Another milestone of the Thailand Public Sector Reform is the law called the Public Organization Act of 1999. This law allowed the establishment of new category of Thai public organizations called the APOs. APOs operate under the supervision of government while maintaining a greater degree of administrative independence. The first APO was Banphaeo Hospital. The hospital was one of the public hospitals ready to transform from public organizations to APOs. In 2000, it successfully became the first APO, still maintaining the status.

Initiation for creating this form of public organizations was discussed by the Public Sector Reform Committee during the premiership of General Chavalit Yongchaiyudh (1996–1997). During the government of General Chavalit Yongchaiyudh, the minister responsible for public sector reforms was the former professor of public law who graduated from France. This minister along with the public reform committee attempted to ease the bureaucratic process with the idea of creating new form of public organizations similar to Quasi Non-Governmental Organizations (QUANGOs), which were quite popular in the United Kingdom during the Thatcher regime. The idea was transferred into a draft bill but the Yongchaiyudh government ended before the law was passed. The Office of Civil Service Commission who acted as the secretary of the Public Sector Reform Committee established during the Chuan Leekpai government (1997–2001)[12] carried forward this proposal by submitting it for consideration to the Public Sector Reform Committee. The Chuan Leekpai government endorsed the proposal and the bill was drafted. The bill was put through the parliament and became the Public Organization Act in 1999.

Credit for creating this new form of public organization should be given to the leader and staffs of the Office of Civil Service Commission who kept on pushing this concept from one government to another until it became the law. In July 2015, there were 39 APOs in Thailand.[13] There were both positive and negative stories about APOS. The early ideas were to create public organizations which are less bureaucratic and perform in the same way as business organizations. At APOs, the compensation package is compatible with business sector and the way of working is similar to the working of the business sector. Critics said that APOs are government offices with high salary and operation costs with performance being the same as those of regular government offices.[14] Another comment is that certain APOs are the dirty hands of corrupted politicians who use them for their personal benefits such as appointing their own people as head of APOs and doing business with those APOs. Some opined that the underperformance of APOs was because APO boards were appointed by politicians, and some APOs have retired officers who resist to deviate from formal rules and regulations.

After more than 15 years of operation, APOs are under the review of the National Reform Council[15] and a reform proposal was prepared by the Committee on Public Sector Management.[16] The reform proposal was later tabled for consideration by the National Legislative Council. Another reform in APOs may happen in the short time frame.

To conclude, it should be noted that the concept of APO was initiated not by the government of the day but by the Public Sector Reform Committee, which comprised both university professors and senior officers. The Public Sector Reform Committee was run mainly by the strong support of the Office of Civil Service Commission, who acted as the secretary of the Public Sector Reform committee. The Public Sector Reform Committee was chaired by the prime minister and comprised senior officers and academicians. Thus, the driver of the reform was not one person but a group of experts and practitioners. The government of the day only gave a 'green signal' to the concept. One, however, cannot deny the leadership of the ruling prime minister who was the one who had final say and the secretary general of the Office of Civil Service Commission who prepared the reform agenda.

ESTABLISHMENT OF OPDC AND
SYSTEM-WIDE REFORMS

The 1997 Constitution clicked the public sector reform process by mandating that public administration functions must be in line with good governance principles. Owing to this mandate, the law of good governance was enacted and named as the 'Royal Decree on Criteria and Procedures for Good Governance of 2003'. Under this Royal Decree, the Public Sector Development Commission was created together with the OPDC. This led Thailand Public Administration to a new stage of development. Following the Royal Decree, new initiatives were introduced to all public agencies. Most, if not all, followed the New Public Management (NPM) principles, which emphasized market mechanism, citizens as customers, entrepreneurial government and performance improvement of the public sector (Osborne & Gaebler, 1992). At present, Thai officers and other public sector employees are relatively familiar with these NPM principles and concepts such as strategy map, strategic planning, strategic thrusts, performance targets and Key Performance Indicators (KPIs). In public human resource management, the officers are also being accustomed to concepts such as performance management, HR scorecards, individual development plan and individual KPIs. For public budgeting, public officers are familiar with strategic performance budgeting. Geographic Information System has been employed for planning and monitoring. In addition, good governance is also a very common term for public employees and government officers. In most government offices, staff are highly likely to note the statements of vision, missions and core values of the organizations posted on the wall of their offices and their websites. Statements similar to 'citizen charter' are also visible in most government offices, including the local administration offices. Citizen satisfaction survey is quite a regular practice for most government offices. The Prime Minister Award, following the concept of the Malcolm Baldrige National Quality Award, was created and recognized by most government offices. There are some examples that reflect the principles and practices of NPM and good governance. What one sees today has gradually appeared in the last 20 years or more, and these are, in a way, evidences of public sector reforms.

In addition to system-wide reform, which has been deployed throughout Thailand's public organizations since 2002, through the initiation of OPDC, a major structural change happened in 2002. Before 2002, there were 15 ministries; however, structural reform in 2002 led to expansion of 20 ministries. Some of these ministries were separated from the existing ones and some were newly established. The new ministries are Ministry of Information and

Communication Technology, Ministry of Culture, Ministry of Tourism and Sports, Ministry of Social Development and Social Security, and Ministry of Natural Resources and Environment. New departments under different ministries were created and reshuffled. This structural reform was for a purpose of making clear owners and responsibilities so as to make the government more efficient. However, critiques said that it was structural changes that only served political interests.

In order to understand how the above-mentioned reforms happened, one should look at how the OPDC had been functioning. By law, the Public Sector Development Commission was authorized to initiate reform agendas and oversee their implementation. This commission was supported by sub-committees, which were tasked to form reform proposals and follow up with their implementation. Implementation was the responsibility of OPDC. Chair of the Public Sector Development Commission, by law, was the prime minister. Members of the Public Sector Reform Commission and members of sub-committees were from public and private sectors and academia. With this structure, reform agendas were not initiated solely by any group of political leaders, high-ranking officers, private sector executives or academicians. They were usually being initiated through discussions and consultations.[17] It must also be noted that the OPDC was quite strategic in implementing its initiatives. Firstly, in the beginning, the OPDC office exercised its authorities to create OPD unit in every government department. This unit was asked to deploy OPDC policies and initiatives in its department and also tabling the department initiatives to the OPDC office. The OPDC office had thus created its own subsidiary unit for implementing its initiatives. Secondly, the OPDC created a bonus-like scheme for government officers based on department's performance. The set of performance indicators were assigned by OPDC. With this bonus-like scheme, those senior officers and department heads were eligible for as many as 12 months of basic salary.[18] This was an effective incentive for driving OPDC agenda. Thirdly, the OPDC had created a prime minister award for high-performance organization and for work improvement and innovation. This PM award was given every year by the prime minister to the government units and government officers who win the contests. This PM award worked very well in generating enthusiasm among government units and officers and had created good innovation for public offices. These three strategies, together with the leadership of senior officers of the office of OPDC, had led the OPDC to be well known among Thai public officers. This public sector movement was not without resistance. Officers complained that the bonus scheme benefitted mainly senior officers. Low ranking officers, who sweated for achieving the OPDC performance indicators, received only a small part of bonus money. Another critic said that it is not the real performance but only putting in the form right.[19]

As of the present, OPDC, amidst rumors of amalgamation with the Office of Civil Service Commission (OCSC),[20] is still pushing its initiatives forward. The bonus-like scheme is not as effective as in the beginning due to smaller amount of bonus allocated by the government. The first head or CEO of OPDC who was professor of public administration has been changed.[21] The second CEO was able to stay only for a short period. Although the reform process is still moving forward, this has slowed down the movement.[22]

REFORM OF EDUCATION SECTOR

Basic education is one of the most important factors in terms of country's competitiveness. Every Thai government has placed basic education on a high priority. This can be seen from the overall budget of the country in the last 25 years, whereby education sector, especially basic education, always received the highest share of governmental annual budget. During the last 25 years, Thai governments have established education-related public organizations with the aim to improve the quality of education. These include establishment of the Office for National Education Standards and Quality Assessment (ONESQA) in 1972[23] to perform as external reviewer for both private and public educational providers to assure the quality of education, and the National Institute of Educational Testing Services to administer national entrance examination, such as O-NET and A-NET, to Thai universities, and N-Net for basic education. Laws were also promulgated to facilitate educational reforms.

For example, the National Education Act of 1999, in pursuance of the 1997 Constitution, was enacted in August 1999 to act as a fundamental law for education reform. The act consists of nine chapters, which are (1) objectives and principles, (2) educational rights and duties, (3) educational system, (4) national education guidelines, (5) educational administration and management, (6) educational standards and quality assurance, (7) teachers, faculty, staff and educational personnel, (8) resources and investment for education and (9) technologies for education. In terms of the education system, this Act resulted in the amalgamation of those ministerial level education-related organizations into one ministry which were under the Ministry of Education. Under the Ministry of Education, there are five offices, which are (1) Office of Permanent Secretary, (2) Office of National Education Commission,

(3) Office of Basic Education, (4) Office of Vocational Education and (5) Office of Higher Education. This amalgamation was done in a hope that coordination among these five offices would become more effective and would in effect help to facilitate implementation of national education policy.[24] The National Education Act of 1999 also gave birth to the ONESQA, which was established not under the ministry of education, but instead, in order to ensure its autonomy, was placed under the office of prime minister. It also placed an emphasis on stakeholder participation by creating school board to monitor school management and school quality. The purpose of the creation of this school board was to create a channel for community and stakeholders to get involved in school policy and management. There are also other initiatives designed and implemented to reform education sector. All of these have been designed and carried on to show that Thai governments have been extremely concerned about education problems.

Looking closer at the Education Reform Movement, concerns over the quality of education have been floating around for years. After the 1992 Black May, when concerns and campaigns for political reform towards democratization were gaining momentum, those in the education sector and others had also raised a point that the country must also place highest emphasis on human resource development so as to create a democratic regime and sustain it. Without morally good and competent human resources, any reforms are unlikely to be successful. With such assertion, waves of education reform had taken place and gained momentum. The government of that day set up a national education reform committee to draft proposal for education reforms, which later became the National Education Act, 1999. After the 1999 Act, laws had been promulgated and education structure and system had been reshaped and reformed by concerned agencies and stakeholders. The outcomes were not as expected. Thailand was ranked relatively low compared to other ASEAN countries. The Public was concerned about this situation. The present military government has also placed high priority on educational reforms, especially on basic education. The draft constitution mandates the government to prepare reform initiatives and pass the educational reform act within two years.

Why did the Thailand educational reform fail? Standing among other reasons is the teacher personnel system. By the National Educational Act of 1999, teachers for basic education were placed in different school districts throughout the country. Teachers who were placed in remote areas would submit a request to be transferred to their home province or to the urban area after 2–3 years. The school district board was authorized to grant transfer, and this was at the sole discretion of school district board. National human resource planning for teachers was difficult. Morale of teachers in rural areas was low and this affect their teaching as well. Without competent and committed teachers, it was nearly impossible to uplift the quality of education.

REFORM OF HEALTH SECTOR

Health reform in Thailand has been cited as one of the most successful stories. Before 2001, health care coverage was extended to mainly those who were under civil service and social security schemes but did not offer coverage to 18.5 million people of the population of 62 million (Towse, Mills, Tangcharoensathien, 2004). These 18.5 million people were previously not insured. The country took a 'big bang' approach to introduce a universal access to subsidize health care services. The idea of universal coverage was formed and floated around 2001. In 2001, the concept was picked up by Thai Rak Thai party and became one of the important party platforms under the name '30 baht to heal all diseases', which led the party to win elections and form the government at that time. This reform resulted in the National Health Security Act, which was passed by the parliament in November 2002. The act created new institutions to regulate the quality and financial elements of health schemes. It preserves all benefits that have been entitled for members of the civil service and social security schemes, but places management of their financing with the National Health Security Office, which runs the 30 baht scheme. The act allows for the civil service and social security schemes to be merged into a single universal coverage scheme by decree, should that become politically acceptable in the near future. The National Health Security Office functions as a 'regulator', and hospitals under the Ministry of Public Health as 'operators'. This reform was in line with the NPM, namely 'steering rather than rowing' (Osborne & Gaebler, 1992), and was a 'big bang' in terms of public sector reform.

Who were the people pressing for this revolutionary reform movement? It is clear that if the Thai Rak Thai party had not 'bought' the idea in 2001, the reform might not have come this far. It was, however, not true to conclude that it would not have been picked up by other political parties. This concept fits very well with the populist policies of the Thai Rak Thai party, which made it go well with the party platform. The idea, however, originated from health experts who had been discussing and proposing this reform for years. It may be fair to say that with support of the Thai Rak Thai party, the reform process took place and became an act. It is also fair to say that the reform process went well due to the fact that health experts actively pursued and helped the idea to materialize. It takes two hands to create sound: politicians and health experts. The story of this health care reform is similar to other reforms taken place since 1997: (1) reform ideas had been floating around for years, (2) the reformists had been awaiting to put them in the hands of policy maker, (3) party leaders had also been looking around for right ideas which fit their policy agenda and (4) when both ideas and agenda maker met, the ideas became reform policies. The story of health care reform was not without resistance. Obstructions laid in the implementation details, including the way to calculate health care per capita, the way to allocate health care budget to hospitals and how to follow up to see whether the health care delivery was up to expected quality, and others. All these detailed implementations were carried out by the National Health Care Office. The success lies with the concerted effort of health care experts who transferred their ideas from one generation to another and kept convincing for support of the politicians who took charge of the Ministry of Public Health.

Table 1.   Reform Initiatives and Its Drivers.

Reform Initiatives	Drivers
Decentralization	Key political leaders, local administration leaders and academicians.
Autonomous public organization	Public Sector Reform Committee with the strong support of the Office of Civil Service Commission. Members of the committee are from both government agencies and academe.
Establishment of OPDC and system-wide reform	Public Sector Development Commission and its sub-committees. Member of the committee are from both government agencies and academe. The first CEO was the public administration professor.
Reform of education sector	National education reform committee led by the education minister under the military government. The minister was the former university professor and former president of a public university.
Reform of health sector	Thai Rak Thai political party government with the reform idea formed by health experts.
Commissioned-type organization	Leaders of higher education sector who are members of parliament as well as those who are involved in bill drafting.

OTHER REFORM INITIATIVES

As mentioned earlier, public sector in Thailand includes not only ministries and departments but also other types of public sector organizations: PE, APO and OPF. It is worth mentioning that for both APO and OPF, the new forms of governance has been introduced into Thai bureaucracy. In ministries and departments, the heads of the organization are the permanent secretary and the director general, respectively. All legal authorities necessary to run the organization are bestowed to the head of the organization as a single leader. On the contrary, these public organizations, including APO, OPF and the agencies, become 'commissioned organizations',[25] i.e., legal authorities which are 'line authorities',[26] given to organization policy and management board. For example, at the office of higher education commission, the authorities concerning higher education standards are, by law, authorities of the higher education commission and not authorities of the secretary general of the office of higher education commission. This is also true for other line authorities and in other 'commissioned organizations' as well as for APO and OPF. This change in organizational governance can be recorded as another public sector reform in Thailand, since decision-making is shifted from a single person to a group of persons.

For any commissioned organization, one can note that it allows for stakeholder participation in its structure.[27] For example, the commission on higher education comprises permanent secretary of the ministry of education, secretary general of the office of basic education commission, secretary general of the office of vocational education commission, secretary general of the office of national education commission, director of the budget bureau office, secretary general of the office of the council of state, secretary general of the office of the national economic and social development board, secretary general of the office of the public sector development, director of the office of national educational standards and quality assessment, and representatives of private sectors, local administration authorities, professional sectors and those who have expertise. The members in the expert category are mostly well-known charismatic persons and retired public officers. This is true for the members of governing board of APO and OPF organizations as well.

This commission-type organization can be called as another reform movement, which brought participation of different stakeholders into governance of public organizations. In addition to participation, it also brought with it the practices of group decision and collective responsibility. Another remark is that governance of this form of public organization gave room to retired officers who still hang on in the system. It is thus another channel for them to share their tacit knowledge and experiences. At the same time, with these retired officers in the governance structure, it means that there are different generations – from baby boomers to generation Z in one organization – which may have both negative and positive impact.

The prototype of this 'commissioned' organization is the university board. In Thailand, since the very beginning, public university is governed by the university board. The structure and composition of a university board differs from one university to another university. It, however, comprises the following three groups: (1) representatives of university administration, (2) representatives elected from university professors and (3) experts from outside the university. This tripartite system, which reflects representation of concerned stakeholders, has been implanted in all public universities since the beginning of the university system in Thailand. The experts who serve as board members carried with them this prototype structure and shared the same with other policy makers on becoming members of the parliament. In this respect, this commissioned organization was created by the experts who had been associated and familiar with university administration for a long time.

OUTCOMES OF PUBLIC SECTOR REFORM INITIATIVES

From the 1992 Black May to the 1997 Constitution and to the present, there are several visible outcomes of reform initiatives. The first one is related to the form of Thai bureaucracy. New organizations created after 1997 are constitutionally independent organizations, APOs and OPF. These new forms of structures gave more flexibility for designing government organizations. The second outcome was the new high-level governance structure or the commissioned organization, which allowed participation of related stakeholders at the policy and management board of public organizations. The third outcome was policies and practices of decentralization. At present, local administration organizations cover every part of the country. People are well aware of the existence of local administration organizations and their authorities, and citizens are extremely active in local elections. The fourth outcome is a system wide reform of public delivery. Today, one can visit the local authority and obtain a citizen identification card in less than half an hour compared with 3–4-month-long wait in the past. This is also true for other registration identifications such as passports and driver licenses. On the other hand, the public sector is getting bigger in terms of both public personnel and budgeting and corruption, although corruption is still a common practice and seems to be getting more serious.

CONCLUSION

Since the 1992 Black May Day to the present, the political landscape of Thailand has swung from military-dominated regime to a campaign for full democracy, from 1992 to 1997, which resulted in the 1997 Constitution, called the people's constitution. After 1997, political stability occurred under a very strong executive and weak legislative. This and other causes led to another military intervention in 2006, which resulted in the 2007 Constitution. The 2007 Constitution granted strong powers to constitutionally independent organizations and the constitutional court, which later created differences between the government of the day and the constitutionally independent organizations. These differences, together with public outcries about politicians' unacceptable activities, led to another military intervention in 2014. Thailand is now in the process of reformation and drafting of new constitution with the hope that with these reforms and new constitution, the country will get back on another normal course.

With these unremitting political conflicts and crisis, the public sector, being another side of the same coin, has been also continuously changing with various reform attempts by different reform champions. The nature of these reform movements can be summed up as follows:

1. Leaderships of these reforms comes from issue experts and senior civil service officers. Experts are from universities and government agencies. These experts may have ideas but no authority. The experts have reform ideas ready to be put in policy packages and submitted to elected governments to be made into national policies. On the another end, political parties are looking for ideas that fit their policy platforms. They may pick up certain policy packages for political campaigns and put into policy agenda on elected to the office. These policy packages were also picked up during military intervention. When the military seized state power, they were not often ready to run the country. They usually looked for ready-to-deliver policy packages and push them through policy agenda. In the educational sector, major reforms included the following: (1) the National Education Act of 1999, which resulted in the amalgamation of three ministerial-level bodies to become a single ministry, i.e., Ministry of Education; (2) single chief executive officer has been replaced by the commissioned officer; (3) in basic education, educational service areas were established throughout the country and education was removed from the supervision of provincial administration; (4) the basic education curriculum was redesigned; and (5) academic standing, with monthly salary, was introduced so as

to motivate teachers to provide quality education. All these educational reforms were mainly initiated and driven by education authorities but certainly with the support from the government. The outcome of educational reform is, however, unsatisfactory. Thailand is ranked at the bottom compared with other ASEAN countries.[28]

In the health sector, a major reform was the universal health care system. The reform agenda was drafted by a group of health policy experts and picked up by the Thai Rak Thai party to become its winning strategy. After the party took office, necessary policy infrastructure, such as the National Health Security Act of 2002 and the National Health Security Office, was developed. Senior officers and health experts at the ministry of public health carried out and made the policy agenda materialized. At present, it can be said that Thailand has been quite successful in promoting the universal health care system. As for the system-wide reform, ideas of public sector reforms had been discussed among senior officers and experts from academe for years before 2002. After the 1997 Constitution, laws related to public sector reforms were enacted. The most important one was the royal decree on criteria and procedures for good governance 2003. This royal decree and the establishment of the commission on public sector development and its office were milestones of the system-wide public reforms. This commission and the office have put forward different packages of reform agenda and actions, mostly based on the NPM concepts, and still initiating and carrying forward new reform agendas. Leadership of this system-wide public reform is similar to other reforms. They are public sector reform experts and senior officers. They, however, waited for the right time to present it when policy agenda was opened.

2. For most reform agendas, strategies for policy delivery are quite similar. Policies were discussed among experts from universities and government agencies. Usually experts from universities were commissioned to conduct research and presented the findings and suggestions to a group of policy makers and practitioners. Outcomes of this commissioned research became a draft policy agenda. At the right political situation, these drafts would be put to policy makers. If picked up by policy makers, then such draft policies were modified to fit political agenda and context and carried into policy window. Public sector reform in Thailand is thus explained not by the orchestrated leadership model but by the jazz-banded leadership model. Different reformers who shared similar reform visions initiated reform agendas in their sectors and shot them through policy agendas when policy window was opened.

3. Since each reform agenda took few years to form and years to get implemented, one may wonder whether there was any resistance to these reform
movements. In Thailand, resistance usually occurred during the implementation stage rathan than at the formulation stage. At the implementation stage,
budget allocation may not be in line with planning. Financial procedures
are usually detailed and tight, which delays the implementation process. In a
country plagued with corruption, these tight and tough procedures are necessary. They slowed down the processes but did not stop policy agenda. For
the policies, such as a set of decentralization policies, which had effects on
public employers, resistance came from line ministries who wanted to secure
their authority and budget and also from employees who did not want to
change their status. These types of resistances were managed through negotiation among concerned stakeholders. It is a rare instance when a political
leader steps in and delivers a final say to get rid of resistance. It is almost
always through long negotiation processes that resistance has been removed.

NOTES

1. Black May (Thai: พฤษภาทมฬ; RTGS: Phruetsapha Thamin) is a common
name for the 17–20 May 1992 popular protest in Bangkok against the government of
General Suchinda Kraprayoon and the bloody military crackdown that followed. Up
to 200,000 people demonstrated in Central Bangkok at the height of the protests. The
military crackdown resulted in 52 officially confirmed deaths, many disappearances,
hundreds of injuries, and over 3,500 arrests.
2. Retrieved from http://www.worldometers.info/world-population/thailand-
population/.
3. Retrieved from http://www.buddhanet.net/e-learning/history/bstatt10.htm.
4. Retrieved from http://www.worldbank.org/en/country/thailand/overview.
5. Retrieved from http://www.zcooby.com/2560-thailand-information-number-
statistics/.
6. Retrieved from http://www.dla.go.th/work/abt/. Accessed on 23 March 2017.
7. Retrieved from http://www.dla.go.th/work/abt/index.jsp.
8. Retrieved from http://www.parliament.go.th/.
9. It should be noted that these four forms of organizations are under the
executive branch. There are also public organizations under legislative and judicial
branches.
10. It should be noted that after the Black May 1992 to November 1997, the
country had nine governments, of which the 9th one led by Prime Minister Chavalit
Yongchaiyudh resigned in November 1997 due to 'Tom Yum Kung' financial crisis.
11. It should be noted that along with the decentralization process such as the
establishment of TAOs, the Ministry of Interior took this opportunity to create the

Department of Local Administration. This department became, budget-wise, the largest department of all departments. This decentralization reform was thus the positive-sum game for the key stake-holders.

12. Appendix C.

13. Retrieved from http://www.opdc.go.th/org.php?url=org3.

14. From personal interview with the APO leaders.

15. Under the Constitution of the Kingdom of Thailand (interim) BE 2557 (2014), the National Reform Council was appointed by the National Council for Peace and Order and comprised not more than 250 members. The National Reform Council was established to study and provide recommendations for reform in the following fields: (1) politics, (2) administration of state affairs, (3) law and judicial procedure, (4) local administration, (5) education, (6) economy, (7) energy, (8) public health and environment, (9) mass communication, (10) social and (11) others. This National Reform Council, after submitting its reform proposal to the National Council for Peace and Order, was replaced by the National Reform Steering Assembly.

16. The Committee on Public Sector Management was tasked to review and make recommendations on public sector reform. Such proposal would then be tabled to the National Reform Council. Upon the endorsement of the National Reform Council, the proposal would be submitted to the government for consideration and action.

17. When the OPDC was first established, I was appointed a member of two sub-committees and this statement is my own observation. In the sub-committee meeting, certain members usually proposed their concerns and wishes for reform movement. Such concerns would usually form into an agenda for discussion, and if endorsed by the meeting would be tabled to the PDC. If the PDC agreed with the proposal, such proposals would then be submitted for cabinet consideration.

18. This bonus-like scheme varied from agency to agency. Some may be granted 1–2 months, while others may receive 12 months. The size of bonus is up to the achievement score. This score is calculated according to the fulfillment measured by Key Performance Indicators established under the annual performance contract signed between the head of the department and the OPDC. This bonus-like scheme is one of the key drivers of reform initiatives.

19. All are my personal observations.

20. As of today, the four central national agencies which were often tasked as a joint secretariat of the national public sector reform committee as well as the national committee responsible for public personnel right sizing are able to maintain their turf by focusing on what they do best. While the Office of Public Budgeting's task is on budgeting, the Comptroller General's Department is tasked on national spending matter, OCSC is responsible for those public personnel matters and OPD is tasked with structural matters.

21. Note that the first CEO of the OPDC was placed back to the OPDC since October 2016.

22. As of today, the government has set up a new office to carry the integrated reform agenda and within four months after the promulgation of the 2017 constitution, the law on national reform must be enacted.

23. Retrieved from http://www.ipst.ac.th/eng/index.php/about-us/fast-fact.

24. It should also be mentioned that with the amalgamation, the commission-type management was also implemented at basic, vocational and higher education levels.

The commission comprises those from private sector, academe and high ranking officers, which made it different from regular public organization led by a single leader. Decisions on basic, vocational and higher education issues were discussed and decided at the commission meetings.

25. These commissioned organizations are Office of Basic Education Commission, Office of Vocational Education Commission, Office of Higher Education Commission and Office of National Education Commission.

26. 'Line authorities' are the authorities concerning mission of the organization which are different from 'staff authorities', which mostly concern personnel, financial and day-to-day authorities.

27. The National Education Act 1999 stipulated that the commissions that appeared in the Act comprises ex-officio, representatives of private sectors, representatives of local administration authorities, representatives of professional sectors and those who have expertise.

28. Retrieved from http://www3.weforum.org/docs/WEF_GlobalCompetitiveness Report_2013-14.pdf.

29. Office of Civil Service Commission. *Civilian workforce in Thailand.* Retrieved from http://www.ocsc.go.th/ocsc/th/index.php?option=com_content&view=article&id =2779&catid=540&Itemid=30.

30. Retrieved from http://www.bb.go.th/bbhome/page.asp?option=content&dsc=% BE%C3%BA.%A7%BA%BB%C3%D0%C1%D2%B3%C3%D2%C2%A8%E8%D2% C2&folddsc=19004 *US$1 = 35.3531 Baht as on April 10, 2016.

31. Compiled from the Royal Thai Government Gazette Website by the author.

REFERENCES

Bowornwathana, B. (2011). History and political context of public administration in Thailand. In E. Berman (Ed.), *Public administration in Southeast Asia: Thailand, Philippines, Malaysia, Hong Kong and Macau* (pp. 29–52). New York, NY: CRC Press.

Kokpol, O. (2012). *Decentralization process in 1990–2010: A case of Thailand.* Retrieved from http://kpi.ac.th/media/pdf/M10_141.pdf. Accessed on December 15, 2017.

Lorsuwannarat, T. (2008). Organizational contexts of autonomy and performance in Thai public sector organizations. *Proceedings of EGPA study group on governance of public sector organizations,* September 19–22, Madrid, Spain.

Osborne, D., & Gaebler, T. (1992). *Reinventing government: How the entrepreneurial spirit is transforming government.* Reading, MA: Adison Wesley.

Towse, A., Mills, A., & Tangcharoensathien, V. (2004). *Learning from Thailand's health reforms.* Retrieved from http://www.ncbi.nlm.nih.gov/pmc/articles/PMC314057/.

APPENDIX A: NUMBER OF THAILAND CIVILIAN WORKFORCE 2004–2013 (IN MILLIONS)[29]

Year	Population	Civilian Workforce	Percentage
2004	65.19	1.48	2.27
2005	64.88	1.98	3.05
2006	65.34	1.92	2.94
2007	65.8	1.94	2.95
2008	66.51	2.04	3.07
2009	66.72	2.04	3.05
2010	67.2	2.11	3.14
2011	67.4	2.26	3.35
2012	64.46	2.22	3.44
2013	64.79	2.19	3.38

APPENDIX B: THAILAND BUDGET EXPENDITURE FOR FISCAL YEAR 1992–2016[30]

Fiscal year	Budget Expenditure (Baht)	Budget Expenditure (US$)
1992	460,400,000,000	13,022,903,225
1993	560,000,000,000	15,840,195,061
1994	625,000,000,000	17,678,789,130
1995	715,000,000,000	20,224,534,765
1996	843,200,000,000	23,850,807,991
1997	984,000,000,000	27,833,485,607
1998	923,000,000,000	26,108,035,788
1999	825,000,000,000	23,336,001,652
2000	860,000,000,000	24,326,013,843
2001	910,000,000,000	25,740,316,974
2002	1,023,000,000,000	28,936,642,048
2003	999,900,000,000	28,283,234,002
2004	1,028,000,000,000	29,078,072,361
2005	1,200,000,000,000	33,943,275,130
2006	1,360,000,000,000	38,469,045,147
2007	1,566,200,000,000	44,301,631,257
2008	1,660,000,000,000	46,954,863,930
2009	1,835,000,000,000	51,904,924,886
2010	1,700,000,000,000	48,086,306,434
2011	2,070,000,000,000	58,552,149,599
2012	2,380,000,000,000	67,320,829,008
2013	2,400,000,000,000	67,886,550,260
2014	2,525,000,000,000	71,422,308,086
2015	2,575,000,000,000	72,836,611,217
2016	2,720,000,000,000	76,938,090,295

APPENDIX C: LIST OF THAILAND
PRIME MINISTERS, 1980–2015[31]

Name	Period	Time in Office
General Prem Tinsulanonda	3 March 1980–4 August 1988	8 years, 154 days
General Chatichai Choonhavan	4 August 1988–23 February 1991	2 years, 204 days
Anand Panyarachun	2 March 1991–7 April 1992	1 year, 36 days
General Suchinda Kraprayoon	7 April 1992–10 June 1992	64 days
Anand Panyarachun	10 June 1992–23 September 1992	105 days
Chuan Leekpai	23 September 1992–13 July 1995	2 years, 293 days
Banharn Silpa-Archa	13 July 1995–25 November 1996	1 year, 135 days
General Chavalit Yongchaiyudh	25 November 1996–8 November 1997	346 days
Chuan Leekpai	9 November 1997–17 February 2001	3 years, 92 days
Police Lt. Colonel Dr. Thaksin Shinawatra	9 February 2001–19 September 2006	5 years, 222 days
General Surayud Chulanont	1 October 2006–29 January 2008	1 year, 120 days
Samak Sundaravej	29 January 2008–9 September 2008	223 days
Somchai Wongsawat	18 September 2008–2 December 2008	75 days
Abhisit Vejjajiva	17 December 2008–8 August 2011	2 years, 234 days
Yingluck Shinawatra	5 August 2011–7 May 2014	2 years, 275 days
General Prayut Chan-o-Cha	24 August 2014	Present PM

CHAPTER 6

LEADERSHIP AND PUBLIC SECTOR REFORM IN VIETNAM

Ha Ngoc Pham

ABSTRACT

This chapter describes how public sector reform (PSR) became important following the 'Doi Moi' (renovation) programme in 1986. Restructuring of state-owned sector was regarded as crucial for ensuring the quality of economic growth, and the Vietnamese government (www.chinhphu.vn/portal/page/portal/English) put considerable effort in PSR. The 8th Party Congress (1996) emphasized the urgent need for a more transparent, capable and modern public sector, including efforts to improve law-making process and capacity, reducing burdensome bureaucracy, fighting corruption, increasing leadership by senior officials and improving public service delivery. The government specifies the national PSR Master programme, and the Ministry of Home Affairs coordinates its implementation among ministries, central agencies and provincial governments. Local political leaders (party leaders) determine reforms based on guidelines of the party and government. The author writes that in spite of ambitious public service reform programmes and some positive achievements, the quality of public sector remains poor. The professional capacity of civil service is low, pay is low, corruption is high and processes and structures seem ill-fitted for the market economy.

Leadership and Public Sector Reform in Asia
Public Policy and Governance, 127–149
Copyright © 2018 by Emerald Publishing Limited
All rights of reproduction in any form reserved
doi:10.1108/S2053-769720180000030006

Reform scope is too broad, the capacity of public agencies and civil servants is limited and existing monitoring, evaluation and reporting systems are weak. In some successes, leaders use appointment and promotion to encourage lower level to implement reforms and training to increase understanding. They believe that Vietnamese leadership has become less proactive and vigorous in practicing or embracing bold reform experiments.

Keywords: Doi Moi; 8th Party Congress; leadership; Vietnam

INTRODUCTION

The literature as well as the actual experiences of public sector reform (PSR) in Vietnam in recent years indicates the critical role of leadership in the process of change and reform in public organizations (Charlesworth, Cook, & Crozier, 2003; Hung et al., 2013; Van Der Voet, 2014; Wong, 2015). Leadership is widely perceived in the Vietnamese society as a decisive factor in the success of any reform. Undoubtedly, there is a close connection between these two streams of research as they have a shared consideration of creating positive change and fostering organizational performance (Wong, 2015).

This chapter provides an overview of the context, characteristics and the development of PSRs in Vietnam since 1986, through which the role of leadership can be seen. To be specific, it discusses how leadership plays its role in determining reform progress, managing risks of reform initiatives and sustaining reforms. These issues are then specifically illustrated by a case study of Da Nang city. Finally, the concern of how to strengthen PSR in Vietnam through leadership is discussed.

Vietnam is a one-party and unitary state with a supreme role of the Communist Party of Vietnam (CPV) in leading the whole country as clearly declared in the 1992 Constitution. Even though party's documents are not legal documents, rule by CPV directive has dominated the society. They have a key role in setting up political-economic policy for development (Beresford, 1988, 2008). In principle, the state power is vested in the state machinery, which includes National Assembly (legislature), government (executive) and court and office of supervision and control (judiciary). In fact, the decisions of CPV are adopted and implemented by a complex system of local and national government. All government agencies are subordinate to CPV at each level (Malesky, Nguyen, & Tran, 2014).

State agencies are organized and operate based on the democratic centralism principle which shapes the hierarchical system of state structure as well as a mechanism of collective leadership. Hierarchical system is characterized by the lower level which must obey all decisions made by higher levels, and collective leadership refers to the outcomes that are determined by the majority vote (Phan, 2012). According to the amended 1992 Constitution, the National Assembly is the highest representative organ and the highest state authority with wide constitutional and legislative powers. The National Assembly is elected every five years consisting of about 500 members. The executive branch of the National Assembly consists of the government, its ministries and ministerial agencies. The prime minister, the head of the government proposes a cabinet, which comprises deputy prime ministers, and heads of all ministries and ministerial agencies (ministers). The judicial branch comprises the people's court and the people's office of supervision and control.

At local level, there has been a strong tradition of 'double subordination' and 'self-sufficiency' in administrative structures (Painter, 2005a). More specifically, local government includes three levels: provincial, district and communal levels. Each level has a people's council and a people's committee. People's council, whose members are elected by citizens every five years, and the committee are its executive but play a more substantial role as the local branch of national government. The head of the people's committee is the chairman (equivalent to a mayor in western local governments), who is in charge of the day-to-day management of each locality. At each level, line departments are established to support people's committee. These organs are directly under the control of line departments at the higher levels (vertical control) and the people's committee at the same level (horizontal control).

In spite of the distinction between the government and the party apparatus in power, separation between the party and the government is not clear and proper. It is observed that Vietnam has come a long way in clarifying responsibilities between party and state, and among different levels of government (Wescott, 2003). However, the line between policy making and policy execution is blurred, and the distinction between a 'party cadre' and a 'state cadre' is unclear (Do & Truong, 2009). This is mainly because almost all key positions in the government are usually occupied by CPV members. For instance, in the administrative structure of all cities and provinces, heads of people's committee are subordinates to the party chief in the local branch of the Communist Party. Chairman of the people's council normally is occupied by the party chief.

In such a political context, PSR is under the leadership of CPV. The implementation of PSR over the whole country is led by the government – the highest state administrative agency. The government issues various documents to translate the party directions into reality, including the directions on PSR. Similar to in many other countries, PSR in Vietnam is a complex process aimed at improving the public administration system and provisions of public services (United Nations Development Programme [UNDP], 2009).

1. PUBLIC SECTOR REFORMS IN VIETNAM

From 1986 ('Doi Moi') to 2000

Since the independence of Vietnam in 1945, PSR was just officially mentioned in the party and state documents until the 6th Party Congress of the Communist Party in 1986. It was considered as a response to the serious socio-economic crisis at the time, aiming at renovating and strengthening the state apparatus. Before the Doi Moi (renovation) programme was launched in 1986, the Vietnamese economy was characterized by a centrally planned economy, which was under the absolute control of the state. Since the beginning of the 1990s, Vietnam's economy has been transitioning towards an open and market-oriented system. The most notable features of this transformation were the restructuring of the state-owned sector and allowing private sector development (e.g., recognition of private property rights, grant of land use rights etc.). As the restructuring of state-owned sector was regarded as a crucial condition to improve the quality of national economic growth, the Vietnamese government put considerable efforts in making the state-owned sector become more effective and efficient.

From 1993–1999, under the resolutions of the Party Congress (7th and 8th Party Congress), the reforms were still paid attention in spite of impressive achievement of Doi Moi. The 8th Party Congress emphasized the urgent need for a transparent, capable and modern public sector which can serve the people better. A wide range of activities were carried out from the central to the local level such as improving the law-making process and capacity, reducing the number of burdensome bureaucracy, fighting corruption, promoting personal responsibility and powers of senior officials, and further economic integration and diplomatic relations with the region and the world. As a result, Vietnam achieved impressive growth and social progress (GDP growth index increased from 3.9 per cent to more than 7 per cent between 1986 and 2000 (Rowley & Truong, 2009). A case in point of a positive effect of Doi Moi policy is the tremendous transformation of agricultural sector. It made a shift from a country facing chronic food shortages to the world's second largest exporter of rice, coffee and pepper (Truong & Nguyen, 2009).

From 2000 to date

In spite of dramatic development in comparison to that in the past, the Vietnamese government understood that Vietnam has been facing a set of new pressures that require more continuing PSR efforts. As a consequence, the 9th Party Congress in 2001 and the 11th Party Congress in 2011 developed a comprehensive PSR framework, namely Master programme on Public Administration Reform (PAR) for the period 2001–2010 and 2011–2020 in response to the following challenges.

- *Lack of professional civil service.* The Vietnamese public sector is usually criticized for the lack of professionalism. There exist poor links between qualifications and job specifications as well as the general requirements of a position and the unclear distinction among people working in state and party agencies and mass organizations This leads to a pervasive phenomenon of *luan chuyen can bo* (cadre transfer) within the political system (among branches/agencies/government levels) which can negatively influence the continuity and stability of administrative system. Besides, due to the absence of transparency in appointment and promotion procedures, ineffective remuneration and lack of incentives for development, Vietnamese government has been facing a challenge in maintaining a qualified contingent of civil servants. The fact shows that the quality of cadres and civil servants is considerably lower than that of their counterparts in the private sector. The public sector lacks competent civil servants who are supposed to identify, prepare projects and manage international investments according to international financial and economic standards (Dinh, 1999, 2002). This weakness can be obviously seen as one of the main reasons for economic downturn during the 2000s.

The problems were expected to be solved with the adoption of a set of new regulations on civil service management along with salary reforms. The amendment of the Ordinance on Cadres and Civil Servants in 2003 and its upgrade to Law on Carders and Civil servants and Law on Public servants in 2008 established a new and more comprehensive framework for civil service management. Most notable features were the clear distinction between civil servants in administrative agencies and public servants in public service delivery agencies, and more autonomy for ministries and provinces in civil service management, especially in recruitment and promotion. In the meantime, strengthening of employment and salary policies remains a priority. Civil service salary is gradually in alignment with market alternatives (ADB, 2005).

- *Organizational problems.* As economic reform has outpaced administrative reform and Vietnam is still in its transition period towards a market economy, the administrative machinery needs to be compatible. The rigid, inflexible and non-operative centralized government with weak defining the mandates and functions of institutions at central and local levels, weak cooperative mechanisms must be replaced. Liberalization and decentralization of economic power is essential for a transition to a market economy, which requires corresponding decentralization in public administration (Minh Chau, 1997).

Revising tasks, functions and organizational structures, and modernizing administrative systems were among the main contents of the Master programme on PAR for both phases of 2001–2010 and 2011–2020. During the period of 2000–2010, the emphasis was put on reorganization of administrative agencies, reduction in the number of burdensome agencies, decentralization and reform of state-owned enterprises. As a result, the number of ministries in the government was reduced considerably from more than 40 (before the year 2000) to 22 ministries (2007 to date). Their working procedures, functions and responsibilities were better defined. Through decentralization process, local governments got more authority in various areas of economic management, organization and personnel, culture, society, health and education (World Bank, 2006).

- *A high level of corruption.* Corruption is a pervasive phenomenon in most of developing countries' public sectors that exist at all levels of government and related to different fields. Corruption can lead to a neglect of output/outcome and a public mistrust in government as well as discouragement of both domestic and foreign direct investments (FDI; Painter, 2014). The most common forms of corruption in Vietnam are paying bribes by creating obstacles, accepting bribes for favour and using public properties for personal interests (Do & Truong, 2009). As giving bribes is generally perceived as a 'habit' of the Vietnamese, the government may face great challenges in dealing with corruption. Moreover, in a booming economy the opportunities for corruption may expand more rapidly than the capacity of the government to tackle it (Painter, 2008).

The past decade has witnessed people's increasing demands for a more transparent, accountable government, and better performance of public sectors. This created pressure on the government for further comprehensive reforms. Anti-corruption continued to be remarked in the Master programmes on PAR for the period of 2001–2010 and 2011–2020 as one of the key tasks. Many solutions for this problem have been proposed such as eliminating red tape, simplifying administrative procedures, increasing financial transparency, monitoring the assets of senior civil servants and their immediate families, processing complaints and denunciations etc. Specifically, Vietnam's anti-corruption law 2005 and the national strategy for preventing and combating corruption towards 2020 were issued and a set of anti-corruption bodies from the central level to local level were established as efforts of the Vietnamese government to tackle corruption. However, corruption remained prevalent during the last decade as international and national indexes have indicated, and combating corruption in Vietnam has become particularly challenging (Thang et al., 2015).

Both Master programmes on PAR for the period 2001–2010 and 2011–2020 aimed at improving the overall quality of public service delivery. However, the later has placed a greater emphasis on strengthening performance and delivering result. Some significant proposals were made, for instance, the introduction and expanded adoption of one-stop-shop model and internationally certified standards (ISO) aiming at serving people better as well as reducing red tape and enhancing transparency. Administrative procedures have been simplified to create more favourable environments for people and enterprises.

- *Need to respond to challenges from global context*: Being a member of regional and international organizations such as ASEAN and WTO and its commitment to international conventions signed, Vietnam has been forced to change its public sector to meet the requirement for these organizational memberships. In addition, in order to fulfill the increasing demands from economic integration process at regional and international levels and effectively dealing with problems raised from a more complex economy, a more competent and accountable government is required. Also, the Vietnamese government needs to review its ways of governing as an attempt to catch up with its neighbouring countries in the ASEAN, especially when concerns about the limitations of competencies of Vietnamese leadership in international economic integration is more growing. Besides, because of the trend of globalization, international ideas and practices related to public administration, such as new public management, ISO accreditation, job description etc. have been transferred to Vietnam in many ways, for example, through international donors (e.g., foreign countries and international organizations; Vasavakul, 2006), there is a need of corresponding changes in administrative machinery.

It was evident that in the end of the 1990s the exhaustion of the gains from Doi Moi reform 1986 combined with economic slowdown after the Asian Financial Crisis 1997 (Abuza, 2002) was one of main reasons for Vietnam to comprehensively reform its public sector. To further economic integration with the region and the world, all areas of public administration need to be improved, which was clearly reflected in both of the recent Master programmes on PAR. Some initial achievements were acknowledged. For example, in regard to regulatory framework, a series of regulations have been passed and amended to create a more favourable business climate for both domestic investment and FDI such as commercial law, the law on FDI, the law on credit organizations, the law on import and export tariffs, the law on value etc. Among these, the law on FDI was considered to be one of the most liberal in the region (Truong & Nguyen, 2009). Moreover, the contents of the regulations are increasingly in accordance with international standards (World Bank, 2004).

An overview of PSRs is summarized in Table 1.

In short, Doi Moi programme which focusses on both administrative and political reforms marked a shift from a closed and central planning economy to a market-oriented socialist economy. Doi Moi leaders demonstrated some remarkable entrepreneurial characteristics in their economic thinking and implementation. The next reforms continued to advocate extensive reforms but stressed the need to maintain socio-political stability, national security and the primacy of CPV. The resolution of the 8th Party Congress opened a new phase to build new regulatory frameworks for the Vietnamese public service. The most recent reforms developed more comprehensive and more ambitious programmes covering four key components of public administration (regulatory framework, organizational structure, civil service and public finance) and contain many elements of new public management such as restructuring, eliminating unnecessary procedures, decentralization and the adoption of modern management practices, empowering managers, focussing on clients, participation and partnership.

The Master programme on PAR for the period 2011–2020 was basically the next step of the Master PAR for 2001–2010 with some new activities and greater emphasis on strengthening performance and delivering results, aiming to take ongoing reform to a higher level. PSR in Vietnam has had mixed results (Ministry of Home Affairs [MOHA], 2010, 2015) and two Master programmes on PAR have been proved to be ambitious programmes (Thang et al., 2015; UNDP, 2009). Indeed, Vietnam's public sector has been undoubtedly reformed; however, some key shortcomings still remain within the public administration system, such as unsystematic and inconsistent regulation

Table 1. Major PSR From 1986 Up To Now.

Period	Main Reform Programmes	Contents	Implications and Evaluation
1986–1991 The 6th National Party Congress	Renovation programme (Doi Moi)	Abolishment of the centrally management system dependent on state subsides Adoption of a multi-sectoral economy Encouragement of FDI and international trade Recognition of private property rights Grant of land use rights	Focus on both administrative and political reforms Marked a shift from a closed and central planning economy to a market-oriented socialist economy Some remarkable entrepreneurial characteristics among Doi Moi leaders
1993–1999 The 7th and 8th National Party Congress	Next stage of Doi Moi	Improvement of law-making process and capacity Reduction in the number of burdensome bureaucracy More vigorous tackle of corruption Senior officials with more accountability Further economic integration and diplomatic relations with the region and the world	Continued advocating of extensive reforms but stressed the need to maintain socio-political stability, national security and the primacy of CPV The resolution of the 8th Party Congress opened a new phase to build new regulatory frameworks for civil servants and public services in Vietnam
2001–2010 The 9th National Party Congress	Master programme on PAR for the period 2001–2010	Reorganization of administrative agencies, decentralization Simplification of administrative procedures Application of modern management tools in improving the quality of public services Modernization of the financial sector State-own enterprises reforms Staff downsizing Continuance of anti-corruption campaign Civil service reform	Developed a more comprehensive but more ambitious reform programme which covers four key components of the public administration (regulatory framework, organizational structure, civil service and public finance)
2011 to date The 11th National Party Congress	Master programme of PAR for the period 2011–2020	Greater emphasis on strengthening performance and delivering results Further simplification and reduction of administrative procedures Decentralization	Continued with the main reform themes of Master programme of PAR for the period 2001–2010

systems, lack of professionalism among civil and public servants, backward operation styles etc. (MOHA, 2010, 2015), that create frustrations and scepticisms among policy makers, government officials, citizens, enterprises and international donors in Vietnam.

2. LEADERSHIP THAT MATTERS FOR REFORM

Leadership in Current Institutional Arrangement of Reform programmes

Each past reform programme was launched by a newly formed team of leaders and at a major plenum of the Communist party. Similarly, current programmes and guidelines for PSR were issued by central government based on the Resolution of the 10th and 11th Party Congress of CPV, then spread down to lower levels. The implementation of these programmes is the responsibility of MOHA. Central line units (ministries) and local authorities (people's committees and local line units) set up their own annual action plan to implement the Master programme on PAR. In each agency, there is one unit in charge of leading the implementation of changes initiated.

Top-level leaders (head or deputy head) at central and local levels are generally responsible for the adoption of PSRs in their agencies/localities, for example, at the provincial level, the chairman of people's committee (equivalent to mayor in the western government system). The assignment of PSR responsibilities and the reporting process are hierarchical and top-down, through various administrative branches from central to provincial, district and commune level.

At central level, Party Congress determines overall PSR policies and then government specifies the national PSR Master programme, which identifies key reform priorities, objectives and solutions for next 5 and 10 years. Government (headed by prime minister) plays a key role in directing the administrative reform of the country. Ministry of Home Affairs is responsible for developing the PSR implementation plans for the government to approve, organizing and coordinating the implementation of PSRs among ministries, central agencies and provincial governments, evaluating reform results from all ministries and localities and reporting to the government (Hung et al., 2013).

At local level, political leaders (party leaders) determine the PSR policies of the locality based on the guidelines and general policies of the party and the government. People's committee, especially the chairman, provides overall guidance and directs implementation of PSRs within their jurisdiction, assigning responsibilities and tasks to local units, monitoring, inspecting and supervising their implementation. Department of home affairs (DOHA) or section of home affairs is responsible for developing the PSR implementation plan for people's committee to approve, organizing and coordinating the implementation of PAR, evaluating reform results from local units and reporting to the people's committee (Hung et al., 2013).

It is noteworthy that there is a strong presumption that reform is a 'top-down' process of command and control in Vietnam as discussed above. However, in practice, there is a noticeable feature in the reform process by which 'reform' follows on after local experiments through breaking the rules (Painter, 2010). In other words, this process includes piloting and assessing the results, building consensus and scaling up. Before the full implementation of any change initiatives, several pilot projects are made in a number of local agencies. For instance, before the one-stop-shop model by the end of 2007 was established in all provinces, in at least one of their departments, this model had been piloted in several districts and line units of Ho Chi Minh City's authority since the early 1990s.

Schmitz, Tuan, Hang, and McCulloch (2015) point out that the reform process in Vietnam since 2005 has been a continuation process of the previous practice of learning by experimenting, which reflects the favour of the Vietnamese leadership in marginal adjustments rather than sudden changes. This 'gradual, step-by-step' or 'learning-by-doing' approach is probably suitable in the context of Vietnam over past two decades because of the ambiguity of the roles and responsibilities in implementing government policies and the goal of political stability. However, in order to address the emerging challenges, it needs to be adjusted.

The importance of leadership in determining reform progress

Traditionally, in Vietnam, leaders do not always communicate openly and transparently with the public, and there is an absence of individual leadership role. Nevertheless, it is evident that the success of several specific reform programmes is built on the contribution of individual leadership role. For example, the significant success of Doi Moi policy during the period of 1986–1999 considerably goes to Party's General Secretary Nguyen Van Linh, being its architect and leader, and Prime Minister Vo Van Kiet being its implementer. Both of them are described as leaders who took participation seriously, committed time and effort to reforms and managed them properly. Vo Van Kiet was elected as prime minister in 1991. His tenure marked the advance of the administrative branch at the expense of the influence of Party's institutions. Representing the reformists, he initiated a large programme of economic reforms. Kiet advocated for further privatizations of state-dominated economy, as well as democratization, reorganized the government structure and urged the broadening of diplomatic ties. In the early 1990s Vietnam gradually recovered from the economic crisis of previous decade. In 1995, the country joined the ASEAN community and normalized relations with the United States, ending 20 years of formal mutual enmity and American embargo after the fall of Saigon (Rama & Võ, 2008). He is described as an architect of economic reforms who was one of the most prominent political leaders that led the Doi Moi reform.

At local level, a research finding of Schmitz (2015) shows that leadership in the reform process varies among provinces. In some provinces, local leadership plays a critical role, whereas in others, central government is a key driver of reforms. Ho Chi Minh City's is an example. Before becoming PRIME MINISTER in 1991, Vo Van Kiet had been Communist Party Secretary in Ho Chi Minh City, where his role in reforms was clearly demonstrated. During his tenure, he was seeking and accepting reform initiatives in numerous ways. For example, he used 'informal' think tank which was expected to make a more important contribution to economic reform than mainstream institutions (Rama & Võ, 2008). In 1976, unsatisfied with the limited technical knowledge of the team in charge of running the city, Kiet established a unit in charge of mobilizing the intellectual resources from the former regime in the south. The main aim of using this unit was to ask for honest advice, confront the views from all sides and to choose in each case the recommendations that seem more appropriate. Another notable case is the contribution of Da Nang's CPV Secretary Nguyen Ba Thanh to the dramatic development of the city through a series of reforms. During his tenure, Da Nang had been widely known in Vietnam as a model city in administrative reforms. We will discuss this case in more detail in the next section.

Leadership and Managing Reform Risks

As widely recognized in change management literature, the resistance to change and reform always exists in every organization, especially in public organizations. In the context of Vietnam, PSR tends to face resistance from various actors who may be insiders or outsiders of public sector. For instance, many managers and bureaucrats with a stake in state business enterprises opposed reforms because of the fear that their protected status would be undermined, or even their control on assets would be denied. For those who work in the fields of land administration, customs, traffic police, tax administration and construction, to whom reforms mean that they have to give up their benefits, are also unwilling to implement reforms.

In addition, the concern of conservatives for stability as a top priority has hindered the government to implement necessary reforms that could result in a period of economic hardships, increased unemployment and socioeconomic inequalities (Abuza, 2002). Other potential risks of reforms, such as conflict of interests among different groups, improper deployment of lower levels, lack of coordination within and among public organizations etc. may negatively affect the effectiveness of reform. There are several effective ways to reduce these risks which can be seen in the reform process such as using appropriate leadership style to undertake reform, establishing a steering group for PSR, being aware of strong leadership traditions in Asia, focussing on the human component of reform process and promoting the existing mutually supportive relationship.

In order to minimize this resistance, leaders or reformers must demonstrate their ability to convince different actors in their organizations, ability to obtain stakeholders' support (both internal and external support) and strong commitment to reform through widespread participation in the reform process. As a head of reformers during the 1990s, Prime Minister Vo Van Kiet was effective in coping with conservatives in the government. Innovators attempted to convince the politburo to consistently continue with the reform programme that was launched since Doi Moi through its fantastic results with dramatic economic growth. He also showed his strong commitment to PSR. At the opening meeting of the National Assembly in 1995, he criticized excessive spending by some ministries, pointed that weak bureaucracy and corruption among government officials as a major barrier to economic development. He stressed that Vietnam had to stop the party interference in government affairs, strongly promoted ministry mergers as a part of PSR and advocated for a greater role for private sector.

Prime Minister Kiet was also an inspiring leader who established a strong sense of urgency. In his speech, he stressed the danger of Vietnam lagging behind its neighbours. He stated that Vietnam had to push for better ties with various countries as a vital step to catch up with them. Similar to other Vietnamese leaders, Kiet also urged for support from international donors. He developed close relationships with international organizations and foreign countries to get necessary financial and technical support for PAR. He was the first Vietnamese leader to travel widely. In both Europe and Asia, Kiet expanded diplomatic and trading ties with many countries and helped to

attract international aid and FDI. During his time as premier, the US embar-
goes against Vietnam were lifted and normal relationships between the two
countries were established (Vuong, 2014).

During its reform periods, the strong tradition of high level of trust and
obligation between leaders and followers in Vietnam was clearly illustrated.
Like many other Asian countries, Vietnamese leaders are traditionally well
respected and followed by organizational members, either as collective or
individual leadership. Especially, in the context of Vietnam where state agencies are organized and operate based on the democratic centralism principle,
the role of leadership is even more emphasized.

The mutually supportive relationship between the provincial executive
(chairman and vice chairmen of the people's committee) and the provincial
party secretary is also key determinant for success of reform in Vietnam.
Government and party leaders tend to be the key people in the provincial
people's committee and leading an alliance seems critical for undertaking
reforms. The more consistent the consensus between the government and the
party, the greater the progress in reforms. The greater the experimentation,
the greater the need to engage the party in discussion. (Rama & Võ, 2008).

Establishing a steering group for PSR is considered as an option for risk
reduction during the time of its implementation. In 1998, Prime Minister Vo
Van Kiet established a steering group for PSR, with prime minister as its chairman, the minister of organization and personnel (now MOHA), the minister of justice, the minister of the office of the government and the head of
the Personnel Administration Institute. The aim of the steering group was to
direct, coordinate and monitor the reform work being carried out by the ministers and the provinces consistent with the directives issued annually by the
prime minister in the government's action programme (Rama & Võ, 2008).
This helped central government to minimize the improper deployment of lower
levels and create a closer coordination between central and local agencies.

Sustaining Reform through Leadership

The public administration in Vietnam has been changing to fulfill the increasing requirements of the society. Under the leadership of CPV, a range of significant reforms were undertaken from the central to the local level based on
the principle of democratic centralism (Hung et al., 2013). Since the 6th Party
Congress, the importance of PSR has been stressed upon and strongly confirmed in the following Party Congress sessions, reflecting commitment of top
leadership in continuing reforms. However, whether or how PSR is sustained

greatly depends on local leaders and managers who are responsible for compliance with the direction, regulations and programme of the central government. The Vietnamese leaders at all levels are well aware that PSR is considered as top priority and a regular and continuing task of public agencies, and it needs to be sustained for a long term. In doing so, the Vietnamese central government seeks the consensus between reformists and conservatives through various ways, uses its appointment and promotion procedures and other managerial tools to encourage local leaders and officials to implement reforms.

The reform process in Vietnam can be explained as an undertaking of basic cooperation among leadership groups, according to which policy changes are driven by the acceptance of new ideas by the leadership rather than by the victory of one group of insiders over another. The early 1990s witnessed a deadlock to come to a consensus within the top Vietnamese leadership on how to proceed with Doi Moi programme of 1986 with very positive initial results (Abuza, 2002). Due to the collapse of socialism across Eastern Europe in the mid-1990s which resulted in division within the CPV and the government and the ideological stuck in a transitional system of market socialism among top leaders, there was a long time of 'reform immobilization'. This hindered higher economic growth at the time when Vietnam needed more reforms to catch up with its ASEAN neighbouring countries.

The Vietnamese leadership used its conventional ways – the consensus principle – to tackle with the conflict. The 7th Party Congress was clearly a compromise for both conservatives and reformers. With many attempts being made, the year of 2002 witnessed the coherence of reformist and conservative strategies of governing to improve transparency within the state and party bureaucracy, and to further economic reforms (Abuza, 2002; Abrami, 2003). That consensus continued to be seen in the 10th, 11th and 12th Party Congress sessions. All CPV resolutions showed the confirmation of fostering reforms to build a modern, effective and efficient public sector consistent with socialist-oriented market economy and international integration. At local and organizational levels, leaders also attempted different ways to reach consensus on reform implementation plans with their staff and different stakeholders such as organizing of workshops and meetings with other public agencies, social groups (farmers, women, youth, etc.) or local enterprises to discuss relevant reform issues, using different dissemination methods (announcement via pubic media, posters, brochures on reform programmes, etc.).

Top Vietnamese leaders also use appointment and promotion procedures and other managerial tools to encourage lower level leaders and officials to implement reforms that are considered as an effective way to sustain reforms. On the other hand, these also assist in enhancing economic investment and growth and thus raising tax income of their localities. At the provincial level, leaders of the people's committees and provincial departments seek promotion to higher positions in the central government or party bodies by implementing reforms. According to Rama and Võ (2008), the local leaders who undertook the early reform experiments were at high positions of the party machinery. Many of them were CPV's provincial level secretaries.

Another effective way to sustain reform, which leaders at both central and local governments also often use, is providing training and guidance on specific reform programmes to managers and employees. Training aims to prepare managers and staff with necessary knowledge, skills and abilities to develop and use policies/programmes successfully. When leaders and subordinates understand how a reform programme operates and get familiar with it, and get more involved in the reform process, they start to appreciate its benefits, which results in the continuity and sustainability of reforms. Thousands of civil servants, including leaders and managers and public employees at all levels, are sent to relevant training courses whenever a specific reform project or programme (e.g., Project 30 on simplification of administrative procedures, one-stop-shop model, programmes on application and development of information technology (IT), etc.) is deployed. Leadership in each central agency or locality usually commits to provide sufficient budget for training and retraining of cadres and civil servants (MCaD, 2010; Vietnamese Government, 2011).

Engaging civil servants and different stakeholders in the reform process also contributes to the sustainability of reforms, because the more they get involved, the longer they commit themselves to reforms. Leadership at each level plays a certain role in encouraging the participation of various government agencies, units and stakeholders, and coordinating them in implementation of reform. For example, at the commune level, the people's committee chairman assigns tasks to his or her staff and coordinates work units in implementing the reform project. He or she chairs meetings with citizens, social organizations (e.g., women union, youth association, etc.) and enterprises, or organizes focus forums (e.g., farmers forum, enterprise forum, etc.) to mobilize the participation of different social groups in discussing relevant reform matters (Hung et al., 2013).

3. CASE OF DA NANG CITY

Da Nang is among the top six richest provinces or municipalities of Vietnam. Its municipal government has obtained very high ranking in terms of education, health services and competitive advantages. Since 1997, its economy has grown rapidly with an annual growth rate of 11.6 per cent, which has even been faster than the growth rate of Ho Chi Minh City and Hanoi. Its industrial and services sectors have been significantly large compared with the national average (Ca, 2014). It has increasingly become an important centre for economic, social, science and technology development.

In the last two decades, Da Nang has been known widely as a model city in administrative reforms. Da Nang is considered a typical example of breaking-the-rule moves as experimental steps for the country. The city's success is closely associated with the talent and determination of its leaders and officials. It is undeniable that the success of Da Nang's reform owes much to the contribution of party secretary and chairman of the People's Council Nguyen Ba Thanh.

During his tenure, being party's chief and chairman of the People's Council at the same time, enabled Thanh to implement reform initiatives quickly (Ca, 2014). Under Thanh's leadership, the main actions taken by the Da Nang Government were providing hard and soft infrastructure, ensuring and enabling environment for business and implementing market-competing measures. Da Nang has made dramatic efforts in socio-economic development. Although Da Nang municipal government was created in 1997, Da Nang has been among the highest performers since the first introduction of provincial ranking in 2005. It was widely observed that Thanh's leadership greatly contributed to the success of reforms.

More specifically, in terms of civil service reform implementation, Thanh was effective in selecting competent people for important tasks and in adopting sound personnel policy. Among the central provinces, Da Nang city is the only one that is successful in attracting well-trained human resources to government agencies. Thanks to many policies to attract talents to Da Nang as suggested by Dr Nguyen Phu Thai, director of the Center for Development of High Quality Human Resources, Da Nang's contingent of public employees has become more powerful. In the past 15 years, the city has attracted more than 1,000 high quality officers and employees. Up to 2013, 20 per cent of the city's government officers were subjected to the talent recruiting policy. Of those, many people occupied leadership positions in public agencies (Vietnamnet, 2013). For example, Dr. Nguyen Hoang Cam, deputy director of the Da Nang department of information and communications, quitted a company in 2006 to work for Da Nang with lower salary because he liked the city leaders' enthusiasm. He has significantly contributed to the achievement of holding country's leading position in the readiness index of ICT application and development in the past five years. It can be said that this policy encouraged their genuine efforts, which in turn will contribute to the success of upcoming reforms.

Thanh was aware of the need of the continuity and sustainability of reforms. Therefore, he always stressed upon the importance of trained personnel in the success of reform, and the need of training for its civil servants and residents. Strong commitment of the leadership is observed in the city training programmes for the future leadership or city residents. In order to meet the increasing demands of skilled labour, the municipal government has begun to cooperate with some foreign organizations to train local residents. Civil servants who are sent abroad for training courses include leaders and managers of city departments and districts (those at the vice head or upward of a division), corps of administrative civil servants (senior experts, principle experts and experts) and officials listed in the source for promotion. The annual budget that Da Nang has devoted to training and retraining of cadres and civil servants was huge.

Similar to many other Vietnamese leaders, Thanh sought to reach a consensus within city government in order to implement effectively reform programmes. In his speech in public, he also stressed upon the urgency of implementing decisive reforms to cure current administrative system. For example, he had a talk with over 4,000 officials of all the levels of Da Nang city at a stadium about city's development strategy and the issues that the city was facing (TalkVietnam, 2012). Such leadership is necessary to reduce the resistance to reform as well as other reform risks.

Leaders and managers at lower levels of Da Nang city also play an important role in the success of reforms. Traditional leadership culture in Vietnam is collective; even though the roles of individual leaders are also emphasized, the success of any reform is associated with a team of leaders. City authority expresses its determination, continuing effort and commitment to create an innovative working environment to promote rapid and dynamic development of the city and to provide people better quality public services. To be specific, the city government issues a number of directives and legal documents, and programmes on reform (e.g., the Da Nang's PAR programmes 2001–2010 and 2011–2020, Decision 43, 2011 on providing information and online public service on websites of government agencies) as well as assigns responsibilities and specific tasks to each local unit, supervising, coordinating and monitoring them during the implementation process of these legal documents and programmes.

For example, significant examples are the application of IT to improve quality of public service delivery and the implementation of the project on developing the city-wide electronic one-stop-shop model. Department of Home Affairs was responsible for developing the project implementation plan for the city people's committee to approve, organizing and coordinate the implementation of the project, evaluating results from local units and reporting to the city people's committee. Head of department of Information and technology was in charge of the overall professional and technical activities, directing, operating, supervising and monitoring all activities of the city department in the field, who is assisted by advisory civil servants (section heads, vice heads and principal experts) and executive civil servants (experts and technicians). Consequently, over the past several years, Da Nang has been recognized as the leading city in the readiness level to apply IT. In 2013, 100 per cent of its agencies and units established their own sectoral and local websites (in 2003, there were only two websites). City units at all levels used electronic one-stop-shop document management software (Ca, 2014).

In addition, in order to minimize possible reform risks as well as ensure the positive effects of PSR, the city government established a mechanism to obtain public opinion and feedbacks on the impacts of administrative reforms on the community. For instance, Da Nang Institute for Socio-Economic Development and Hotline for Public Administrative Services were created to conduct surveys on public services in the city (Ca, 2014). These examples show the role of leadership in deploying and sustaining reforms as well as avoiding possible risks that may occur during the reform process.

4. CONCLUSION

In spite of ambitious programmes for PSR over past decades and some positive achievements, as widely observed in practice, the quality of public sector remains poor and still hinders overall socio-economic development. One of the main reasons for the slow pace of change is that the scope of reform is too broad as it covers all key elements of public sector, meanwhile the capacity of implementing public agencies and individual public servants is still limited. Even though PSR is considered a top priority and a regular and continuing task of public agencies, its implementation in both central and local levels has not been properly carried out. Moreover, the weakness of the existing monitoring, evaluation and reporting system also contributes to the ambiguous results of PSR.

It remains to be seen whether the PSR process in Vietnam can attain its predetermined targets, but in order to achieve PSR results as desired, strengthening of leadership from the top to the lowest level of government during reform process, undoubtedly, is one of the key solutions. The awareness of Vietnamese top leaders of this solution was also shown in the 2011–2020 PAR Master programme as a key guideline for PAR implementation.

Indeed, leaders are widely perceived to play a critical role in leading PSR in Vietnam. However, in practice, their role is mainly to ensure the compliance of regulations and rules regarding PSR among subordinates. The role of leader in motivating people and managing the reform process seems to be neglected. Also, it is observed that after the initial success of reforms, Vietnamese leadership has become less proactive and vigorous in practicing or embracing bold experiments on reforms (Khuong, 2015). To deal with these matters and to promote the effectiveness of leadership in PSR, the following recommendations should be taken into consideration.

First, both central and local leaders should be selected and trained carefully to ensure capable people being selected for important tasks. As suggested by Khuong (2015), these leaders should articulate a clear vision for the country's development as well as local development. More importantly, at a critical time, they need to be aware of the urgency of implementing decisive reforms to catch up with other peers. They should also reflect ability to communicate, convince, cooperate and cope with resisting actors. To obtain these leadership skills, leaders at all levels should participate in training courses more proactively and effectively on related leadership issues. Moreover, some key actors who are in charge of civil and public servants training and development such as MOHA and provincial department of home affairs and National Academy of Public Administration should be the pioneer in reforming the training system for civil and public servants.

Second, as suggested by Wong (2015), it is of significant importance to recognize the tradition of strong leadership in Asia and the high level of trust and obligation between leader and followers. Therefore, any public administration reform in Vietnam should allow the leaders to lead. However, in the new economy, the role of the government, especially the leadership role, should be changed from 'controlling role' to 'enabling role' to create a favourable environment for all stakeholders in the economy to participate in and develop.

Third, the 'gradual, step-by-step' or 'learning-by-doing' approach in implementing PSR as favoured by almost all Vietnamese leaders has been appropriate in the context of Vietnam over the past two decades when it was evident that the roles and responsibilities in implementing government policies remain ambiguous. However, this approach seems to be no longer appropriate in a rapid changing world because of the lack of long-term strategy for change.

Fourth, leadership continuity and stability should be considered to ensure a professional civil service and the success of any reform. It is evident that in Vietnam there is a popularity of *luan chuyen can bo* (cadre transfer) within the political system (among branches, agencies and government level), which can lead to decrease in the continuity and stability of administrative system.

It can be concluded that leadership, either collective or individual, really matters for PSR. Whether the PSR process in Vietnam can reach its predetermined targets greatly depends on how proactive and effective leaders at all levels practice their roles.

REFERENCES

Abrami, R. M. (2003). Vietnam in 2002: On the road to recovery. *Asian Survey, 43*(1), 91–100.

Abuza, Z. (2002). The politics of reform in Vietnam, 1986–2000. In *Vietnam: Current issues and historical background* (194 pp). New York: Nova Publishers.

ADB (Asian Development Bank). (2005). Strategy and Program Assessment, Vietnam: Private Sector Assessment, Hanoi.

Beresford, M. (1988). *Vietnam: Politics, economics, and society.* London: Marxist Regimes Series, Pinter Publisher.

Beresford, M. (2008). Doi Moi in review: The challenges of building market socialism in Vietnam. *Journal of Contemporary Asia, 38*(2), 221–243.

Ca, T. N. (2014). Regional economic development and perspectives for the electronics sector in Vietnam: The case of Da Nang. In F. E. Hutchinson (Ed.). *Architects of growth? Subnational governments and industrialization in Asia* (pp. 149–170). Singapore: Institute of Southeast Asian Studies (ISAS) publications.

Charlesworth, K., Cook, P., & Crozier, G. (2003). *Leading change in the public sector: Making the difference.* London: Chartered Management Institute.

Dinh, Q. X. (1999). The state and the social sector in Vietnam: Reforms and challenges for Vietnam. *ASEAN Economic Bulletin, 16*(3), 373–393.

Dinh, Q. X. (2002). Public administration and civil service reforms in Vietnam. In D. P. Chi & T. N. Binh (Eds.), *The Vietnamese economy: Awakening the dormant dragon* (2003, pp. 245–267), London: RoutldgeCurzon.

Do, X. T., & Truong, Q. (2009). The changing face of public sector management in Vietnam. In C. Rowley & Q. Truong (Eds.), *The changing face of Vietnamese management* (pp. 187–220). *London: Routledge.*

Hung, N. K., Poon, H. Y., Hoa, D. D., Dung, T. N., & Nguyen, X. N. (2013). *Practices and key learning from PAR planning and implementation at the provincial level.* The framework of the Danish-funded Good Governance and Public Administration Reform Program, Phase 1 (GOPA 1, 2008–2011), Hanoi, Vietnam.

Khuong, V. M. (2015). Can Vietnam achieve more robust economic growth? Insights from a comparative analysis of economic reforms in Vietnam and China. *Journal of Southeast Asian Economies (JSEAE), 32*(1), 52–84.

Malesky, E. J., Nguyen, C. V., & Tran, A. (2014). The impact of recentralization on public services: A difference-in-differences analysis of the abolition of elected councils in Vietnam. *American Political Science Review, 108*(01), 144–168.

MCaD (Management Consulting and Development). (2010). *Report on building the training roadmap up to 2020 and training plan up to 2015 for civil servants in Ho Chi Minh City administration.* Hanoi: MCaD.

Minh Chau, D. (1997). Administrative reform in Vietnam: Need and strategy. *Asian Journal of Public Administration, 19*(2), 303–320.

Ministry of Home Affairs. (2010). *Report on review of implementation of public administration reform in the phase 2001–2010.* Hanoi: MOHA.

Ministry of Home Affairs. (2015). *Report on review of implementation of public administration reform in the phase 2011–2015.* Hanoi: MOHA.

Painter, M. (2005). The Public Administration Reform Agenda in Vietnam: Foreign Transplants or Local Hybrids?. In J. Gillespie & P. Nicholson (Eds.), *Asian Socialism and Legal Change: The Dynamics of Vietnamese and Chinese Reform* (pp. 267–287). Canberra: Asia-Pacific Press, Australian National University.

Painter, M. (2008). From command economy to hollow state? Decentralisation in Vietnam and China. *Australian Journal of Public Administration, 67*(1), 79–88.

Painter, M. (2014). Myths of political independence, or how not to solve the corruption problem: Lessons for Vietnam. *Asia & the Pacific Policy Studies, 1*(2), 273–286.

Phan, T. L. H. (2012). *Reforming local government in Vietnam. Lesson learned from Japan.* Ph.D. dissertation. Japan: Nagoya University, Graduate School of Law.

Rama, M., & Võ, V. K. (2008). *Making difficult choices, Vietnam in transition.* Washington, DC: International Bank for Reconstruction and Development (IBRD).

Rowley, C., & Truong, Q. (Eds.). (2009). *The changing face of Vietnamese management.* London: Routledge.

Schmitz, H., Tuan, D. A., Hang, P. T. T., & McCulloch, N. (2015). Drivers of economic reform in Vietnam's provinces. *Development Policy Review, 33*(2), 175–193.

TalkVietnam (2012, March 6). *Da Nang's mayor model – Hope and obstruction.* Retrieved from www.talkvietnam.org.

Thang, N. V., Thang, N. B., Thanh, Q. L., Canh, Q. L., (2015). *Local governance, corruption and public service quality: Evidence from a national survey in Vietnam.* A Joint Policy Research Paper on Governance and Participation Commissioned by Asia Pacific Institute for Management (the National Economics University) and the United Nations Development Programme (UNDP) in Viet Nam, Ha Noi, Vietnam, December 2015.

Truong, Q., & Nguyen, T. T. (2009). The changing face of strategy management in Vietnam. In C. Rowley & Q. Truong (Eds.). *The changing face of Vietnamese management* (pp. 187–220). London: Routledge.

United Nations Development Programme (UNDP). (2009). *Reforming public administration in Vietnam: Current situation and recommendation.* Hanoi: National Political Publishing House.

Van der Voet, J. (2014). The effectiveness and specificity of change management in a public organization: Transformational leadership and a bureaucratic organizational structure. *European Management Journal, 32*(3), 373–382.

Vasavakul, T. (2006). Public administration reform and practices of co-governance: Towards a change in governance and governance cultures in Vietnam. In *Active citizens under political wraps: Experiences from Myanmar/Burma and Vietnam* (pp. 143–165). Chaing Mai.

Vietnamese Government. (2011). *Report on summary of results of PAR for the period of 2001–2010.* Hanoi.

Vietnamnet. (2013, 18 April). *20 percent of Da Nang's civil servants are employed as talents.* Retrieved from www.vnn.vn.

Vuong, Q. H. (2014). Vietnam's political economy: A discussion on the 1986–2016 period. *CEB Working Papers Series,* N°14-010, Université Libre de Bruxelles, Brussels: Belgium.

Wescott, C. G. (2003). Hierarchies, networks and local government in Viet Nam. *International Public Management Review, 4*(2), 20–40.

Wong, W. (2015). Public managers must also be leaders: The hollowing out of leadership and public management reform in Hong Kong. In E. Berman & M. S. Haque (Eds.), *Asian leadership in policy and governance* (Vol. 24, pp. 261–284). Bingley: Emerald.

World Bank. (2004). *Vietnam development report 2005 – Governance*. New York, NY: World Bank.

World Bank. (2006). *Vietnam development report 2007 – Vietnam aiming high*. New York, NY: World Bank.

CHAPTER 7

LEADERSHIP AND PUBLIC SECTOR REFORM IN THE PHILIPPINES

Alex Brillantes and Lizan Perante-Calina

ABSTRACT

In this chapter the authors discuss that despite public sector reform being a primary concern of successive national leaders of the Philippines, 'massive – and sometimes impressive – reorganization plans have not met their declared objectives'. They note that intractable and stubborn problems of Weberian bureaucracy, such as excessive rules and regulations, overlapping structures and procedures, inefficient procedures, lack of coordination, excessive partisan politics and corruption, remain. They examine how leadership can play a pivotal and key role in addressing these problems. Specifically, they argue that reforms should be multi-dimensional, going beyond reorganization and shifting organizational boxes and encompassing changes in behaviour, perspectives and attitudes. Using a concept of 'phronetic leadership', they examine three cases of national, local and civil society leaders, as well as a survey of university leaders. They conclude that leaders can make a difference by developing capacities of themselves and of others, and pushing the boundaries of continuous improvement. However, to be sustainable,

Leadership and Public Sector Reform in Asia
Public Policy and Governance, 151–178
doi:10.1108/S2053-769720180000030007

public sector reforms have to be complemented by reforms of institutions,
structures and procedures and anchored in behaviour, values and a common
vision that is communicated well and owned by all.

Keywords: Bureaucracy; partisan politics; corruption; leadership;
the Philippines

Like many countries in the Third World, the public sector in the Philippines
has been hounded by issues and challenges in governance. These include
corruption and accountability concerns, excessive rules and regulations
resulting in slow, unresponsive and inefficient procedures and the much
blamed 'bureaucratic red tape', overlapping structures and procedures,
lack of coordination due to the so-called 'silo mentality' prevalent in the
bureaucracy and excessive partisan politics.[1] Many of these issues and
challenges – characteristic of 'bureaupathology'[2] and bureaucratic malaise –
may be attributed to the failure of, or lack of, leadership. Of course, others
have attributed these challenges to lack of resources, including financial
resources, certainly a common problem in developing countries, and also
lack of capacities in the bureaucracy. While this is certainly true, this chapter zeroes in on leadership concerns and how leadership in public sector
reform can indeed play a pivotal and key role in addressing the perennial
problems confronted by the public sector at various levels. It examines the
experiences of leaders of national government agencies, local governments
and higher education institutions.

The Philippine political administrative history has shown that public sector reform has always been a primary concern for every administration in the
Philippines, from Manuel Quezon (the first Filipino to head a government of
the entire Philippines between 1935 and 1944) to the present Rodrigo Duterte.
The general goal is to streamline the bureaucracy and to respond promptly
and implement administrative reforms to address corruption and inefficiency
in the delivery of government services. A major leadership challenge has been
sustaining avowed public sector reforms largely because of changes in administration and a Filipino tendency referred to as *'ningas kugon'*.[3]

Public sector reform is a mechanism that introduces innovations in public
management to induce modification, transformation, change and reforms in
several aspects. Reforms vary; they may be any of the following: size reduction
of public sector personnel, streamlining of business processes, curbing bureaucratic red tape and corruption, decentralization, fiscal and economic reforms
and performance management, among other reforms in the social, economic

and political realms. All these faces of reform, ranging from financial to management reform, aim to bring about 'long-term productivity improvements in public sector and better service to the community' (Scott, 1994, p. 5).

The impetus for reform may either be internal or external to the public agency or institution. A primary impetus for reform is leadership. Leadership has mostly been considered an internal force. The drive for reform can also come from the government's politico-administrative structure, internal experiences and frustrations with excessive red tape, inefficiency and lack of accountability. However, calls for reform in the organization have many times been influenced by variations in the extent of organizational hierarchy of institutions, whether it is flat or tall organization, and again, leadership, more specifically whether the leadership style is centralized or decentralized or participatory, again pointing to the critical role of leadership for reform.

The Philippines' public administration system is divided into two tiers – the national and sub-national local governments. The national government comprises various agencies and offices attached to the three core branches of the government, namely the executive, the legislative and the judiciary, that co-exist with each other under the principle of checks and balances. The second tier consists of local governments, which have been exercising the powers devolved to them following the Republic Act 7160 (local government code [LGC]). Being hierarchical, the entire administrative system is replete with rules, regulations, procedures and policies to rationalize its functions, services and authority.

Aside from internal factors, there are also external pressures that stimulate reforms. As cited in the World Bank report on *Doing Business in Philippines*, in 2016, the country ranked 99 among 190 economies in the cases of doing business. It remained unchanged from 99 in 2015. Ease of doing business averaged 121.22 from 2008 until 2016, reaching an all-time high of 144 in 2009 and a record low of 97 in 2014.[4] Many of the indicators used to measure the ease of doing business basically assess procedures[5] and the accompanying institutions that enable (or disable) the performance of such function. That the Philippines ranks very low in the ease of doing business suggests that still much more has to be done to ease the doing of business in the Philippines by streamlining processes and procedures. Nevertheless, the leadership of the three branches of the government, namely the executive, the legislative and the judiciary, has seen some reform measures implemented for the benefit of the country and its citizens.

The demand for reforms in the politico-administrative system can – and many times must – come from the citizens themselves. As stakeholders many times considered formally 'eternal' to the system, it is imperative that citizens continue to demand better service delivery. The public can scrutinize – within the context of continuous monitoring and evaluation – the kind of services that the government provides. For one, the public expects efficiency, account-ability, transparency, productivity, responsiveness, professionalism and value-for-money services from the government. The citizens – as taxpayers – have the right to demand for leadership and direction from the government. With the growing bottom-up demand for better service delivery, accountability and transparency from both internal and external drivers, public sector reform initiatives and good leadership are crucial towards the attainment of good governance.

Other countries in Asia and all over the world are similarly implement-ing reforms in the public sector. The growing globalization standards require transforming systems in government to help the country keep up with the increased level of standards in other countries. Genuine public reform is not only inevitable, it is imperative. It is not only crucial for the overall develop-ment of the country but also vital in the sustained regional and international relations of the country with its neighbours in the Association of Southeast Asian Nations (ASEAN) region as well as with other countries for significant political and economic relationships.

Leadership matters for reform: The current era: After the ouster of the Marcos dictatorship in 1986, then President Corazon Aquino proclaimed what was referred to as a 'revolutionary government' with a freedom consti-tution. The 1986 Freedom Constitution that set aside the 1973 Constitution of Ferdinand Marcos is counted as a major public sector reform initia-tive that helped shape the Philippine bureaucracy. The shift of the coun-try's politico-administrative system from Marcos' 20-year term from 1965 to 1986 to a democratic government with the installation of President Corazon C. Aquino (1986–1992) opened the country to the introduction of several changes in the political-administrative state. The 1986 Freedom Constitution was enacted as a provisional constitution to protect the human rights of the people. Aquino then convened the constitutional commission for the crafting of the 1987 Philippine Constitution, which was ratified on 2 February 1987 and now stands as the supreme law of the land. Major institutional reforms were made for changing structures, institutions and processes. The president was granted certain powers to include the removal of officials from office and reorganize the bureaucracy, and an institutional arrangement of reform was installed that allowed local governments to do the same by virtue of decentralization, which will be further discussed in this chapter.

Another major policy of reform document is the Administrative Code of 1987 (Executive Order (EO) No. 292). This code embodies the major structural and procedural principles and rules of governance; it functions as an enabling law of the constitution, which acts as a guide and framework on how government institutions function towards a balanced public administrative system. These two above-mentioned landmark reform frameworks have contributed to making the politico-administrative system responsive to the rapidly changing times. They are now the bases of all other laws that the country has enacted after 1977. Looking back, 1986 stands as a watershed in the Philippine history: It was the year when the Filipino people regained their freedom from almost two decades of Marcos' dictatorship and the restoration of formal structures and processes of a democratic ('post dictatorship') government.

PUBLIC SECTOR REFORMS, REORGANIZATION AND PRESIDENTIAL LEADERSHIP

The post World War II Philippine political administrative history shows that reforming the public sector has been a primordial concern of the leaders of the country.[6] The bedrock of these reforms was the reorganization of government labelled variously by presidents as 'streamlining', 're-engineering', 'reinventing', 'rationalizing' and 'right sizing' the government. Call it what they could, these reorganization initiatives included strategies such as decentralization of the bureaucracy (that will be discussed in the next section), private sector participation – and even sometimes leadership – in governance. Parenthetically, these could be located within the framework of New Public Management (NPM) that at one time has become increasingly popular among public administration academics and practitioners.

The milieu of reorganization in the Philippines frequently targeted the recalcitrant elements in the bureaucracy. Reorganization as a handle for reform always espoused the restoration of efficiency, economy and effectiveness (the 3Es) in the government. Of course, public sector-oriented practitioners and scholars, consistent with the new public administration paradigm of the sixties, always advocated a fourth 'E', which was *equity*. It must be noted that the reorganizational agenda of Philippine presidents that specifically stated the 3E imperatives were those of Elpidio Quirino in the 1950s, Ferdinand Marcos in the early 1970s upon the proclamation of martial law and Corazon Aquino in the mid-1980s.

It is within this context that one of the first acts of President Corazon Aquino upon assumption of office was the issuance of EO No. 5 creating the Presidential Commission on Government Reorganization (PCGR). The issuance was a prompt response to the necessity of effecting necessary and proper changes in the organizational and functional structures of Philippine bureaucracy. EO No. 5 highlights five fundamental philosophies of governance – promoting private initiative, decentralization, cost-effectiveness, efficiency of frontline services and accountability. With the creation of PCGR, reforms were introduced in an extensive and comprehensive approach taking into consideration the two major pieces of government documents – the 1987 Constitution and the Administrative Code of 1987.

When Aquino's term of office expired, a military leader was installed into office in the person of President Fidel V. Ramos (1992–1998), who introduced EO No. 49 that streamlined and restructured the bureaucracy by adopting a homogeneous grouping of functionally related government agencies in consonance with the Administrative Code of 1987.

The next president, Joseph E. Estrada (1998–2001), a former local chief executive, issued EO No. 165 (re-engineering the bureaucracy for better governance programme) at the start of his term. EO No. 165 aimed to develop an efficient, result-oriented and innovative bureaucracy that will support effective governance and sustainable socio-economic growth. It also aimed to fast track management and financial reforms to make the bureaucracy more responsive to the needs of the general public and evolve efficient and effective organizations operating within available resources.

In 2001, Estrada was ousted for alleged corruption and malversation of public funds. The Vice president, Gloria Macapagal-Arroyo (2001–2010), succeeded him. She issued EO No. 366 (rationalization plan) that defined the government's proper role in society, and focussed on core governance functions to improve its performance. In this regard, reforms would transform the bureaucracy into an efficient and result-oriented structure.

The administration of President Benigno Aquino III (2010–2016) was guided by EO No. 18 (rationalizing the office of the president). The said Executive Order basically provided guidelines to improve and systematize government's operations by (a) focussing its efforts on its vital/core functions and priority programmes and projects, and channelling resources to these core public services and (b) minimizing areas of overlap and redundancies within and among departments/agencies.

Under the administration of President Rodrigo R. Duterte, EO No. 1 (re-engineering the office of the president towards greater responsiveness to the attainment of development goals) was issued on 30 June 2016. Just the same with other issuances, the said executive order is germane to the provisions of the Administrative Code of 1987, providing continuing authority to the President to reorganize the administrative structure of his office (Section 31, Chapter 10, Title III, Book III of EO No. 292). Duterte also underscored the need to 'right size' the bureaucracy in his state of the nation address in 2017.

Table 1 summarizes the various reorganization initiatives introduced by different presidents of the Philippines from 1898 to 2017.

The above-mentioned reform initiatives introduced through presidential leadership (although variations of reorganization such as re-engineering, reinventing or rationalizing or right sizing) are manifestations of a strong role, and yes, leadership, by the executive department, playing a significant role in effecting institutional arrangement of reform programmes. Being the highest policy-making body, the executive department has the crucial role in steering reforms.

Notably, a number of specific presidential-driven reforms to improve the national government offices include performance-based bonus (PBB), open government partnership, accountability mechanisms, civil service reform road map, including the strategic performance management system, among others.

Exemplary performance in the delivery of services has been recognized through the PBB. Implemented in 2012, the PBB is 'merit-based incentive programme aimed to institute a culture of excellence in public service across the bureaucracy' (www.gov.ph/pbb/). A monetary reward or bonus is granted to individual employees as well as to government offices. Aside from this, the Salary Standardization Law was also implemented, providing for annual increase in the salaries of civil servants across the bureaucracy (Joint Resolution No. 4 series of 2009).

The Civil Service Commission (CSC), as the central personnel agency, has developed a road map towards a strategic human resources and organizational development. The CSC, through its present mechanism called the Philippine governance system (PGS), was driven to adopt an effective and efficient human resource management and development for the Philippine bureaucracy by 2015. It also aimed high to be Asia's leading centre of excellence for strategic human resources and organizational development by 2020–2030.

Anchored on the core values of love of God and country, excellence and integrity, the CSC now seeks to realize its vision by 2030 with its eight strategic initiatives that were carefully selected to complement its objectives and measures. These strategic initiatives are: (1) *strategic performance management system*: the human resource mechanism that measures office

Table 1.   Reorganization and Public Sector Reform Initiatives in the
Philippines (1898–2013).

Type of Government Reorganization	Period	President	Reorganizational Law	Philosophy
Pre-government survey reorganizational commission (pre-GSRC)*	1936–1945 1946–1948 1947–1953	Manuel Quezon Manuel Roxas Elpidio Quirino	Government survey board Reorganization committee Reorganization commission	Less spoils, Filipinization Economy, efficiency
Government survey reorganizational commission (GSRC)	1954–1956	Ramon Magsaysay	Republic Act No. 997	Economy, efficiency
Presidential commission on reorganization (PCR)	1969–1986 1970 1972	Ferdinand Marcos	EO No. 281 Presidential decree No. 71 Integrated Reorganization Plan (IRP)	Economy & efficiency, economic-social development
Presidential commission on government reorganization (PCGR)	1986–1992	Corazon Aquino	EO No. 5	De-marcosification Decentralization Economic Rationality and social justice
Streamlining of the office of the president	1992–1998	Fidel V. Ramos	EO No. 149	Economic growth, social equity and national solidarity and unity
Re-engineering the bureaucracy for better governance Program	1998–2001	Joseph Estrada	EO No. 165	Efficiency, innovation, effective governance and sustainable socio-economic growth
Rationalization plan	2001–2010	Gloria Macapagal-Arroyo	EO No. 6	Efficiency and effectiveness
Rationalizing the office of the president	2010–2016	Benigno Aquino III	EO No. 18	Economy, efficiency effectiveness and transparency
Re-engineering the office of the president	2017–present	Rodrigo R. Duterte	EO No. 1	Greater responsiveness to the attainment of development goals

Source: Gonzales, J. & Deapera L. (1987); updated by Brillantes and Perante-Calina.

*Pre-GSRC consists of the following: (1) Government Survey Board (1936); (2) Reorganization Committee (1947); and (3) Reorganization Commission (1950)

**PCR as extended in 1972, consequently attached to the Office of the President until its abolition in February 1986.

performance and serves in setting standards for alignment of individual and organizational objectives; (2) *anti-red tape*: massive conduct of the report card survey and conferment of the seal of excellence; (3) *ISO certification*: certification of CSC exams, adjudication of cases and training programmes; (4) *restructuring*: functional competencies-based re-engineering; (5) *resource generation and management:* generate financial resources through traditional means; (6) *information, communication and technology (ICT)*: strengthening ICT; computerized exam programme; digitization of statement of assets and liabilities net worth (SALN); information technology-based reporting system, call centre ng bayan, website enhancement; (7) *marketing*: branding CSC through marketing its programme; honour awards programme, civil service academy, computerized exams and the anti-red tape act; and (8) *HR accreditation*: HR plan, competency standards, regional training enhancements and comprehensive wellness programme (CSC Reform Agenda 2012).

The CSC endeavours to be more citizen- and client-centred; strategic in terms of formulating and implementing policies; more result-oriented than overly focussed on procedures and to be more empowering and entrepreneurial. These thrusts came about after the PGS examined the following four areas: (1) roadmap, vision and mission from another perspective; (2) strategies for the CSC to be more relevant; (3) fresh insights and inspiration to propel CSC beyond its traditional mandates and relationships and (4) the opportunity to revisit and reaffirm personal and organizational values (CSC Reform Agenda 2010).

Indeed, the above-mentioned presidential reform initiatives are manifestations of a strong leadership in the executive department, playing a significant role in effecting institutional arrangement of reform programmes. As the top policy initiator and maker, the president, supported by the executive department has the crucial role in steering reforms.

PUBLIC SECTOR REFORMS, DECENTRALIZATION AND LOCAL LEADERSHIP

At the local level, local governments being front liners in the delivery of services, have been restructured through a system of decentralization. With the enactment of LGC in 1991, local government units came to enjoy local autonomy so that the services at the lower level became more receptive to the needs of local constituents. The code provides for mechanisms to attain local autonomy such as greater people participation, innovativeness and creativeness, local–national relationships and expanding leagues of local governments.

Over the years, decentralization has paved the way for a number of best practices in local governance mostly contributed by exemplary leadership of municipal and city mayors and provincial governors. The practices reflect how leadership matters taking into account the strong institutional framework, culture and values in a certain locality. Decentralization and local autonomy contributed to the emergence of outstanding leaders at the local level as evidenced not only by Galing Pook Awards that confers recognition to outstanding and innovative local governments in the country but also to local leaders through the Local Government Leadership Awards (LGLA), where the key role of transformational leaders in the process of local development are recognized.

Innovations at the local level have been sustained by the local leaders who built upon the operational capacity to succeed in reform implementation. Indeed, the more important question is: How do leaders sustain the gains of decentralization after 25 years since 1991? It is in this context that developing new capacities of local leadership is imperative because of their strategic position as frontline leaders in local governance.

Two years after the enactment of the LGC, the local government academy of the department of interior and local government, together with the Asian Institute of Management, launched the Galing Pook Awards Programme that recognized innovations and excellence at the local level. The programme, inspired by the innovations in Local Governance of the Kennedy School of Government of Harvard University and the Innovation in Public Service of the Institute of Public Administration of Canada, aimed to recognize and document outstanding local government programmes at the local level. Galing Pook has been conducted for over two decades and continues to be among the most prestigious awards for local governments. It has in fact been referred to as the 'Oscars' of local governments.

Our own study on local governance[7] has a specific chapter entitled 'What Makes Excellent Leaders: The Local Government Leadership Award' that focussed on the key role of leadership that enabled innovations at the local level. More specifically, the book cited the following key success factors – empirically based – for local innovations:

- A hospitable policy environment;
- A 'triggering crisis' such as flood, fire, etc;
- Aggressive local government;[8]

- Aggressive civil society;[9]
- Inadequacy of financial resources;
- Response to a demand for specific basic services such as water, power, etc;
- Attendance in a local and international training;
- Enabling national government programmes; and
- Initiated by a university or local academic institution.

More importantly, our work looked deeper into the reasons behind the sustainability of innovative programmes. Topmost among these reasons was *leadership*. Other reasons included ownership by local bureaucracy, people participation and support, harnessing ICT, muti-sectoral cooperation, media and information dissemination, support and ownership of leagues of local governments, and support of international stakeholders.

Indeed, leadership did matter for local governments that have become paragons of governance innovations at the local level.

Looking deeper into the role of leadership and reflecting upon the so-called 'question behind the question'[10] not only in bringing about innovations but equally important in sustaining innovations, we conclude that leadership can also be contextual. Our cases of outstanding leaders include Bayani Fernando, former mayor of the city of Marikina for many years, whose strong, authoritarian – but effective – leadership made a name for his city as one of the most innovative cities in the Philippines that became a hall-of-fame awardee of Galing Pook. Then there was another outstanding personality, former local chief executive Jesse Robredo, whose local government, Naga City, was also conferred the Galing Pook award for many times, making it a Galing Pook Hall of Fame Awardee as well. One of the major conclusions of the *innovations* as it related to leadership was that the context of leadership styles must be considered. For instance, depending upon the circumstances and the imperatives of the times and events, leadership could be very participative (as was the case of Robredo) or it could also be highly authoritarian (as in the case of Fernando), and could even be plotted in a continuum, with each side of leadership approach (participative to authoritarian) on both ends of the continuum. However, both could certainly bring about good – and responsive – governance as their Galing Pook awards attest.

THREE 'PHRONETIC' LEADERS IN THE PHILIPPINES

We were part of an international study group of scholars that documented the experiences of leaders in the ASEAN region and Japan. Phronetic leadership draws its origins from the work of Aristotle and Plato, also referred to as leadership based on practical wisdom, and used by Ikujiro Nonaka writing about the imperatives of a 'wise leader' (Nonaka & Hirotaka, 1995).[11] We identified such phronetic leaders in the Philippines. The concept of 'practical wisdom' came from the idea of phronesis, one of the three forms of knowledge identified by Aristotle,[12] and six properties of 'wise leadership' are described and operationalized. Practical wisdom is experiential knowledge that facilitates individuals to make ethically sound decisions.[13] Nonaka points out that phronesis is a virtuous habit of making judgements and taking actions that serve the common good. While Nonaka's phronetic leadership paradigm is mostly from successful companies in the private sector, it has been argued that leadership need not be sector-specific and is actually universal. Hence, phronetic leaders being what they are may also be found in the public sector.[14] Following are the six abilities of phronetic leaders:

1. Ability to make judgement on goodness
2. Ability to perceive reality as it is
3. Ability to create *ba* (or a community brought together by a set of common interests)
4. Ability to articulate the essence[15]
5. Ability to exercise political power
6. Ability to foster phronesis in others.[16]

In the Philippines, our team documented three cases of phronetic leaders from national and local governments and also from civil society,[17] who demonstrate the above abilities. These leaders, also referred to as 'transformational' leaders due to their accomplishments in actually reforming and transforming their organizations, are as mentioned:

1. Tomas Africa of the National Statistic Office (NSO), a national government agency
2. Feliciano Belmonte, mayor of a local government
3. Antonio Meloto, a civil society leader and founder of Gawad Kalinga.

The NSO[18] is the primary statistical arm of the Philippine government mandated to collect, compile, classify, produce, publish and disseminate general purpose statistics and to carry out and administer the provisions of the Civil Registry Law. This case[19] of the NSO under the stewardship of its leaders (who occupied the positions of administrators), Tomas Africa, and succeeded by Carmencita Ericta, illustrated dramatic improvement in the national agency's services. Africa served as administrator for over a decade (1989–2001) and likewise did his successor Ericta (2001–2014). The NSO leaders Africa and Tomas made remarkable contributions to the success of the agency's reform initiatives.

When administrator Africa was appointed by the president in 1989, service delivery in the agency was considered by the public as anything but efficient. There were long queues of clients for getting authenticated civil registry documents. The waiting period took weeks before they could get their requested documents. They had to line up for many hours just to file the request, and afterwards line up again for long hours to get it, or sometimes, only to be told to come back another time. NSO employees were overworked, embarrassed and wanted to improve their surroundings and services.

Both Africa and Ericta using their 'oido'[20] (translated as hands-on) in management put importance to NSO's human resources. As leaders they see the potential of others and foster goodness in them. They led and encouraged NSO people to think of doable solutions to their problems. Together, they worked with them in drawing up plans that they could implement on their own. More importantly, they always attributed success to NSO people, emphasizing that '*we were all in it together*'.[21]

The leadership and management style of the two administrators introduced gradual changes in the way the services are delivered to the clients. As a result, in 1991, the NSO received the Philippine Quality Award for Performance Excellence Level 1. By June 2002, civil registry copies were released within a day or the next day. Today, it only takes a few minutes to transact with the NSO.

Needless to say, with many changes and improvements implemented in the NSO over a period of two decades, it has now become one of the best agencies in government, and has served as a paragon for good governance for many. Morale and pride among the employees has been restored. All these are mostly due to leadership – transformational, phronetic and otherwise.

Another case that examined leadership and management practices was that of former Quezon City mayor Feliciano 'Sonny' Belmonte, who served as mayor of Quezon City, one of the biggest cities of the country, for close to nine years (2001–2010). Earlier on, before he became an elected mayor of his city, Mayor Belmonte served as the head of other national government corporations[22] before he became a mayor and has now moved on to be the Speaker of the House of Representatives of the Philippines.[23]

Quezon City (QC) is one of the cities in Metro Manila. It has the largest population (3.18 million in 2012) and the largest area in the region

(161.13 sq km). When mayor Belmonte took the helm of leadership in 2001, the city was deeply buried in debt. The city government had a bank debt of PhP 1.25 billion and suppliers and contractors were claiming PhP 1.96 billion. The state of the city's poor population was bad with high incidence of drug abuse, juvenile delinquency, child labour, unemployment and illiteracy.

With Belmonte as the mayor of Quezon City, a dramatic turnaround in the city government was achieved. The city's 2001 income of PhP 3.64 billion became PhP 9.16 billion in 2009. After nine years in office, he left a financially robust city government that was not only debt-free but also had savings of more than PhP 1 billion. He put in place programmes for poverty alleviation, livelihood, education and sustainable development, among others, that helped a lot in improving the lives of city's residents. As a leader, he was unconventional and not afraid to experiment and try new frontiers. He was instrumental in increasing the city's tax rates despite the probable backlash due to the move's unpopularity. Despite this, Belmonte immediately put the money to good use, i.e., improved infrastructure and services, which was easily realized by all.

Belmonte received various awards, including the LGLA for Most Outstanding City Mayor (2003).[24] He also received for the City the Galing Pook Award for Effective Fiscal Management (2003), the Galing Pook Award for Outstanding Government Programme for the Molave Youth Home Programme (2005) and the Galing Pook Award for the Payatas Dumpsite Transformation Project (2008).

The third case of phronetic leadership was that of Antonio 'Tony' Meloto, a private individual who founded Gawad Kalinga (GK); it has been recognized nationally and internationally as one of the most successful and empowering civil society groups in the country that introduced remarkable innovations in helping the poor, thereby complementing government's efforts in reducing poverty in the country.[25] Gawad Kalinga, which means 'to give care', is a non-government organization that aims to build homes and better quality of life using volunteerism and the spirit of *bayanihan*[26] (cooperation). The first community that Gawad Kalinga built was for 43 families in Manila. It has since grown internationally with projects in Cambodia, Indonesia and Papua New Guinea. Today, Gawad Kalinga is proud to state that it has built around 200,000 houses in over 2,000 communities with around 20,000 regular volunteers, 250 employees and 500 companies collaborating with it. Apart from literally building houses, the more important accomplishment of Gawad Kalinga was its ability to build communities of practice. Similar to the Gawad Kalinga volunteers, residents of Gawad Kalinga communities are grounded in good old fashioned patriotism and love for country and self-less dedication. One primary ideology Gawad Kalinga is '*Una sa serbisyo. Huli sa Benepisyo*'.[27]

Under Meloto's leadership, Gawad Kalinga was able to uplift the poor. He harnessed the energies of volunteers – motivated mostly by good old fashioned love for country and patriotism – coming from different sectors – academe, business and the government, and also from different countries. Because of his accomplishments, and perhaps more importantly, his following,[28] Meloto was offered cabinet berth by different presidents of the country. However, he refused, recognizing that his 'comes from my not desiring power'. As a testament to his – and the movement's accomplishments – Meloto was recognized nationally and internationally, and was conferred many awards, more notably of which are: 2006 Ramon Magsaysay Award for Community Leadership, 2006 Outstanding Filipino Award for Community Service, 2010 Reader's Digest Asia Philippines' Most Trusted Award, 2010 Ernst & Young Social Entrepreneur of the Year and the 2012 Skoll Award for Social Entrepreneurship.

The three exemplifying cases of leadership and management that could be emulated by executive officials of public organizations are the National Statistic Office, Quezon City and Gawad Kalinga. An essentially basic feature of a successful leadership is the sustainability of reforms initiated even without the physical presence of leader. This has been seen in the case of NSO, Quezon City and Gawad Kalinga. They nurtured younger leaders and developed succession plans.[29] Leadership is fundamental because it does matter in sustaining innovations. 'Sustaining innovations as the key to stability is understanding the fact that when the leader is out of the picture, the reforms and innovations introduced by this leader remain' (Brillantes, 2014).

Admittedly, there are several constraints in leadership. However, in dealing with different situations, leaders are confronted with challenges in governance (i.e., corruption and accountability concerns, expected inefficiencies and mediocrity that characterize many governments, etc.) It is certainly not the intention of this chapter to romanticize leadership in public sector reform. As our framework suggests, leadership is only a handle, a lever, albeit a major lever for public sector reforms. That being said, taking from many focussed group discussions and interviews with our leader-respondents for this chapter, the following are the concerns they continue to encounter as leaders, and perhaps reveal that, in spite of them being phronetic leaders, there continue to be many challenges that they have to confront and sometimes fail to overcome:

1. In spite of many victories (big and small) that phronetic leaders are able to attain, there continues to be endemic corruption and lack of accountability at various levels of government. Corruption has been so deeply embedded and institutionalized that it has become an accepted fact of life of public sector. The challenge is not to eliminate it (because as experience has shown this is practically an impossible task) but to minimize and lessen its impact, negative effects and, at the practical level, minimize the costs of corruption. This has been a realistic and attainable goal of our leaders.

2. Apathy in the bureaucracy and cynicism of people has been another constant challenge confronted by phronetic leaders, also sometimes referred as 'change agents'. 'Here we go again' has become a common refrain among the jaded elements in the bureaucracy and among the citizens when new leaders come in, fired with a desire to bring about reforms. Cynics – in and out of the bureaucracy – have doused cold water upon the enthusiasm of the so-called change agents. In one institution we have dealt with, skeptics in the bureaucracy said: 'Commissioners come and go, but we remain'. This has become a source of discouragement for some leaders, and unfortunately has led to the non-sustainability of reforms initiated by some leaders.

3. Then there is the perennial lack of financial resources that led to the failure of reform initiatives. This has always been a challenge, causing leaders to experiment and adopt innovative means to augment limited finances, ranging from contracting out to privatization to partnerships with private and other sectors. Admittedly, not all experiments have succeeded.

4. And finally, another major challenge encountered by phronetic leaders that have tripped their initiatives and innovations was the lack of capacities – human resources – in the bureaucracy itself. Hence, programmes to develop internal capacities – both human and organizational – have been initiated by leaders. These include visioning and team-building exercises, constant training, exposures and even immersion of officials and staff in the bureaucracy.

Africa, Ericta, Belmonte and Meloto are the four phronetic leaders in the public sector who transformed their organizations simply by being wise leaders.[30] Phronetic leadership, variously known as wise leadership or even leadership characterized by practical wisdom, certainly would be very useful and practical for executives and leaders, be they operate in the firm or at national, local or even international levels.

LEADERSHIP IN ACADEMIA: A SURVEY OF STATE UNIVERSITY AND COLLEGE PRESIDENTS

As part of this chapter's efforts to provide more Philippine context to public leadership, we decided to conduct an indicative survey[31] of presidents of public higher education institutions also referred to as state universities and colleges (SUC). The survey sought to draw their insights as leaders at the helm of public institutions seeking to implement much needed reforms in their SUC. The survey, entitled 'Innovations and Excellence: Leadership and Public Sector', requested the respondents to answer a short set of 10 questions. The questions were about aspects of leadership and on general organization and management.

On aspects of leadership, the SUC presidents responded the following questions:

- What would you consider among your outstanding accomplishments as a leader so far?
- What are the biggest challenges you encountered, and how did you handle those challenges?
- What are the factors behind the success of your leadership, and the qualifications needed to become an effective leader?
- Based on your experience, what would you consider are the qualifications needed to become an effective leader?

On general organization and management, the questions to the respondents included the following:

- What reforms or innovations did you introduce upon assumption of office and during your incumbency?
- What could best explain the success of the reform you introduced in your university?
- What were the major obstacles, if any, in the implementation of reforms in your organization?
- How important was support from the national government or other agencies for the success of the reform? What support did they provide?
- How important was support from other sectors (national and local government, donors, etc.)? Can you give examples?
- How do you ensure the continuity of your reform in the future?

In analysing the responses of our SUC presidents-leaders, we utilized our governance reform framework that included 'leadership' as a fundamental area of reform.

More specifically, our enhanced governance reform framework, which has been built upon our earlier work,[32] identified five areas that should be considered in designing and implementing of public sector reforms. The five areas are: (1) reforming institutions, structures, processes and procedures; (2) reforming values, behaviour and mindsets, which we called metanoia[33] to suggest a new way of looking at things, adopting a shift in paradigms; (3) enabling mechanisms for leadership – duty bearers; whom we suggest should be 'phronetic', using what Aristotle referred to as 'practical wisdom'; (4) enabling mechanisms for citizens engagement who may be referred to as 'duty bearers' and (5) communication. All these are driven – and bound together – by a common vision. The Philippines has adopted AmBisyon Natin 2040, which is the first of the four medium-term plans that will work towards realizing the collective vision of Filipinos over the next 25 years.[34]

These areas of reform occur within the context of rapid globalization without neglecting the local context ('think global, act local'), hence *glocalization*, and a world whose relationships among nations are characterized by a combination of cooperation and competition, hence *coopetition*. This is more significant considering the institutionalization of regional bodies such as the ASEAN marked by cooperation and competition among its members.

This is shown in Fig. 1, which we called Public Sector Reform Framework 4.0.

Fig. 1.   Reform Governance Framework 4.0.

The following is a discussion on the responses of our SUC president-leaders taken from our public sector reform framework.

Accomplishments as SUC president–leaders: Among the outstanding accomplishments of SUC presidents are the accreditation of academic courses; more access to higher education (i.e., adoption of socialized tuition scheme and scholarship programmes); resource generation for development of facilities and institutional core processes (i.e., establishing of procedures for human resources, maintaining previous organizational structure and quality assurance). According to the presidents, some main, enabling mechanisms have improved interpersonal and working relationships; proper placement of personnel; empowering faculty and staff; career development (e.g., training and the corresponding promotion) and potential linkages (e.g., industry–community–university–local government linkages). They also improved participation of faculty engagement in planning and decision-making; increased participative and consultative management, and increased faculty participation in national and international conferences, especially in sharing research outputs. They also emphasized changing the values and behaviours of faculty, staff and employees needed to transform universities which respect the rights of colleagues. To this end, they used clear vision, mission and goals and transparency in communication and relationships was the top concern of SUC presidents. The aim was to establish a two-way communication approach in conveying the plans and strategies of the university.

Biggest challenges of SUC president-leaders: Among the biggest challenges that SUC presidents encountered include political interventions in the appointments, wherein the endorsement of political leaders matters most. This means that the freedom of appointing authority is somehow influenced by such dynamics which is prevalent in public personnel management. Minimum qualification requirements for the position then would suffice. The second major challenge identified by SUC president leaders were the strict and rigid requirements – and interpretation – of audit rules and procedures of the Commission on Audit. Other challenges encountered by SUC presidents were the following: meagre funding if not shortage; management and improvement of physical landscape, facilities; bureaucratic system that hampers the procurement process; improvement of facilities, and systems and procedures; resistance to change; and death threats, white paper/poison letters circulation.

Factors behind successful leadership and qualifications needed to become an effective leader: Leadership by example and communication leads to successful leadership but knowledge, skills, expertise and experience are key ingredients in attaining success and efficiency in an organization.

Reforms and innovations: The presidents noted many reforms such as streamlining of organizational structures, strengthening of procurement systems, administration and production, school site development, manual of operation, computerization of enrolment, full application of procurement laws, monitoring and evaluation of programmes and the adoption of build-operate-transfer (BOT) schemes. In organizations such as SUC, which is public, the area of administration and management is to focus on reform and innovation. Key enabling mechanisms for leadership were communication, professionalism and transparency in budgeting. Financial resources play a vital role in the implementation of reform, training, facilities and equipment, as well as in improving and promoting quality education to improve standards, including support from the lead agency, i.e., national government agency, which is the Commission on Higher Education.

However, implementing reforms faced many threats such as the inadequacy of financial resources to implement reforms, political intervention, conflicting rules of key government agencies (i.e., commission on audit, commission on higher education and department of budget and management) and limited experts in the field of research and extension service. Other threats involved were resistance to change, traditional senior faculty and staff and the culture of entitlement (i.e., preference of Filipinos to claim rights rather than to abide the duties and obligations to enable the organization to which they belong achieve its mandate).

To ensure continuity of reform in the future, continuous review and revision of the programmes implemented is needed, along with capacity building and strategic planning. There is also a need for support from stakeholders, provision of incentives and rewards to outstanding employees, proper communication of plans and reforms and openness are also important in ensuring continuity of reform measures.

In such a case, leadership really matters. Introducing reform measures is not an easy task; it takes a lot of things to consider, from functionary to organization. Knowledge management is likewise very important in making innovations. There are considerable number of state universities that have introduced innovations because of some factors such as leadership, relevant training and skills and their capacity to introduce innovations (e.g., budget, income, number of enrollees and external support). That is why we have to go back to the question: 'Are leaders born or made?' The debate continuous, especially in the public sector as there are a number of challenges faced by them, including budget constraints, the hierarchical nature of organization and the people to manage. However, learning as a process and continuous capacity building programmes should be emphasized by the public sector.

CONCLUSIONS

Leadership and public sector reforms are two intertwined – and inseparable – concepts. The Philippine political administrative history has shown that the role of leadership in public sector reform cannot be overemphasized. Our history has shown that no less than the country's chief executive – the president – has been at the tip of the spear of public sector reforms. All chief executives of the country – from Roxas to Quirino in the late 1940s and 1950s, to Macapagal and Marcos in the 1960s and 1970s, to Aquino and Ramos and Estrada in the 1980s and 1990s, to Macapagal-Arroyo, Aquino and Duterte in the contemporary Philippines – have put public sector reform through the reorganization of executive branch as primordial in their executive agenda.

Still the following question at the back of our mind remains: Considering the many efforts and movements to reform the public sector, why should we be more hopeful whenever a new reorganization plan is initiated and affected? The mere fact that reorganization has been topmost in the chief executive's agenda suggests the following two issues. First, the earlier massive – and sometimes impressive – reorganization plans have not met their declared objectives as has been shown in Table 1.

The so-called classic 3Es have always been invoked: economy, efficiency and effectiveness (the fourth E, equity, was later added considering the 'public' nature of public sector reform), hence the need to say: yes, reorganize again. Second, public sector reform is a dynamic, continuous and live process considering the need to respond (or react, depending on one's perspective) to demands of a rapidly changing environment brought about by globalization, including global warming, global trade wars, information technology, etc. The reform imperative is also a recognition of the intractable and stubborn nature of the bureaucracy, considering the entrenched nature of hierarchic bureaucratic institutions' rules, norms and processes that are hallmarks of any Weberian bureaucracy that by nature are resistant to change.[35] These by themselves are not bad, considering that the Weberian values are supposed to promote professionalism, continuity and stability in the bureaucracy. This dynamics of the imperatives for change and reform and the need to protect the status quo have become contradictory forces that could have cancelled out and neutralized each other.

It was within the above context that over the years we developed our framework for public sector reform. We have argued that reforms have to be multi-dimensional, going beyond reorganization and shifting organizational boxes.[36] Reforms should encompass changes in behaviour, perspectives and attitudes, and these have to be implemented and *led* by leaders. This is where implementation becomes crucial, sometimes framed within what has been called 'political will'. However, reforms have to be owned and embraced by the stakeholders, including, and perhaps most especially, the citizens. This is where the active engagement of citizenry would come in, with vigilant stakeholder citizens demanding – and monitoring – the reforms in the bureaucracy. All these reforms have to be moving towards a common vision[37] as articulated by the leaders in consultation with the stakeholders of society. Finally, communication is imperative if only to create massive awareness, and in a language popularized in the 1970s, 'conscienticize'[38] the people.

Aiding in our discussion and analysis of public sector reforms were actual leadership cases that we drew from the bureaucracy, including cases from national and local governments (the NSO successfully transformed by its administrators Tomas Africa and Carmencita Ericta), and a local government transformed by its mayor Feliciano Belmonte. We also included the case of a civil society leader, Antonio Meloto, whose movement, Gawad Kalinga, successfully uplifted communities from poverty.[39] The chapter also conducted a survey among leaders (presidents) of state universities and colleges to elicit their ideas on leadership and public sector reforms in the public higher education system.

Drawing from the above cases, we end by citing some emerging lessons for scholars in leadership and public reforms. These include the following:

- Leadership does matter. Leadership is a critical handle in the designing and implementation of reforms in the public sector.
- Practical wisdom – or grounded leadership – is central for effective leadership. The long-term and sometimes ideal vision must be grounded by practical realities.
- Leadership in the public sector must be inclusive within the context of effecting ownership and buy in by the stakeholders (referred to as a 'ba' or communities of practice bound by a common vision of improving their sector).
- Leaders are sensitive to the needs of their communities. This is where they are able to articulate the essence of relying on 'oido', some kind of a sixth sense that knows what is goodness.
- Leaders are risk-takers, not afraid to go into terra incognita, after having made necessary analysis and weighed the consequences, and after having counted the costs, grounded on the pursuit of common good.
- Leaders are political animals, as in Aristotle's 'political animal' sensitive to the realities of struggle, conflict and debate, and compromise towards the common good.

- Leaders develop other leaders. They mentor others. They develop support for reforms. They are not threatened by younger leaders who they mentor, who will not only share the vision to pursue public sector reforms for the common good but, more importantly, sustain the reforms.
- Leaders develop capacities of themselves and of others. Leaders recognize the imperative of continuous improvement, including their own improvement. Leadership means lifelong learning.
- However, leadership is not enough. To be sustainable, public sector reforms driven by leaders have to be complemented by reforms in other areas, including institutions, structures and procedures and reforms in behaviour and values, anchored and on a common and vision owned by all and communicated to the people.

NOTES

1. These issues and concerns have been culled from the many workshops and training programmes we have been conducting throughout the country over the past several years. Leadership (poor, inadequate or its lack) has always been cited among the challenges of governance.

2. *Bureaupathology* is concerned with the dysfunctional and irrational aspects of bureaucracy, and can be defined as the set of problems that arise from exaggerated bureaucratic controls. Elements of bureaupathology include routinization, reliance on regulations and resistance to organizational changes. The term was apparently coined by Victor Thompson in the early 1960s (see https://everything2.com/title/bureaupathology; https://clarotesting.wordpress.com/tag/bureaupathology-the-denigration-of-competence-edward-j-giblin/).

3. A Filipino term that refers to the general tendency of initiating projects (many times highly visible project for 'optics') but not completing them because of lack of resources, or more significantly, lack of monitoring by the public, loss of interest by the stakeholders, and equally important, lack of push ('political will') by the leadership.

4. https//tradingeconomics.com/Philippines/ease-of-doing-business

5. These include dealing with construction permits, paying taxes, starting a business and trading across borders.

6. This section is drawn from the article by Brillantes and Perante-Calina (2016).

7. Brillantes (2003).

8. We have since reflected on this work a decade and a half ago (2003) and suggested that the more appropriate terms would be 'daring' and 'enterprising' local government rather than 'aggressive' that has negative connotations.

9. Similarly, this could be more appropriately described as an engaged, zealous and persevering civil society rather than 'aggressive' for the same reasons cited above.

10. A phrase used by Dr Kenneth Elison, when we worked with him, and he led a series of studies that conducted rapid field appraisals on the state of local governance

after the implementation of the local government code in the Philippines in the early to mid-1990s.

11. Professor Ikujiro Nonaka is Professor Emeritus at Hitotsubashi University, Tokyo, Japan; Xerox distinguished faculty scholar, University of California-Berkeley; the first distinguished Drucker scholar, Claremont Graduate University and proponent of the Nonaka Leadership Socialization, Externalization, Combination, Internalization framework for the ASEAN leaders in public and private sectors.

12. The three types of knowledge identified by Aristotle are *Episteme* (scientific), *Techne* (skill and crafts) and *Phronesis* (wisdom).

13. Nonaka points out that there is a similar term in Japanese called *toku*, which means the virtue that helps a person take up *common good and moral excellence as a way of life*. This is not unlike the classic *bayanihan* spirit of the Filipinos, where communities come together for a common good.

14. This is reminiscent of the NPM paradigm that argued that many private sector organizational and leadership approaches may actually be applied to the public sector, an argument for the universality of some of the principles in human behaviour in organizations, human resources, organizational development and leadership.

15. This might be a variation of what we referred to earlier when we quoted Ellison who emphasized that analysis – and extending this, leadership – should be able to always look at the 'question behind the question'. Nuancing and not taking things always at the face value, which is also central to critical thinking, is a basic ability to a phornetic leader.

16. This is essentially the ability – and desire – of a leader to mentor others. It has been said that the success of a good teacher – and again this may be extended to leadership – is her students. A leader is secure and not threatened by the accomplishments of younger leaders who follow him.

17. These cases were part of a research study conducted by the authors with the Philippine Society for Public Administration (PSPA) for the National Graduate Institute for Policy Studies. This was part of a bigger 'Research Project on Leadership and Management Development in Asian Countries' organized by the Graduate Institute for Policy Studies in Tokyo and with support from the Japan International Cooperation Agency.

18. The NSO is one of the major statistical agencies of the Philippine Statistics Authority (PSA). Under the Philippine Statistical Act of 2013, which reorganized the Philippine statistical system creating the PSA, the agency is constituted from among the existing personnel of the major statistical agencies, i.e., the NSO, the technical staff of the National Statistical Coordination Board, the Bureau of Agricultural Statistics and the Bureau of Labour and Employment Statistics.

19. The case was prepared by Magdalena Mendoza, vice president of the Development Academy of the Philippines (DAP) together with Ma. Cristina Valte and Krichelle Ching, both from DAP.

20. A phronetic leader is able to grasp the essence. This is central to 'oido'.

21. A phronetic leader creates and enables a 'ba' – a community characterized by a common belongingness.

22. Philippine Airlines and the Government Service Insurance System.

23. The case was prepared by Dr. Eduardo Gonzales, Dean of the Asian Center of the University of the Philippines (UP) together with Zita Calugay of the National College of Public Administration and Governance, UP.

24. The award was conferred jointly by the UP, Local Government Academy of the DILG, the Ateneo School of Government, the De La Salle University and the Senate of the Philippines. This has been considered as one of the most prestigious awards for local government chief executives (mayors, governors etc.) considering that the panel of judges include presidents of top universities of the country (UP, Ateneo University, De La Salle University, University of San Carlos and the Mindanao State University) with the primary author of the local government code, Senator Aquilino Pimentel, Jr, as the chair of the awards body.

25. Alex Brillantes, Jr. and Lizan Perante-Calina of the PSPA prepared the case of Meloto as a civil society leader.

26. A Filipino concept we referred to earlier that literally means promotion of a common spirit and community for a common good.

27. Literally, 'First to render service. Last to receive benefits'. GK workers in the community help build houses for others first before their own. This is like the biblical leadership spirit of 'he who is first should be last' (The Bible, Matthew 20:16). Humility and servant hood (hence 'servant-leadership') as a cornerstone of the leadership ethics of Meloto and GK community leaders.

28. Perhaps, with an end in view of converting this followership into political power.

29. At the GK specifically, Tony Meloto put in extra effort to develop succession leaders. A phronetic leader develops phronesis in others.

30. In the interviews with these phronetic leaders, we concluded that they simply exercised practical wisdom, knew the essence and simply did what they felt they should do for the common good (*oido*) anchored on integrity, without any 'handbook' or guidelines for leadership. They were phronetic leaders without even knowing they were phronetic leaders. And this is true for many executives at the firm level.

31. Our access to these university and college presidents from all over the country was facilitated by the fact that one of the authors of this paper was a commissioner of the Commission on Higher Education. As such he served as the chairperson of 22 state universities and colleges and also had some frequent interactions with the Philippine Association of State Colleges and Universities (PASUC). There are 112 SUC in the country. We had 31 responses (or almost 1/3 of the presidents) in the indicative survey of SUC presidents. Note though that the responses are indicative and there is no intention to draw statistical significance.

32. Brillantes, Fernandez, and Perante-Calina (2013b).

33. *Metanoia definition*: A fundamental change in character or outlook, especially repentance; *metanoia* means afterthought, from *meta*, meaning 'after' or 'beyond' and *nous*, meaning 'mind'. In Classical Greek, *metanoia* meant 'changing one's mind about someone or something'. Retrieved from https://www.collinsdictionary.com/dictionary/english/metanoia

34. The National Economic Development and Authority describes AmBisyon Natin as follows: 'AmBisyon Natin 2040' represents the collective long-term vision and aspirations of the Filipino people for themselves and for the country in the next 25 years. It describes the kind of life that people want to live, and how the country will be by 2040. As such, it is an anchor for development planning across at least four administrations. *AmBisyon Natin 2040* is a picture of the future, a set of life goals and goals for the country. It is different from a plan, which defines the strategies to achieve the goals. It is like a destination that answers the question '*Where do we want to be?*' A plan describes the way to get to the destination; AmBisyon Natin 2040 is the vision

that guides the future and is the anchor of the country's plans. *AmBisyon Natin 2040* is the result of a long-term visioning process that began in 2015. More than 300 citizens participated in focus group discussions and close to 10,000 answered the national survey. Technical studies were prepared to identify strategic options for realizing the vision articulated by citizens. The exercise was benefitted from the guidance of an advisory committee composed of government, private sector, academe and civil society. Retrieved from http://2040.neda.gov.ph/about-ambisyon-natin-2040/

35. Then there is of course the dark side of excessive rules and procedures that have become fertile grounds for discretion and abuse among bureaucrats, leading to corruption in the bureaucracy.

36. Over the years we have heard jaded and exasperated officials articulate hopelessness in the continuing reorganizations, with someone stating that the 'reorganizations in government were like rearranging the chairs in the sinking Titanic'.

37. In the Philippines, the latest vision for public sector reforms has been incorporated in the broad *AmBisyon 2040*, crafted by the Benigno Aquino government and embraced by the Duterte government through the National Economic and Development Authority. This is like the *Wawasan 2020* (Vision 2020) in Malyasia under the leadership of then prime minister Mahathir Muhammad that has brought Malaysia to where it is today. Fundamental public sector reforms undergirded the efforts.

38. 'Conscientization' is social concept, grounded in Marxist critical theory that focuses on achieving an indepth understanding of the world, allowing for the perception and exposure of perceived social and political contradictions. It was developed and popularized by Brazilian thinker Paolo Freire. Retrieved from http://www.definitions.net/definition/conscientization. This was very popular during the revolutionary movement in the Philippines during the anti-dictatorship movement that resulted in the ouster of Marcos.

39. These three leadership cases were earlier written from the phronetic leadership paradigm of Aristotle and utilized by Japanese scholar and thinker Ijujoro Nonaka.

REFERENCES

Alfiler, M., & Corazon, P. (1995). *The political-administrative accountability continuum in Philippine public service, conquering politico-administrative frontiers. Essays in honor of Raul P. de Guzman* (p. 401). L. V. Carino (Ed.). The Philippines: UP College of Public Administration and the University of the Philippines Press.

Asian Development Bank. (1995). *Governance sound development management, our framework policies and strategies.* Manila, Philippines: ADB.

Behn, R. D. (2001). *Rethinking democratic accountability, why do we mean by accountability, anyway?* (p. 23). Washington, DC: Brookings Institution Press.

Brillantes, A., Jr. (2003). *Innovations and excellence, understanding local governments in the Philippines.* Quezon City: Center for Local and Regional Governance, National College of Public Administration and Governance, University of the Philippines.

Brillantes, A., Jr. (2014). *Accountable, responsive and inclusive governance, Philippine governance digest* (1st ed.). Quezon City: Philippine Society for Public Administration and Center for Leadership, Communication and Governance.

Brillantes, A., Jr., & Perante-Calina, L. (2013a). *Antonio Meloto: Empowering the poor towards sustainable and innovative Filipino community.* Research Project on Leadership and Management Development in Asian Countries. Philippine Society for Public Administration (PSPA) for the National Graduate Institute for Policy Studies (GRIPS) and Japan International Cooperation Agency (JICA).

Brillantes, F., & Perante-Calina, L. (2013b). *Framework for governance.* Presentation at the 2013 Making Reform Happen (MRH) Policy Workshop in Southeast Asia and Korea, Public Sector Reform Since the Late 1990s. Center for International Development, Korea Development Institute and Korea Research Institute, University of New South Wales, Siem Reap, Cambodia.

Brillantes, F., & Perante-Calina, L. (2016). *Dynamics, issues and concerns of the Philippine politico-administrative system: Decentralization and reorganization, comparative politics in ASEAN* (pp. 353–400). Bangkok: Semadhama – ASEAN and Asia Studies Center National Institute of Development Administration, Information for National Library of Thailand, ASEAN and Asia Studies Center (AASC),National Institute of Development Administration (NIDA), Comparative Politics in ASEAN.

Brillantes, A., Jr., & Perante-Calina, L. (2018). *Antonio Meloto: Empowering the Filipino poor toward sustainable and innovative communities.* In Hirose Nishihara, A., Matsunaga, M., Nonaka, I., Yokomichi, K. (Eds.), Knowledge Creation in Community Development, Institutional Change in Southeast Asia and Japan (pp. 107–128). Switzerland: Palgrave Macmillan

Carino, L. V. (1989). *Accountability, corruption and democracy, a clarification of concepts.* Seminar on 'Promoting accountability in the public service', Eastern Regional Organization for Public Administration and the Public Service Department, Kuala Lumpur, Malaysia, 24–25 October 1990.

Carino, L. V. (1993). Administrative accountability: A review of the evolution, meaning and operationalization of a key concept in public administration. In V. A. B. Ma, C. P. Alfiler, D. R. Reyes, & P. D. Tapales (Eds.), *Introduction to public administration in the Philippines: A reader* (p. 451). Quezon City: College of Public Administration, University of the Philippines Press.

Fukuyama, F. (1986). *Trust: The social virtues and the creation of prosperity.* New York, NY: Free Press (Good Citizenship Movement. *Modules on good citizenship values. References for values formation.* Gonzales, Eduardo, and Calugay, Zita).

Gonzales, J. & Deapera, L. (1987). A Review of Philippine Reorganization. *Philippine Journal of Public Administration,* Volume XXX1, Number 3 (pp. 257–278). University of the Philippines, Diliman: Quezon City.

Hughes, O. E. (1998). *Public management and administration, an introduction* (2nd ed., p. 230). London: Macmillan.

Lane, J. E. (Ed.). (1997). *Public sector reform, rationale, trends and problems* (pp. 2–6). London: Sage.

Mendoza, M. L., Valte, M. C., & Ching, K. A. L. (2013). Research project on leadership and management development in Asian countries. In *Co-creating the census Serbilis: Case study of the national statistics office.* Philippine Society for Public Administration (PSPA) for the National Graduate Institute for Policy Studies (GRIPS) and Japan International Cooperation Agency (JICA).

Mendoza. (2018). *Co-Creating the census serbilis, a study of the Philippines National Statistics Office.* In Hirose Nishihara, A., Matsunaga, M., Nonaka, I., Yokomichi, K. (Eds.), *Knowledge Creation in Community Development, Institutional Change in Southeast Asia and Japan* (pp 143–172). Switzerland: Palgrave Macmillan.

Nachura, A. B. (2002). *Outline reviewer in political law* (p. 250). Manila: RJVL Printing Press.

Nonaka, I., & Hirotaka, T. (1995). *The knowledge-creating company, how Japanese companies create the dynamics of innovation*. New York, NY: Oxford University Press.

Nonaka, I., Toyama, R., & Hirata, T. (2008). *Managing flow, a process theory of the knowledge-based firm*. London: Palgrave Macmillan.

Peters, G. B. (2007). Performance-based accountability. In A. Shah (Ed.), *Performance accountability and combating corruption*. Public *sector governance and accountability series* (pp. 15–16). Washington, DC: World Bank.

Philippine Society for Public Administration. (2015). *The state of decentralization and democratization towards development: A rapid field appraisal*. Diliman, Quezon City. Alampay, Cureg, Lamarca, Salvosa, Carinugan, Antonio, Go, Barcillano, Rico, Limson, Fernandez, Ochotorena, Garcia, Isolana, Samonte, Tomaquin, Tomaquin-Malong, Tanggol, Comilla and Nangpuhan.

Scott, I. (1994). Public sector reform: A critical overview, trends and development. *Asian Journal for Public Administration* (Hong Kong), *5*.

Tantuico, F. S., Jr. (1994). *Accountability+performance, central pillars of democracy* (pp. 63–66), Publication No. 22. Mandaluyong City: Fiscal Administration Foundation (FAFI).

Ursal, S. B. (1999). *Readings in Philippine state audit, a collection of lectures, observations and writings of a COA commissioner* (pp. 37–51). Asian Graphics Printing.

LAWS

National Budget Circular No. 542, 29 August 2012.

INTERNET SOURCES

www.businessdictionary.com
http://www.coa.gov.ph/Gen_Information.htm
https://www.collinsdictionary.com/dictionary/english/metanoia
http://2040.neda.gov.ph/about-ambisyon-natin-2040/
http://www.opm.gov/html/glossary.asp)
http://www.unescap.org/pdd/prs/ProjectActivities/Ongoing/gg/governance.asp.

CHAPTER 8

LEADERSHIP AND PUBLIC SECTOR REFORM IN SINGAPORE

David Seth Jones

ABSTRACT

This chapter discusses reforms to increase customer-centredness, public consultation (including professional, business and community associations), whole-of-government approaches (a case of trafficking in persons), increased budget, personnel and procurement delegation to departments and increased role of statutory boards (autonomous agencies). According to the author the driving force behind public sector reforms emanates from the inner core of ministers, most particularly the prime minister and deputy prime minister, working in close conjunction with senior permanent secretaries, directors of boards and government-linked companies. In Singapore, power is concentrated in the hands of political executives and senior levels of civil service. Ministers set the policy agenda and make final policy decisions on important issues. The administrative service is the elite service (of about 250 persons) within the civil service that shapes policy, especially permanent secretaries and deputy secretaries. Objections to reforms are often avoided through inputs to the reform process by key stakeholders and experts of relevant fields from inter-ministerial and inter-agency committees and through public consultations. Singapore has achieved an exceptional level

---

Leadership and Public Sector Reform in Asia
Public Policy and Governance, 179–205
Copyright © 2018 by Emerald Publishing Limited
All rights of reproduction in any form reserved
doi:10.1108/S2053-769720180000030008

of prosperity, and according to the author civil service is guided by practices of meritocracy (e.g., in promotion) and strict accountability through audits and anti-corruption steps.

Keywords: Political executive; meritocracy; accountability; anti-corruption; Singapore

INTRODUCTION

Singapore has achieved a level of prosperity and public provision that has earned it the label of a fully developed country. The economy continues to grow based on high end production and services, its income per head being one of the highest in the world and public provision in terms of health care, education, housing and infrastructure is of a high standard. The government and the public sector have played an important role in the transformation of Singapore in formulating policies that spurred economic growth and improved standards of public provision and by implementing these polices through efficiently managed administrative institutions.

The chapter examines the system of government, and the structure and features of public sector. It then considers five sets of reforms in the public sector that promote client-centredness, public consultation, 'networked government', decentralization of operational responsibility and a shift to a business model in service delivery. An important consideration is how the reforms have changed the leadership styles in government agencies. Two case studies are used to illustrate these reforms and their impact on leadership style. The conclusion summarises the impact of reforms on leadership styles in the public sector, and then assesses how far leadership has in reality substantially changed as a consequence.

GOVERNMENT AND THE PUBLIC SECTOR

System of Government

The system of government in Singapore is based on the Westminister parliamentary model but with an elected president as head of state. Instead of being purely titular, he/she now exercises limited executive powers. The executive itself consists of a cabinet of ministers (currently 18) assisted by junior ministers (senior ministers of state and ministers of state) and parliamentary secretaries, collectively responsible to a 99-member unicameral parliament. The criteria of appointment to the cabinet are stringent. Those appointed are often talent-spotted through informal feedback, with recognition given to professional achievements and high academic attainments.

Within the framework of the parliamentary model, the system of government in Singapore has been characterised over the years as moderately authoritarian. This is linked to both the existence of a dominant party system, in which the People's Action Party (PAP) has held power since June 1959, with at best only limited opposition, and moderate curtailments on individual freedom, especially in the press and electronic media. In fact, the only governance indicator used by the World Bank on which Singapore does not have a high global percentile score is voice and accountability '(42.86 in 2015) (World Bank, 2016a). This may, however, underestimate currently a subtle shifting in Singapore's political culture, marked by increased electoral support for opposition parties in the last four years, and the greater leeway given to public debate on important issues.

The Structure of the Public Sector in Singapore

The central vein of the public sector in Singapore is the civil service. It consists of 16 ministries employing currently 83,713 officers (including a small number employed in organs of state), compared with 61,032 officers in 2001 (an increase of just over 33%) (Department of Statistics [DOS], 2012, 2016). The civil service is responsible for policy formulation (at its senior and middle levels), and certain areas of policy implementation such as education, policing and employment protection. The range of implementation responsibilities of the civil service has, though, narrowed in recent years as more have been transferred to statutory boards (see below).

Another important part of the public sector are statutory boards (sometime referred to as statutory authorities or statutory corporations). Statutory boards are operationally autonomous government corporations, and as such legal entities in their own right. They are separate from the civil service but affiliated to a parent ministry and accountable to a minister. Statutory boards are governed by a board of directors appointed by the government (Quah, 2010; Sin, 1990; Worthington, 2003). They are responsible, amongst other things, for specialist, professional and technical services, regulation of businesses and infrastructure operators, control of urban zoning, building and land allocations, and various forms of licensing

(Saxena, 2011). As will be discussed later, many boards have been increasingly managed as business entities.

Also part of the public sector and subject ultimately to government control are so-called government-linked companies (GLCs) in which the government holds an exclusive or majority stake through a holding entity or company. The main holding entity is Temasek Holdings, but other holding entities include statutory boards and Minister for Finance Inc. GLCs are required to compete with private sector companies and make profits. Down the years, they have played a key role in Singapore's industrial and infrastructure development, although in recent years the government has reduced its shareholding in many of these through a programme of divestment (Jones, 2006).

Features of Public Sector

Executive Domination

The Singapore public sector is characterized by the concentration of power in the hands of political executives and senior levels of the civil service. Ministers in the government set the policy agenda and make final policy decisions on important issues (Ho, 2003). A crucial role in shaping policy is undertaken by top civil servants in the elite administrative service, especially permanent secretaries and deputy secretaries. Middle-level administrative officers and senior officers in the professional and specialist schemes of service conduct policy research and analysis (Ho, 2003; Jones, 2002a). It is noticeable how Ministers when speaking in parliament emphasize how closely they work with their top civil servants, seeing them as part of a policy team and working in partnership with them. The belief remains that to relax the dominant role of the executive and the senior civil service could undermine the standards of governance and compromise the core values upon which the prosperity and stability of Singapore have been built

Meritocracy

Singapore's public sector has been described as a meritocracy. At the heart of the meritocracy is the administrative service. It is the elite service within the civil service. Although its numbers are small (about 250 officers), it exerts a crucial influence upon the formulation and implementation of policy in different ministries and statutory boards. As such, it dominates senior positions in the civil service and enjoys an exclusive monopoly of the two highest positions, viz. permanent secretary and deputy secretary. Administrative officers are, as well, seconded to senior positions in statutory boards. Those below the rank of permanent and deputy secretary also conduct important policy-related work (Jones, 2002a; Public Service Division [PSD], 2008).

Reflecting the influence of the meritocratic system, membership of the administrative service is reserved for the so-called 'brightest and best'. These are, in the main, returning scholarship holders with good degrees from prestigious universities. Previously, if they passed a rigorous and selective interview, they were directly recruited to the administrative service. However, in 2002, it was decided to end the system of direct entry. Scholarship holders are now required to join the so-called Management Associates Programme (MAP) as a preliminary to entry to the administrative service three or four years later. In addition, those who were not scholarship holders are too given an opportunity to join the MAP. Only appointees who proved themselves in their different postings in the MAP, including non-scholarship holders, are appointed to the administrative service. This meant that proven ability in the job has become a determinant of entry in the Service, showing a departure from the traditional meritocratic criteria, which gave precedence to educational qualifications (Chan, 2009; Public Service Commission [PSC], 2002; PSD, 2008).

At the start of their career, administrative officers are subjected to rigorous appraisals that entail ranking them within a relevant cohort of fellow officers, and providing a career potential rating known as the current estimated potential. In the meritocratic system, those with high ratings and rankings are identified as the so-called 'high-flyers', and rise through the ranks rapidly, some becoming deputy secretary in their thirties and a few becoming permanent secretary even before the age of 40. During their career they remain generalists being rotated through several ministries and statutory boards (Jones, 2002a; Ong, 2011; PSD, 2008).

Meritocracy is also evident in other graduate schemes of the civil service, comprising professional and specialist schemes, with a close correlation between qualifications and point of entry into those services. However, in 2014, it was decided to start entry of non-graduates, who had shown potential but not reflected in their academic attainment, to graduate schemes. This further represents a shift in meritocratic system, which is more oriented towards the practical ability on job (PSD, 2014).

Strict Accountability
The Singapore public sector is subjected to be a rigorous system of accountability centred on three watchdog bodies: (1) the Auditor-General's (AG)

office, (2) the Corrupt Practices Investigation Bureau (CPIB) and (3) the Public Service Commission (PSC).

The AG audits the public accounts of ministries, some statutory boards, government funds, certain GLCs and government-regulated accounts. Audits of statutory boards are often undertaken by commercial auditors on behalf of the AG (2016). Two types of audit are carried out. One is the annual compliance audit (known as the financial statements audit) to determine whether expenditure and revenue collection of a government entity are in accordance with the relevant statutes and legal procedures, and also to assess whether a proper disclosure of accounts has been published, reflecting fairly and accurately all the financial transactions undertaken. It assesses the adequacy of record keeping and the effectiveness of internal controls to prevent non-compliance and irregularities (AG, 2011, 2014). In addition, from time to time, the AG undertakes an in-depth audit, known as a selective audit. This provides a more detailed assessment of compliance, and highlights too 'excess, extravagance or gross inefficiency leading to waste, and whether measures to prevent them are in place' (AG, 2011, 2016). Any lapses highlighted in the annual report are taken seriously, and it is incumbent on the entity concerned to put to right the shortcomings referred to.

The second watchdog body is the CPIB, which is part of the Prime Minister's Office, and responsible for implementing the Prevention of Corruption Act (PCA). Its task is to investigate complaints regarding alleged corruption by public officers, and any other evidence that indicates malpractice and misconduct. The CPIB has wide powers of investigation, and thereby spares no effort to unveil corrupt dealings. If there is insufficient evidence to mount a prosecution, suspected officials may be referred to their head of department for disciplinary action with the concurrence of the public prosecutor. The CPIB and the PCA have played a key role in making Singapore one of the least corrupt countries in the world (Corrupt Practices Investigation Bureau, 2017a, 2017b; Quah, 2003).

The third watchdog is the PSC, which was set up in 1951 to uphold the high standards of integrity and competence in the civil service and statutory boards. Its functions are to make appointments to the administrative service, determine promotions at the most senior levels of the civil service and award scholarships to students with high academic attainment with the intention that on completion of studies they will work at a senior level in the public sector (Saxena, 2011, pp. 56–57). It also 'considers the suitability of candidates' for appointment as CEOs of major statutory boards, and also for rank promotions within the CEO post. On top of these functions, the PSC has been the main disciplinary body in the civil service. It deals with cases of misconduct and authorises sanctions against civil servants for breach of their ethical and professional obligations. In 2015, it dealt with 74 cases, and the main types of misconduct were stated as immoral behaviour and indebtedness and insubordination/noncompliance with orders. Sanctions taken against errant officers include dismissal, demotion and monetary fines (PSC, 2016, 2017).

RECENT REFORMS OF PUBLIC SECTOR AND IMPACT ON PUBLIC LEADERSHIP

Reforms to Create Customer-Centredness

In recent years, important initiatives have been implemented to make the Singapore public sector more customer-centred so as to better respond to the needs of the public and provide a high standard of service on a day-to-day basis. These initiatives have entailed the following:

- Improving transparency by providing a greater range of information and guidance to members of the public about regulations, schemes and entitlements.
- Trimming red-tape and paperwork and reducing time taken in the submission and processing of requests, applications and claims.
- Improving interaction between public agencies and members of the public, achieved by training counter officers in customer-help skills.

The objectives of better customer service were incorporated into the Public Service for the 21st Century (PS21), published in May 1995, a government statement to outline the future of the Singapore Public Service (Haque, 2009; Quah, 2010; Saxena, 2011).

One aspect of customer-centredness has focussed on improving dealings with the public on a day-to-day basis. Here important roles have been played by the Service Improvement Unit (SIU), set up in 1991 and the Service Quality Committee (SQC) of PS21. One of the results of their work has been the trimming of red tape and paperwork in the dealings of government agencies with the public, an example being the now streamlined procedures in applications to purchase a Housing and Development Board apartment (HDB, 2012). Further results of the work of the SIU and SQC have been to reduce the processing time taken and to ensure that counter staff are amenable to the public, provide relevant advice and display a generally courteous and helpful attitude. The latter have led to the training of counter staff in customer-help skills, and the offer of financial incentives to be courteous and helpful (Quah, 2010; Saxena, 2011).

The other aspect of improved customer-centredness is streamlining bureaucratic procedures that businesses must follow, thereby helping to create a business-friendly environment. These procedures cover registering a business, securing a property title, obtaining export and import permits, paying taxes, reporting company results, and hiring and firing employees. According to the World Bank's Ease of Doing Business Survey of 2016, Singapore is ranked 2nd out of 190 countries for overall ease of doing business. This assessment for the most part covers regulatory requirements, bureaucratic procedures and red tape, which can impede doing business across different business activities. It is evident from the survey that such regulations and procedures have been kept to a minimum by the Singapore government. For example, only three bureaucratic procedures are involved in starting a business (obtaining a business registration), taking 2.5 days to complete, ranking Singapore at 6th place in the global ranking of ease of starting a business (World Bank, 2016b). Several agencies have been involved in creating a pro-business environment. One of them is the Accounting and Corporate Regulatory Authority (ACRA), a statutory board, which is responsible for business regulations (2017a).

Improved customer service and more efficient and faster operations have been made possible through the development of e-government. A wide range of online services are now available which benefit the public and business sector alike (Quah, 2010). These services provide information and guidance, entail streamlined procedures and enable transactions and payments. Of particular benefit are simply constructed and user-friendly single-access portals. For example, BizFile is a portal managed by ACRA, which provides online services to register a business, apply for a company name, incorporate a business, register an amalgamation and file annual company returns and financial statements. Another portal EnterpriseOne provides an online business licensing service in which it enables and processes online applications for licences for specific business sectors such as retail, manufacturing, construction, food and beverage sales and wholesale distribution. In addition, it provides a wide range of advice and step-by-step guidance on planning, starting and managing a business. Both portals also allow online payments for the transactions undertaken (ACRA, 2017b; Hawksford, 2017).

These reforms stem from both a policy commitment by the government to establish a customer-centred public sector and entail specific operational measures to implement that commitment. They are predicated on a leadership style at the operational level which is essentially client-centred and empathetic instead of being narrowly bureaucratic and top-down. At the same time, managers and officials cannot deviate from the rules laid down by and ignore the resource constraints of their agencies in responding to client expectations.

Public Consultation

An important recent reform affecting the exercise of public leadership is the promotion of public consultation through an e-government programme known as Reaching Everyone for Active Citizenry@Home (REACH). It was set up in 2006, having superseded the Feedback Unit. Through REACH's web portal, consultations are regularly undertaken on a wide range of policy issues, and the feedback given provides an important input into the drafting of laws, regulations and schemes. At the outset, proposals are drafted (e.g. amendments to an existing statute) by a ministry or statutory board and disseminated online. The public at large and stakeholders (such as business and professional associations, professional and commercial firms, community groups and voluntary organizations) are then invited to give feedback. The feedback most often comprises suggestions on how the proposals could be improved or amended, but may also entail requests for assurance that adverse outcomes from the proposed changes will not arise. Responses from the public and stakeholders may be submitted online, but in a few cases dialogue and focus group sessions are held usually with business and professional groups. The ministry or statutory board in due course considers the suggestions made in response to each proposal and accepts them entirely or in part, or rejects them. It also provides clarifications in response to queries raised. In 2016, 29 formal consultations were undertaken (REACH, 2017).

Consultations are also undertaken to elicit open-ended feedback from the general public on issues of concern through online discussion forums, blogs and e-polls conducted under the REACH web portal. The number of feedback inputs submitted has increased significantly since REACH was set up (see Table 1). A discernible rise was recorded after the 2011 general

Table 1. Number of feedback inputs sent to government agencies through REACH, 2006—2011.

Year	2006	2007	2008	2009	2010	2011
No. of feedback inputs	9,400	17,000	17,000	26,900	32,000	52,000
% increase		45	0	58	19	63

Source: REACH (2011).

election, with the monthly number of inputs averaging 260 after the election (June–November 2011) compared with 153 before it (January–May 2011) (REACH, 2011).

The question arises whether such consultations make much difference and can influence how leadership is exercised by ministers and policy makers. Based on two criteria to assess the impact, viz. the response rate and the number of changes suggested by respondents which are accepted, it is evident that the impact varies considerably. In a number of recent consultations, as a result of the feedback given, few substantive changes have been made to proposals to amend legislation or policy, and those made mostly concerned technical and procedural matters. A good deal of feedback involved clarification of proposals, and assurances that suggestions made were already covered in the proposals, or 'may be considered' in the final drafting of the legislation. In other consultations, the feedback has had an impact and responses to suggestions have been positive. For example, the Ministry of Finance (MOF), which has undertaken regular public consultations since 2004, has replied favourably to many of the responses. In one recent consultation in 2016, in conjunction with ACRA, on proposed changes to the Companies Act, Limited Liability Partnerships Act and Accountants Act, it made 14 revisons to the proposed legislation in response to the feedback given (Ministry of Finance [MOF], 2016).

Various reasons may be given to explain how a ministry or statutory board assesses the responses to consultations under REACH. It is more likely that responses will be accepted if there exists reasonable unanimity amongst those submitting them. Lack of unanimity reduces the chances of acceptance. The second reason is budgetary and practical implications of some of the suggestions made, with ministries and statutory authorities possibly reluctant to accept suggestions which are impractical or too costly.

The third factor determining acceptance or rejection is whether the responses exceed the limits of change set by the government leadership, and bring into question core values and priorities. As explained in one consultation on taxation by the MOF in 2010, 'the reason (for the rejection) was they (the responses) are not consistent with the legislative drafting conventions or the policy objectives for the proposed legislative changes' (MOF, 2010a). This suggests that the priority in public consultations is to improve the operational aspects of a policy rather than to alter its principles, goals or core content.

This points to an important limit to Singapore's public consultation exercises. They do not involve any major questioning of core values of the leadership and the direction of policy. Rather they cover practical issues and the day-to-day details of policy. This public consultation represents bottom-up leadership, but only up to operational level.

'Networked Government' or 'Whole of Government' Approach

Another recent public sector reform is called the 'networked government' or 'whole of government' approach. This stems from the recognition that many policy issues are multi-faceted and involve different agencies. According to the *Singapore Public Sector Outcomes Review* published in 2010, the purpose of this approach was to 'transcend Ministry boundaries', and for public agencies 'to work hand in glove to address any given issue effectively'. In doing this, 'agencies have agreed on a set of common outcomes, with which their priorities have been aligned' (MOF, 2010b; S. Rajaratnam School of International Studies, 2008). This requires public sector leaders to adopt a holistic view of multi-faceted issues which transcend different policy areas and involve several agencies. It is necessary for such agencies to work together, agreeing common outcomes, sharing information and expertise and engaging in joint operations.

The 'networked government' approach is reflected in various inter-ministerial and inter-agency committees and working groups set up to examine policy and operational issues and to make recommendations accordingly (PSD, 2008). The membership of such committees and working groups comprises ministers and senior and mid-level officials drawn from different agencies, who work together in gathering and analysing evidence, submitting proposals and engaging in joint actions. In such cases, sharing of expertise and knowledge, and the articulation of different perspectives, increases the chances of reaching balanced and workable decisions. Recent examples of such cooperation include the inter-ministerial committees on construction safety, sustainable development, climate change, terrorism, the ageing of the population and trafficking in persons (TIP), which will be further discussed below.

A 'networked government' approach is also relevant when a matter involves several agencies and there is uncertainty about which one is primarily responsible. In such cases, feedback and demands from stakeholders such as members of parliament, community and business associations, and members of the public may elicit denials of responsibility and 'buck passing' from each agency, resulting in inaction. This typically arises on issues relating to the upkeep and maintenance of commonly used amenities and living areas such as parks, roads, footpaths, drains and other public amenities. The Singapore government took this matter in hand and established the Municipal Services Office in the Ministry of National Development in 2014. This body adopts a 'networked government' approach to identify the relevant agencies jointly responsible for such amenities and obtain their collaboration in responding to public concerns and feedback (Ministry of National Development, 2014; Sim, 2014; Yap, 2014).

The upshot of adopting 'networked government' is to prevent any one agency dominating the policy agenda on a particular issue, and encourages consensual or collegial leadership amongst different agencies in which divergent views are reconciled and cooperation is secured. So far, although the approach of 'networked government' has been mainly applied to clearly multi-faceted issues, it remains to be seen whether it will be applied to issues which are less overtly multi-faceted and obviously fall within the brief of one agency but which still impinge on the interests of other agencies, such as taxation, food security and public transport.

Case Study of 'Networked Government' and Public Consultation:
Policy to Combat Trafficking in Persons
Singapore's recent policy to combat TIP provides examples of how government leaders seek to develop a policy by both adopting a 'networked government' approach and conducting a public consultation. TIP involves using people locally born or from another country for the purpose of forced labour, prostitution and other forms of sexual exploitation, and the sale of human organs. It involves coercion or exploitation or both, and fetches lucrative gains for the traffickers and others involved in the process. In Singapore, the most common type is TIP from another country, nearly all from Southeast Asia and China, and the evidence has indicated that it had grown significantly in recent years.

Although several laws existed in Singapore that prohibit TIP, they were not sufficiently comprehensive. They did not cover the range or reflect the complexity of TIP offences, which remained ill-defined, nor did they stipulate penalties commensurate with the offences. Furthermore, not much has been done to build enforcement capacity, while low priority had been given to awareness campaigns, prevention and rehabilitation of victims. Another problem was the dearth of reports of TIP which could provide evidence to start an investigation (Singapore Inter-Agency Taskforce on Trafficking in Persons [SITTP], 2012). Moreover, although TIP was a type of crime which naturally concerned several agencies, there had been little effort to bring them together so as to iron out a common strategy, share information and expertise and engage in joint investigations, public awareness initiatives and rehabilitation programmes.

However, in consequence of regional and international pressures, the government decided in 2010 to take action to deal with TIP. One influence was the ASEAN Declaration on Transnational Crime in 1997, which committed member states, including Singapore, to a common effort in fighting transnational crime. TIP was highlighted as one of the most serious of these crimes. Subsequently, various action plans and work programmes under the Declaration have been drawn up (Sovannnasam, 2011). A second catalyst for action was the report of the Philippine Embassy in Singapore in 2008, stating that trafficking in Filipinos in Singapore 'continues unabated' (Uy, 2008, p. 1). The third influence was the US Government's Trafficking in Person's Report of 2008, which stated that the Singapore government was not doing enough to combat TIP (charges which were denied) (US State Department, 2008).

As a result of this increasing concern, the SITTP was set up in 2010 to identify measures to combat TIP. Reflecting the 'networked government' approach, members of the SITTP were drawn from nine government agencies: Ministry of Home Affairs (MHA), Ministry of Manpower (MOM), Singapore Police Force (SPF), Immigration & Checkpoints Authority (ICA), Ministry of Community Development, Youth & Sports (MCYS), Ministry of Health (MOH), Ministry of Law (MOL), Ministry of Foreign Affairs (MFA) and Attorney-General's Chambers (AGC). The lead agencies were the MHA and MOM. The taskforce was committed to, in its own words, 'an holistic perspective on the TIP situation', in which it would 'identify and implement whole-of-government strategies to combat TIP more effectively, both locally and internationally' (SITTP, 2012).

The remit of the taskforce was to draft a national plan of action, which was completed by March 2012, to be implemented over the following three years. Priority was to be given to the following:

- Defining in more detail human trafficking and determining appropriate penalties to be incorporated into new legislation (main agencies MOL and AGC).
- Strengthening enforcement through expediting investigations and prosecutions and setting up a specialized enforcement unit (main agencies ICA, SPF and AGC).
- Raising awareness amongst public officers, the business community and the general public about TIP (main agencies MOM and MHA).
- Undertaking training programmes for relevant officers on detecting trafficking, prosecuting offenders and enhancing care services for victims (main agencies MOM, MCYS, SPF and MOL).
- Rehabilitating victims of TIP and setting up care centres (main agency MCYS).
- Improving the collection of data, with reports to be regularly compiled about trends and developments in human trafficking (ICA, MOM and MHA).
- Achieving 'stronger collaboration with foreign governments and embassies' with the intention to 'engage enforcement agencies of source countries for joint investigation and sharing of information' (main agency MFA) (Durai, 2012, p. 3; Ministry of Manpower [MOM], 2014; SITTP, 2012).

The above priorities reflect the responsibility of the taskforce to set out both 'strategic outcomes and implementation plans'. In other words, it could make policy-level decisions and draft operational details as well. Many of the measures recommended by it have now been incorporated into legislation, the Prevention of Human Trafficking Bill passed by the Singapore Parliament in November 2014. It was tabled as a private members bill in cooperation with the taskforce and received strong support of and was recommended by two ministers of state of the MHA and MOM (Singapore Parliament, 2014).

It can be seen from the above that combatting TIP involves several issues requiring specialist inputs from different agencies. No single agency in itself can do it all. However, it is necessary that the agencies come together and agree upon a common strategy. Equally important, given the interconnected nature of the issues, is that they provide advice and information to each other, and where possible they share certain responsibilities. For example, in reha-bilitation, it is necessary that the MCYS and MOH liaise with each other, and together are privy to information from the SPF on the background, circum-stances and physical condition of the victims. Similarly, it is incumbent on the SPF and ICA to liaise with each other on the movement of both traffickers and victims. In enforcement work, it is useful for MOM inspectors to cooperate with the SPF when investigating businesses suspected of using forced labour or engaging in sexual exploitation. The MFA must play a role in connecting ICA, MOM and SPF with their counterparts in ASEAN states and China. In fact, the minister for state who introduced the second reading of the bill to prevent human trafficking in October 2014 spoke of how different agencies can work together and the importance of this in combatting TIP (Singapore Parliament, 2014; Ministry of Manpower [MOM], 2014).

All this points to the value of a 'networked' or 'whole of government' approach, which breaks down the barriers between agencies and ensures common commitments, mutual cooperation and increased capacity in terms of resources and expertise. It essentially reveals a public leadership style that values inter-agency consensus and collegiality in which no ministry or agency can dominate the agenda at the expense of others. This applies at both policy and implementation levels.

The policy to combat TIP also involved public consultation. In March and April 2014 feedback was canvassed from about 300 individuals to guide the drafting of the above-mentioned bill. The submissions in the feedback came from civil society representatives, academics, business representatives, representatives from religious organisations, grassroots leaders, students and members of the public (Ministry of Home Affairs [MHA], 2014; MOM, 2014). The response of the taskforce to the feedback was mixed. It accepted suggestions for both prosecution of any person or business in the supply chain profiting from TIP, in addition to the traffickers themselves, and stiff sentences to be meted out to all the culprits, especially if the victims were children. It also accepted suggestions for specific protection and support services to be accorded to victims. On the other hand, on a key issue of how wide to cast the net in defining a TIP offence, the taskforce urged caution and sought only intervention in the 'most egregious trafficking cases'. Overall, the feedback seemed to have had an impact in strengthening at the operational level both enforcement and rehabilitation provisions of the Bill (MOM, 2014).

Decentralization and the Corporate Model in Public Sector Leadership

Over the last 25 years, the public sector has been decentralized, with key operational responsibilities delegated to ministries, operational departments in ministries, statutory boards and even GLCs. In consequence, operational managers have become important leaders in their own right, and not just unquestioning policy implementers. This has occurred in a number of ways.

Budget Delegation
One is the delegation of budget management to ministries under the Block Vote Budget Allocation System. When it was introduced in 1989, it was announced that 'ministries will be delegated greater authority to manage their budget allocations' (Ministry of Communications and Information [MCI], 1988). Under this arrangement, the target of total expenditure for each ministry is set as a percentage of GDP. After approval of the budget of each ministry by Parliament, 'the ministry is given flexibility and autonomy to spend the allocated funds according to its stated objectives and to manage the allocation between the various programmes and activities' (MCI, 1988). It thus has the freedom to transfer funds and manpower from one programme or activity to another without approval from the MOF (Jones, 1998).

Delegation of Personnel Matters
Delegation has been also extended to the matters concerning personnel. In the past, functions of personnel within the civil service were mainly the responsibility of the PSC together with two other service commissions (viz. the Education Service Commission, and the Police and the Civil Defence Services Commission), and also the PSD. The permanent secretaries and heads of departments in line ministries could exercise only limited personnel functions delegated by the PSC, relating to the recruitment and promotion of the lowest grades (PSC, 1993).

However, in January 1995, important responsibilities concerning personnel were delegated to the ministries. The main ones were recruitment and promotions, which were transferred from the PSC and other service commissions, to a three-tier system of personnel boards. These reforms gave permanent secretaries and departmental managers greater control over recruitment, promotions and conditions of service in their own ministries than previously. Where necessary, they have now the freedom to offer improved terms and career opportunities to attract job applicants (the main exceptions being the recruitment of administrative officers and their promotion to Grade 7 or above, which are still the responsibility of PSC) (Jones, 1999, 2002a; Quah, 2010).

Delegation of Procurement

In 1996, the Central Procurement Office was abolished, resulting in the termination of centralized purchasing, with the exception of bulk tenders for common user products. Consequently, line ministries and statutory boards became government procurement entities (GPEs) in their own right, responsible for their own purchasing. Subsequently, GPEs were given more control over purchasing goods and services and managing quotations and tenders (Jones, 2002b).

The delegation has enabled line ministries and statutory boards themselves to perform the entire range of functions of purchasing goods and services and hiring contractors for public works. These include deciding the type and quantity of goods, services and works to be acquired, choosing the method of tender (open, selective or limited tender), drafting product specifications and designs, drawing up the contract, and setting the estimated procurement value and the time frame for delivery or project completion. They are also responsible for issuing tender notices, forwarding invitations to tender, evaluating submissions, making recommendations and making the final selection. In the case of selective tendering, they may set the criteria for qualification and determine which bidders qualify. Similar discretion in selection applies to two-stage open tendering. In the case of limited tenders, a ministry or statutory board is free to choose the suppliers who can be requested to submit tender proposals (Jones, 2002b, 2007).

Increased Prominence of Statutory Boards

Another aspect of a more decentralized leadership in the public sector is the greater autonomy exercised at the policy implementation level. This has occurred through the increased prominence of operationally autonomous statutory boards as the main instrument of policy implementation. As mentioned above, they are corporations and thus legal entities in their own right, separate from the civil service. Their numbers have risen from 37 in 1989 to presently 64 with a payroll of 59,470 (DOS, 2016).

Statutory boards now apply the bulk of business regulations and implement a wide range of support services to business entities and the public, and in doing so exercise a significant degree of autonomy. In addition, they draft operational rules that govern such regulations and services. In fact, when a major policy initiative is announced in the budget, the MOF will often state that the operational details will be drafted by the relevant statutory board. Statutory boards also enjoy freedom to determine their internal management. This includes autonomy in personnel matters, such as recruitment, promotions, performance appraisals, salary scales, scholarship awards and terms and conditions of service of various employment schemes. They also enjoy freedom to manage their own budgets and undertake their own procurement. The key operational managers in statutory boards have thus assumed major leadership responsibilities as policy implementers (Jones, 2006).

In addition, many statutory boards have adopted a business model, further reinforcing their operational independence. They generate their own revenue from the fees, charges and rentals (if they own property), which importantly is not remitted to the Consolidated Revenue Account. Instead it is retained to cover all or part of their expenditure. In case only part is covered, the shortfall is met by operating grants from the government (Jones, 2006).

As in any business, the accumulated surplus is treated as retained earnings to finance future capital expenditure, but with income tax levied on any annual surplus made. Also, to fund capital expenditure, boards may raise their own finance through bank loans or by issuing debt in their own name. The bonds issued usually have maturities of 10–25 years. Capital grants may still be given by the government where necessary, part of which may take the form of the so-called 'equity injection' from the Minister for Finance Inc. By this means, the government becomes a shareholder in the statutory board and is entitled to dividend return on the shares issued to it.

Also reflecting the business model, statutory boards are required to follow the Statutory Board Financial Reporting Standards issued by the Accountant-General, which are similar to the accounting disclosures of any profit-making business. The statutory standards set out the format of statutory board accounts which must cover a statement of income and expenditure, a balance sheet (disclosures of the assets, liabilities and equity), changes in equity and cash flow, as do the accounts of any business. It mandates the adoption of accrual rather than cash accounting, commonplace in the private sector but not in the public sector (Accountant-General's Department [AGD], 2014). One of the key elements of accrual accounting is the recognition of yearly depreciation of assets as an annual expenditure. This is then balanced by spreading the capital grant used to purchase an asset, over each year of the useful life of asset, so as to match annual depreciation (known as deferment of capital grant). In each of these years, the deferred grant is recognized as annual income and is entered in the income and expenditure account (AGD, 2014; Jones, 2005).

Another important feature of statutory boards is the creation by some of them of subsidiary companies, in which they are exclusive shareholders. Appended to their name is the term 'group' to reflect the ownership. The subsidiaries perform specialist commercial services on behalf of the statutory board and are able to compete for both public and private sector contracts. One statutory board which has created subsidiary companies is JTC Corporation (JTC was formerly named as Jurong Town Corporation), a major industrial infrastructure provider in Singapore. One of its subsidiaries, Ascenadas, in 2011 won a contract through competitive tender to build an extension to a large bio-medical complex in Singapore (JTC Corporation, 2011, 2016). Some statutory boards through their subsidiaries have invested in joint ventures in other countries, usually involving infrastructure projects (Jones, 2014).

In consequence of the business model, statutory board directors and managers have assumed a leadership role similar to that of any company director or manager, concerned with achieving good returns on their services and resources, raising capital to invest for the future, ensuring efficient use of resources, and assessing new projects on an economic cost-benefit basis.

However, the foregoing analysis has referred to how statutory board directors and managers may exercise leadership through their operational autonomy. As a limit on their autonomy, they must adhere to the policy priorities set by the government leaders and senior policy makers, and are ultimately accountable to the minister as stated earlier. To cement government control, all members of the board of directors are appointed by the government, as stated above, with many holding senior positions in the civil service and the higher reaches of the public sector, so being closely identified with the governing elite. In addition, the appointment of CEOs of major statutory boards are vetted by the PSC. Underpinning the ties to the government is the practice of seconding members of the elite policy-making group in the civil service, viz. the administrative service, to work in a statutory board for two or three years. Throughout his/her career, an administrative officer may in fact serve in two or three statutory boards.

Case Study of Decentralization and the Corporate Model:
The Land Transport Authority

The Land Transport Authority (LTA) is a good example of the trend towards a more decentralized system of public sector leadership and a more corporately managed public sector. It was set up as an autonomous statutory board in 1995 out of three centrally governed departments or divisions in the civil service (Registry of Vehicles; Roads & Transportation Division of the Public Works Department; and the Land Transportation Division of the Ministry of Communications), plus an existing statutory board (Mass Rapid Transit (MRT) Corporation). LTA's remit is to develop and manage road infrastructure, and to develop and regulate various aspects of public transport system (MRT and Light Rail Transit (LRT) networks, bus operators and taxi operators) (Land Transport Authority [LTA], 2016).

A key priority in its road transport policy is the building of expressways, tunnels, overpasses, inter-sections and multi-tiered roads to meet the needs of a growing population and a rapidly developing economy. The constraint is the scarcity of land for road development in a small and densely populated country. The second priority is to provide major incentives for the travelling public to use public transport in view of the shortage of land space and the density of population. Such incentives include providing a well-resourced, integrated and properly managed public transport system, charging affordable fares and increasing the cost of private vehicle ownership and usage. The last mentioned includes electronic payment for using certain roads at certain periods of each week day and various measures to make vehicles expensive, such as high vehicle registration fees and payment for a certificate entitling an individual to own a car, which is determined by competitive bidding (LTA, 2013, 2016).

Activities in the road development and management programme of the LTA includes planning road projects, procurement (hiring of construction contractors and consultants for road building) and on-going maintenance. The activities in the public transport programme include planning, procurement, hiring of contractors and consultants to build the MRT and LRT networks, licensing of MRT, LRT, bus and taxi operators and the regulation of these operators. The operators are either private sector companies or GLCs. The regulation of operators is based on the terms of the licence and various laws and statutory regulations governing land transport. In addition, the LTA administers electronic road pricing, vehicle registration and the ownership entitlement scheme. While it owns the physical assets of MRT and LRT networks, the operators are responsible for on-going maintenance (LTA, 2013, 2016).

Similar to other major statutory boards, the LTA enjoys operational responsibility. It determines key measures and drafts regulations in the implementation of land transport policy, which was most recently enunciated in the Land Transport Master Plans of 2008 and 2013. It is also responsible for day-to-day operations, including conducting construction and consultancy tenders (in respect of road, MRT and LRT projects), awarding operating licences for MRT, LRT, and bus and taxi services, and monitoring the performance of operators (LTA, 2013, 2016).

The LTA's operational autonomy goes hand in hand with its corporate- and business-related models. Its accounts are set out and disclosed as if it were a business, with statement of cash flows, statement of income and expenditure and balance sheet (disclosures of assets, liabilities and equity). The accounting principles followed are accrual rather than cash-based, in accordance with business accounting principles, two important elements of which is recognition of depreciation cost and treatment of capital grants from the government as deferred income. In 2012–2013, depreciation costs were S$633 million (41% of operating expenditure) (KPMG, 2016; LTA, 2016).

As with any business, the LTA levies charges at point of delivery, the revenue obtained is retained rather than remitted to the Consolidate Revenue Account as tax. The revenue contributes to funding operational expenditure together with a 'management fee' (in effect an operating grant) from the government (the LTA is treated as managing the public transport system on behalf of the government). In 2015–2016, the 'management fee' was about 80% of the total income. Any surplus in its operating account can be retained and accumulated (KPMG, 2016; LTA, 2016).

In accordance with the business model, capital expenditure in the LTA is funded in part from the accumulated surplus, which totalled S$873 million at the end of FY 2015–2016, and through borrowing based on bond issues. As with any business, the LTA can borrow money by issuing bonds in its own name. Presently, the debt issued amounts to just under S$4 billion (at face value), mainly comprising short- and medium-term bonds of 5–15 years maturity (KPMG, 2016).

This is supplemented by capital grants from the government. Reflecting the corporate approach, part of the grant takes the form of an 'equity injection' from the Minister for Finance Inc. This means that as a holding company it can claim a dividend return on the surplus made by the LTA. By the end of FY 2015–2016, the 'equity injection' totalled S$218 million with S$111 million shares issued to the Minister for Finance Inc during the stated financial year alone. As with any company, income tax is levied on the surplus. At the end of FY 2015–2016, the LTA was due to pay S$1.35 million in income tax (KPMG, 2016).

Furthermore, the LTA has established three wholly owned subsidiary companies which undertake specialist and commercial functions (none of them are of course the operating companies it regulates). The LTA, therefore, performs the role similar to any commercial holding company. One of the subsidiaries is MSI Global Pte. Ltd., which undertakes consultancy work on land transport in both Singapore and overseas. Currently, it is involved in three projects in Thailand, one in China and one in the Republic of Ireland. Since its inception in 1995, it has a lengthy track record of overseas consultancy projects, including those in China, Denmark, Egypt, Saudi Arabia, UAE, the United Kingdom and Vietnam (KPMG, 2016; LTA, 2017).

Nevertheless, in spite of its operational autonomy, and the independence and flexibility associated with a business model, the LTA is still subject to a degree of government control, and of course must adhere to the policy framework governing land transport. This control is exercised through the Ministry for Transport and the board of directors, who are all government appointees and ultimately accountable to the ministry. Not surprisingly, most are closely linked to the governing elite. Of the present board of 13 members, five are or were top civil servants, and six are directors or CEOs of other statutory boards, while six members have served on government advisory or consultative committees. Nearly all board members concurrently hold three or more appointments (LTA, 2013). What's more, certain senior staff members who occupy key policy and management positions are seconded from the civil service (mainly drawn from the administrative service).

Government control is further compounded by LTA's dependence on government financial support in the form of a 'management fee', capital grants and 'equity injections'. Even the bonds it issues are redeemed on maturity by a government grant (known as a long-term grant). Such dependence gives the government that more extra leverage in determining how policy is implemented, and monitoring how various grants are spent (KPMG, 2016).

Thus, the LTA is an example of the trend towards a more decentralized public sector in which operational autonomy may be exercised within a policy framework laid down by the government. It also shows how the business model of policy implementation and service delivery further compounds that autonomy.

LEADERSHIP INFLUENCES ON PUBLIC SECTOR REFORMS

The driving force behind public sector reforms is in the main a top-down process. It emanates from the inner core of ministers, and most particularly the prime minister and deputy prime minister. They work in close conjunction with senior permanent secretaries (staff grade) and CEOs and directors of large statutory boards and other corporate leaders of GLCs. This nexus of political, bureaucratic and corporate leadership is further entrenched by inter-locking directorships by which certain persons hold a multiple of top directorship positions. The leadership elite is ably supported in promoting change by members of the administrative service and top managers of statutory boards and GLCs (Jones, 2016).

Objections to reform are often avoided through inputs to the reform process from key stakeholders and experts in relevant fields from inter-ministerial and inter-agency committees and from public consultations based on the REACH programme. In keeping with a pragmatic approach, compromises and accommodations are made where there are good reasons to do so. The use of media, parliament and community grass roots organisations, such as Resident Associations, town councils and Citizens Consultative Committees, must also be considered as helping to disseminate the policy and secure public support for key objectives (Ho, 2003; Jones, 2016; Saxena, 2011).

CONCLUSION: IMPACT OF REFORMS ON PUBLIC SECTOR LEADERSHIP

Summary of Changes in Leadership Style

Client-Centred and Consultative Leadership
The reforms to create customer-centredness have made civil servants and statutory board personnel more responsive to the needs of the public and business community. This represents a shift amongst public managers towards client-centred leadership and a shift away from conventional top-down bureaucratic leadership.

Similarly, the focus on consultation has lessened the narrowly bureaucratic top-down approach in the public sector. It allows professional, business and community associations and members of the public a say in framing the details of policy mainly at the operational level as shown in the case study of combatting TIP, which involved public consultation.

Operational Leadership
The reforms to decentralize the public sector have resulted in the delegation of significant operational responsibilities in the areas of budget management, procurement, personnel functions and most of all service delivery and

business regulation through statutory boards. Thus, public sector managers have become operational leaders in their own right to determine the implementation of policy.

Corporate Leadership

Decentralization has been accompanied by the adoption of a corporate or business model in the provision of services in statutory boards. The business features of statutory boards have further reinforced their autonomy since their directors and managers are bound to respond to the requirements of the organization as a business entity as much as to top-down hierarchical policy directives. This has allowed statutory board directors and managers to exercise their leadership in a similar way to company directors and managers.

Consensual Leadership

The introduction of the 'networked government' approach has resulted in a more consensual leadership style (what may be termed collegial) in the public sector, especially applicable to multi-faceted policy issues. This involves spreading the responsibility of tackling an important policy issue across several agencies, ensuring a common strategy, pooling of expertise, frequent communication and day-to-day cooperation. The case study of combatting TIP illustrates (as well as consultative leadership as mentioned above) a consensual leadership style implicit in the 'networked government' approach.

Assessing the Impact of Reforms on Leadership Style

However, it should be recognized that the impact of reforms on leadership styles in the public sector has been variable. Certainly, progress has been made in creating a more client-centred bureaucracy, especially through the streamlining of procedures, reduction in red tape and the availability of user-friendly online services. Similarly, the consultation exercises have influenced policy proposals in a number of areas. However, the shift to client-centred and consultative leadership largely involves operational measures to implement policy rather than core policy. Thus, when the needs of a client group conflict with key policy commitments, it is likely that the latter will prevail. Indeed, it is noteworthy how few of the consultations questioned the principles and core priorities of policy, with the bulk of them focussed on the specifics of implementation.

Decentralization in the public sector has also been important and led to more pronounced operational leadership in ministries and statutory boards instead of all-pervasive hierarchical control. This has been reinforced by a shift to a business model in many statutory boards, resulting in a more independent corporate style of leadership. Nevertheless, the changes are not as far-reaching as one may suppose. Managers in line ministries and statutory boards enjoy greater autonomy only in operational matters and must adhere to the centrally determined and top-down policy agenda, and remain accountable to senior policy makers. As with the reforms promoting customer-centredness and consultation, the change in leadership style is confined to the implementation of policy rather than to its formulation.

Taken in the round, the adoption of more client-centred, consultative, operational and corporate leadership styles does not signal any major departure from core policy principles or any lessening of the domination of the policy agenda by the executive and senior policy-making elite.

The progress in creating networked government and consensual leadership in the public sector has been discernible. The approach has been followed on issues which are obviously multi-faceted and, clearly, cannot be handled by one agency alone, such as combatting TIP. It remains to be seen whether the approach will be adopted on less multi-faceted issues, which involve one agency but still significantly impinge on the interests of other agencies.

REFERENCES

Accountant-General's Department. (2014). *Statutory board financial reporting standards effective as at 1 January 2014*. Singapore. Retrieved from http://www.assb.gov.sg/fr-assb_frs_1Jan2014.html.

Accounting and Corporate Regulatory Authority. (2014a). *About us*. Singapore. Retrieved from https://www.acra.gov.sg/About_ACRA/?indexar=1.

Accounting and Corporate Regulatory Authority. (2014b). *Online services*. Singapore. Retrieved from https://www.acra.gov.sg/online_Services/.

Auditor-General. (2011). *What is public accountability?* Singapore.

Auditor-General. (2014). *Report of the auditor-general for the financial year 2013/2014*, Singapore.

Auditor-General. (2016). *Report of the auditor-general for the financial year 2015/2016*, Singapore.

Chan, T. (2009). *PSD: MAP your future as a leader*. Singapore: Public Service Department. Retrieved from http://community. jobscentral.com.sg/.

Corrupt Practices Investigation Bureau. (2017a). *About corruption*. Singapore. Retrieved from http://www.cpib.gov.sg.

Corrupt Practices Investigation Bureau. (2017b). *About CPIB*. Singapore. Retrieved from http://www.cpib.gov.sg.

Department of Statistics. (2012). *Yearbook of statistics Singapore, 2012.* Singapore: Ministry of Trade & Industry.

Department of Statistics. (2016). *Yearbook of statistics Singapore, 2016.* Singapore: Ministry of Trade & Industry.

Durai, J. (2012). Singapore to fight human trafficking in 'a more strategic' way. *Straits Times,* March 21, p. 3.

Haque, S. (2009). Public administration and public governance in Singapore. In P. S. Kim (Ed.), *Public administration and public governance in ASEAN member countries and Korea* (pp. 246–271). Seoul: Daeyoung Moonhwasa Publishing Company.

Hawksford. (2017). *GuideMeSingapore: Singapore Incorporation Guides,* Singapore. Retrieved from https://www.guidemesingapore.com/business-guides/incorporation-guides.

Ho, K. L. (2003). *Shared responsibilities, unshared power: The politics of policy-making* in Singapore. Singapore: Eastern Universities Press.

Housing and Development Board. (2012). *HDB info-web: Buying a flat.* Singapore. Retrieved from http://www.hdb.gov.sg/.

Jones, D. S. (1998). Recent budgetary reforms in Singapore. *Journal of Public Budgeting, Accounting and Financial Management, 10*(2, Summer), 279–310.

Jones, D. S. (1999). Public administration in Singapore: Continuity and reform. In H. K. Wong & H. S. Chan (Eds.), *Handbook of comparative public administration in the Asia-Pacific basin* (pp. 1–21). New York: Marcel Dekker.

Jones, D. S. (2002a). Recent changes in Singapore's administrative elite: Responding to the challenges of a rapidly growing economy. *Asian Journal of Political Science, 10*(2, December), 70–93.

Jones, D. S. (2002b). Procurement practices in the Singapore Civil Service: Balancing control and delegation. *Journal of Public Procurement, 2*(1, Summer), 29–54.

Jones, D. S. (2005). Recent changes in the financial management of the Singapore Civil Service: The adoption of resource accounting, internal charging and revenue retention. In A. B. L. Cheung (Ed.), *Public service reform in East Asia: Reform issues and challenges in Japan, Korea, Singapore and Hong Kong* (pp. 105–125). Hong Kong: Chinese University Press.

Jones, D. S. (2006). Financial reforms of statutory bodies in Singapore: Control and autonomy in a centralized state. *Public Organization Review, 6*(3), 259–276.

Jones, D. S. (2007). The features and recent reforms of government procurement in Singapore. In L. Knight, C. Harland, J. Telgen, G. Callender, K. Thai, & K. McKen (Eds.), *Public procurement: International cases and commentary* (pp. 117–137). Oxford: Routledge.

Jones, D. S. (2014). Infrastructure financing and development in Singapore. In F. Zen (Ed.) *Financing infrastructure in ASEAN member states – Fiscal landscape and resource mobilisation* (pp. 327–350). Singapore: Economic Research Institute for ASEAN and East Asia (ERIA).

Jones, D. S. (2016). Governance and meritocracy: A study of policy implementation in Singapore. In J. S. T. Quah (Ed.), *The role of the public bureaucracy in policy implementation in five ASEAN countries* (pp. 297–369). Cambridge: Cambridge University Press.

JTC Corporation. (2011). *News release: JTC awards ascendas with 'shell-plus' laboratory development tender for biopolis expansion.* Singapore. Retrieved from http://www. jtc. gov.sg/ News/Press-Releases/Pages/20110524%28PR%29.aspx.

JTC Corporation. (2016). *JTC corporation annual report, 2015,* Singapore.

KPMG. (2016). *Land Transport Authority and its subsidiaries: Financial statements for the year ended March 31.* Singapore.

Land Transport Authority. (2013). *Land transport masterplan, 2013*, Singapore.

Land Transport Authority. (2016). *Land Transport Authority annual report, 2015/2016*, Singapore.

Land Transport Authority. (2017). *About LTA*, Singapore. Retrieved from http://www. lta.gov. sg /content/ltaweb/en/about-lta/.

Ministry of Communications and Information. (1988). *Budget statement, 1988*, Singapore. Retrieved from http://www.mof.gov.sg/news-reader/.

Ministry of Finance. (2010a). *Summary of responses – Public consultation on draft Income Tax (Amendment) Bill 2010, Singapore*. Retrieved from http://app.mof.gov.sg/.

Ministry of Finance. (2010b). *Singapore public sector outcomes review: Meeting challenges of tomorrow with a whole of government approach*, Singapore.

Ministry of Finance. (2016). *MOF and ACRA publish responses to public feedback on proposed changes to the Companies Act, Limited Liability Partnerships Act and Accountants Act.* Singapore. Retrieved from http://www.mof.gov.sg/news-reader/.

Ministry of Home Affairs. (2014). *Public consultations: Public consultation on the prevention of human trafficking bill.* Singapore. Retrieved from http://www.mha.gov.sg/get_news_file.

Ministry of Manpower. (2014). *Newsroom: Summary of feedback for Private Member's Bill on Prevention of Human Trafficking*, Singapore. Retrieved from http://www.mom.gov. sg/newsroom/press-releases/2014/summary-of-feedback-for-private-members-bill-on-prevention-of-human-trafficking.

Ministry of National Development. (2014). *Municipal services office to improve service delivery.* Singapore. Retrieved from http://app.mnd.gov.sg/Newsroom/.

Ong, P. (2011). *Opening address by Mr Peter Ong, head, civil service, at 2011 administrative service dinner and promotion ceremony, March 28*, Singapore. Retrieved from http://www.psd.gov.sg.

Public Service Commission. (1993). *Public Service Commission annual report, 1993.* Singapore.

Public Service Commission. (2002). *Management Associates Programme (MAP) background factsheet.* Singapore. Retrieved from http://a:psd.gov.sg/data/ MAP%20factsheet.doc.

Public Service Commission. (2016). *PSC annual report, 2016.* Singapore.

Public Service Commission. (2017). *Functions of the PSC.* Singapore. Retrieved from http:// www.psc.gov.sg/content/psc/default/psc_funcs/.

Public Service Division. (2008). *National goals, global perspectives: The Singapore Public Service.* Singapore: Public Service Division. Retrieved from http://www.psd.gov.sg.

Public Service Division. (2014). *Public service improves career prospects for non-graduates.* Singapore. Retrieved from http://www.psd.gov.sg/content/psd/en/media/.

Quah, J. S. T. (2003). *Curbing corruption in Asia: A comparative study of six countries.* Singapore: Eastern Universities Press.

Quah, J. S. T. (2010). *Public administration Singapore-style.* Bingley: Emerald Group Publishing.

REACH. (2011). *What Singaporeans are talking about in 2011.* Singapore. Retrieved from http:// www.reach.gov.sg/portals/0/MediaRelease/.

REACH. (2017). *REACH public consultations.* Singapore. Retrieved from http://www.reach.gov. sg/YourSay/EConsultationPaper.aspx.

S. Rajaratnam School of International Studies. (2008). *Networked government & homeland security workshop: Conference report.* Singapore.

Saxena, N. C. (2011). *Virtuous cycles: The Singapore public service and national development.* Singapore: United Nations Development Programme and Civil Service College.

Sim, W. (2014). Municipal services office to open Oct 1, says Grace Fu. *Straits Times*, August 24. Retrieved from http://www.straitstimes.com/news.

Sin, B. A. (1990). Statutory board privatization: Some issues of accountability and control (1). *Malayan Law Journal, 2* (June), 50–57.

Singapore Inter-Agency Taskforce on Trafficking-in-Persons. (2012). *National Plan of Action (NPA) 2012 to 2015*. Singapore.

Singapore Parliament (2014). *Singapore parliament reports vol. 92* (November 3). Singapore.

Sovannnasam, U. (2011). ASEAN efforts in dealing with transnational crime. In Y. Y. Lee (Ed.), *ASEAN matters: Reflecting on the Association of Southeast Asian Nations* (pp. 77–84). Singapore: Lee Kuan Yew School of Public Policy, National University of Singapore, and Institute of Policy Studies.

US State Department. (2008). Trafficking in persons. report, Washington D.C. Retrieved from http://www.state.gov/j/tip/rls/tiprpt/2008/.

Uy, V. (2008). Trafficking of Filipinos to Singapore on the rise. *The Inquirer* (Manila), May 3.

World Bank. (2016a). *Worldwide governance indicators 1996–2015*. Washington D.C. Retrieved from http://www.doingbusiness.org/data/exploreeconomies/singapore.

World Bank (2016b). *Doing business: Measuring business regulations, 2017*. Washington D.C. Retrieved from http://www.doingbusiness.org/.

Worthington, R. (2003). *Governance in Singapore*. London: Routledge Curzon.

Yap, C. (2014). What municipal services unit aims to achieve (letter to Forum page). *Straits Times,* August 30. Retrieved from http://www.straitstimes.com/news.

CHAPTER 9

LEADERSHIP AND PUBLIC SECTOR REFORM IN MALAYSIA

Loo-See Beh

ABSTRACT

This chapter highlights how Malaysia has experienced a successful economy through different stages since independence. The development, administration and institution-building phase was followed by reform initiatives throughout the years. Master Industrial Plans, 5-year development plans and other mid-term plans are used, which include governance and performance management reform. Today, public service reform continues to evolve with emphasis on better services, e-government and one-stop clearance centres. Under the Government Transformation Programme launched in 2010, seven National Key Results Areas have been identified, e.g., reducing crime, fighting corruption, improving education, and raising living standards of low-income households. Within this, political transformation programme, digital transformation programme, community transformation programme and social transformation programme have been created that advance public sector reforms. This chapter shows that while states and leaders remain powerful actors, leaders recognise a need to reform and overcome unethical and inefficient bureaucratic dysfunctions, or keep them at a minimum. Leaders manage such problems

Leadership and Public Sector Reform in Asia
Public Policy and Governance, 207–230
Copyright © 2018 by Emerald Publishing Limited
All rights of reproduction in any form reserved
doi:10.1108/S2053-769720180000030009

by using transparency to address problems of vested interests, stringent audits and punishing civil servants for criminal breaches of trust, removal of ministerial control over government-linked companies and removing resisting actors. Yet, more reforms in shepherding public service renewal are needed in sustaining reforms and reputations of public institutions. The author calls for increased values-based leadership that is inclusive at the highest levels.

Keywords: 5-Year development plans; government transformation programme; bureaucracy; values-based leadership; Malaysia

PREAMBLE

Malaysian economy has been successful since independence through modernisation, state-led development in agriculture and industry, trade liberalisation, manufacturing and export-led growth, privatisation and human capital development. Malaysia's political system is a constitutional system founded upon the British Westminster model of parliamentary democracy that blends with constitutional monarchy. It determines the powers of the legislature, the executive and the judiciary. In Malaysia, there are 1.4 million civil servants in 28 schemes under the public services department. They include federal public service, state public services, the joint public services, education service, judiciary, legal service, police and armed forces. The public sector comprises persons and organisations engaged in the delivery of public goods and services to citizens, and the state is the key actor in the development process. Naturally, private sector and civil society play their important roles alongside the public sector in the pursuit of economic and social development.

This chapter discusses public service leadership and accountability, and selected brief public sector reforms undertaken in past five years as there have been numerous writings on government-led policies under previous premierships that endowed various perils and developments from historical, economic and social reviews (e.g., Beh, 2007a, 2007b, 2011; Lim, Gomes, & Rahman, 2009; Phang & Beh, 2006; Wain, 2009) as well as how leaders manage risks in political survival and sustaining reforms through legitimate leadership. At a broader level, the chapter focusses on leadership conceived broadly to work towards desirable goals and outcomes that would benefit all stakeholders and that leadership could fundamentally be contextual and intricate in the country and leadership aspects that could bring about better quality.

In state–society relations in Malaysia, the leader or government is always the head and thus fewer contingents upon the society's demands resulting in the diminishing or weakening of public decision-making as experienced in many developing countries in contrast to developed ones. The culture during Mahathir Mohamed's reign of 22 years has built a subdued society in a leader–follower relationship, typical of eastern philosophy constantly reiterated by his successors to seemingly champion the disgruntlement of a privileged segment of society (Beh & Kennan, 2013; Wain, 2009). Often, leaders in the country fail to recognise that they must show the capacity to effect public purposes and accountability to the polity to the acceptable level of leaders' good governance of the western model. Leadership in the country is unfortunately too often seen as a kind of control mechanism where options are few in behavioural options as the literature on the dark side of social capital makes clear in favour of highly orchestrated coopera-tive actions and fostering isolation, and resentment in some. Social capital is unevenly distributed, creating vast cultural and political inequalities in Asia and, in particular, Malaysia (Beh & Kennan, 2013). No doubt, good leaders in office are needed at all levels of government and management. Globalisation indirectly challenged its practice of governance in Malaysia. Subsequently, government policies had to reflect principles of transparency, accountability, equity and to a certain extent issues deemed sensitive and rarely discussed publicly prior to this wave of change. The focus as in any other public service is to make the civil service more efficient so that more processes can be completed in a shorter time in which the speed of delivery is improved without sacrificing quality, and the onus always lies with public leaders to increase capacity to manage change (Aucoin, 2012). Inclusive state–citizen partnerships for effective service delivery and to perform their democratic functions will always be a continuing evolution process and challenge in the development of public governance capacity in the country.

In terms of inter-governmental relationships, the federal structure of government in Malaysia tends to be heavily biased towards the central level concentration of powers. States and local governments operate within a framework of subordination to the federal level where federal laws supersede those of the states in addition to much reliance of finance and non-existence of local government elections. Centralisation is further enforced by the argu-ment for national unity integration and political stability, although adminis-trative decentralisation is well coordinated.

REFORMS IN PUBLIC POLICIES AND
MODERNISATION IN BUREAUCRACY

It is clear that many reforms, including civil service reforms, have taken place in the country. Malaysia has made remarkable progress since its independence in 1957. Among others, the Government's industrialisation policy introduced in the early 1970s enabled the nation to advance to an upper middle income nation in 1992. Prior to the 1997–1998 Asian financial crisis, Malaysia's economic growth rate hit the 10% in 1973, 1976, 1988 and 1996. Countries such as Republic of Korea and Singapore that were in the same growth rate have now ascended to high income nation status.

The government has introduced a series of administrative reforms to cope with challenges in the global environment. The development administration and institution building phase began after independence until the 1980s followed by reform initiatives with clear emphasis on innovations and industrialisation till 1990. The political leadership under Tun Mahathir Mohamed moved the reform agenda to enhancing and accelerating ethnic Malays participation in the economy and public administration through all policies in addition to the new economic policy (NEP) evident till today. This phase also introduced the privatisation of state enterprises. Many plans and policies were introduced and refined over time in light of modernisation, including demands of better governance and performance management reforms over each leadership change with emphasis on industrialisation and export orientation. Successful master industrial plans, 5-year development plans alongside other mid-term plans have been introduced and transformed to fit into national objectives and achieving investment and growth within cross-agency collaborations and improvements throughout many years of implementation (Institute of Strategic and International Studies, 2011).

Subsequently, since then till present, public service reform continues to evolve alongside many perennial problems and challenges with emphasis on better counter services, e-government, one-stop clearance centres for better facilities, courtesy and services. Public bureaucracy has undergone many changes with better public accountability and transparency throughout various administrations under previous and current premierships. In the citizens' perspective, generally those reforms and public performance of public agencies have much improved in terms of effectiveness and efficiency over the years in addition to utilisation of improvements and advancements of information technology (Commonwealth Secretariat, 2006).

Under the current leadership of Prime Minister Dato' Seri Mohd Najib, the national transformation policy was introduced comprising creative and innovative ideas and programmes with clear targets and milestones. Under this policy is the government transformation programme (GTP) launched in 2010. The main objectives are to ensure that socio-economic disparities are addressed, and accessibility to social amenities is improved. Seven national key results areas (NKRAs) have been identified, namely reducing crime, fighting corruption, improving education via student outcomes, raising living standards of low-income households, improving rural basic infrastructure, improving urban public transport and addressing the rising cost of living. The next section relates briefly the various recent programmes.

Under the GTP, there are specific domains: economic transformation programme (ETP), political transformation programme (PTP), digital transformation programme (DTP), community transformation programme and social transformation programme (STP).

The ETP launched in March 2010 focusses on industries with comparative advantage via strategic reform initiatives (SRIs) on public finance, government's role in business, human capital development, public service delivery, international standards and liberalisation, and narrowing disparities. Following these efforts, private investment in nominal terms increased by 16.6% to RM111.8 billion in 2011 and RM139.5 billion in 2012. The growth in private investment was led by investment in construction, manufacturing and services.

To further balance the nation security's needs and freedom, the PTP was launched in 2011 to enable citizens to assemble peacefully and voice their concerns, where Section 27 of the Police Act was replaced by the Peaceful Assembly Act 2011. In addition, Section 15 of the University and University Colleges Act (1974) was amended to allow students to join political parties upon attaining the age of 21 years. Amendments to the Printing Press and Publications Act also sees print media no longer required to renew their printing press licences and publication permits annually, although the government still has the discretion to stop their permits at any time as evidenced from time to time.

The DTP launched in October 2011 is anchored on three strategic thrusts, namely shifting from supply to demand, consumption to production and low-knowledge to high-knowledge activity. The eight projects under the first wave of the digital Malaysia programme are the Asian e-fulfilment hub; enabling e-payment services for SMEs and micro enterprises; shared enterprise services; development of on-demand customised online education; microsourcing to generate income for the bottom 40% of households (B40); facilitating societal uplift; establishing a trusted mobile digital wallet platform and growing the embedded systems industry.

The latest being the STP launched on 3rd February 2013 which was introduced to strengthen core values, work culture and attitudes among Malaysians as well as inculcate the spirit of volunteerism, excellence, moderation, tolerance, respect and inclusiveness among youth in the nation-building process. Various positive developments indicate some growth trajectory and may endure a prolonged period of reform, disruption and change often alongside public service renewal to develop capacity, institutionalise change and account for results.

Under the present leadership, on 5th July 2011, the Malaysian government announced six SRIs, a critical component of ETP. Essentially, there are six SRIs: (1) competition, standards and liberalisation; (2) public finance; (3) public service delivery; (4) narrowing disparity; (5) government's role in business and (6) human capital development. SRIs are delved deeper into economic aspects coordinated mostly by the performance management and delivery unit consisting of four main thrusts: (i) creation of a competitive investment environment; (ii) development of a quality workforce; (iii) transformation of government so as to improve its service delivery to support private sector and be fiscally sustainable and (iv) narrowing of disparities. Local industry players are urged to adopt new technologies, skills and international standards in quality and sustainability in order to be internationally competitive.

It may be premature to make a precise judgement about their impacts, but some of the highlights of GTP's achievements in 2014 (Malaysian Government, 2014) include the following:

- Helping 24,646 low-income individuals raise their monthly incomes by RM300 in any three months during the year via Citizens Aid 1Malaysia (BR1M).
- Continuing to improve corruption perception index ranking, moving up to 50th position in 2014 from 53rd in 2013.
- Reducing crime by 12.6% and increase safety.
- Improving quality of education via back to school assistance programme and Book Voucher 1Malaysia.
- Delivered 485 km of rural roads, connected 8,195 households to clean and treated water and 14,299 households to reliable electricity supply.
- Increasing commuter usage of public transport through effective monorail transport system.
- Ensuring greater access to more affordable goods via the set up of *Kedai Rakyat 1Malaysia* (1Malaysia Citizen Shop) programme.
- Improving quality and affordable basic healthcare services for the poor through the Clinic 1Malaysia with 51 clinics as in 2014.

It would be too cumbersome to describe all achievements but details are available in the above-mentioned 2014 report, being the latest. Among other achievements include various guidelines which have been drawn up under the Malaysian Competition Commission to enforce the Competition Act and Competition Appeal Tribunal. Six industry sub-sectors were identified based on competitive advantage and the potential to be a global leader in exports, namely medical devices, pineapple, production of carrageenan from seaweed, halal pharmaceuticals, green technology and cyber security are currently in place.

There have been many policies in improving the quality of life of citizens, raising living standards of low-income households, improving rural development, assuring quality education, improving urban public transport, etc. Below is the discussion of one administrative reform which has successfully eradicated poverty and restructured society demographics and ownerships, that is, NEP, still on-going.

Since independence in 1957 and more prominently after 1970 with the NEP, there has been a larger shift of Malays and Indians from rural to urban areas due to urbanisation, closing the economic gap, especially between the Malays and the Chinese ethnic (Beh, 2007b; Chitose, 2003). The aim of the NEP was to end the identification of economic function by ethnic. The rationale was that 42% Malay households in Peninsular Malaysia fell within an income bracket of less than RM200 per month compared with only 10.4% of Chinese households; 9% of the Chinese had household incomes of RM400 or more compared with 4.3% of Malay households. While Malays held the political weight, the Chinese controlled the country's commercial activities. In terms of ethnic diversity, from 1957 to 1991, Malays comprised 50–58% of total population in Malaysia, Chinese 30–37% and Indians 10%. Today as of 2014 estimates, the demographic has changed with Malays and other native *bumiputera* 65%, Chinese 26%, Indians 7% and the remaining other smaller ethnic of the total 30 million. The NEP is an umbrella policy committed by the government since the Mahathir's administration, illustrating a relationship of social, economic and political dominance where the state machinery is employed. In the early days the Malays concentrated in rural areas of the eastern and northern areas in small-scale farming, rubber plantation, fishing and till present very much involved in politics. The Chinese used to work in the mining sector when it was still active but now concentrate in manufacturing, service sectors and in urban areas engaged in business and professional occupations. The Indians work in rubber industries in rural areas, while the urban Indians in small-scale commercial sectors. Each group has its own distinct culture, language and religion (Institute of Strategic and International Studies, 2011).

Hence, in the 1970s the Outline Prospective Plan for the period 1971–1990 established the implementation of the NEP comprising four 5-year development plans, which covered a period of 20 years (1971–1990) and the policy has continued till today in spite of the change of name to National Development Policy in the year 2000. The NEP is a policy favouring Malays to attain economic gain and equality between ethnic groups with a target of 30% ownership of equity in the hands of Malays and bumiputera by 1990, with 40% held by other Malaysian ethnics and 30% by foreigners. In order to attain the goals of NEP, the government gave special and preferential treatment to the Malays, most notably in education, employment access and promotion, leaders in all industries, contracts, licences, import permits, shares, scholarships and ownership assets. The policy has been successful in re-creating the socio-economic distribution to achieve its double objectives of 'poverty eradication' and 'restructuring the society'. Although the objectives have been achieved, yet the government feels it should be a continuing process in spite of all the overarching statistics given by many scholars and industry experts on the achievement and overwhelming success of the NEP encompassing all other policies.

Eradication of poverty has been implemented via the NEP by raising and improving economic conditions and the quality of life of the poor by the provision of free/subsidised social services, increasing productivity and income levels by expanding productive capital, increasing opportunities for intersectorial movements out of low productivity areas and activities. Most of the rural development strategies incorporate poverty eradication programmes such as new land and in-situ development; provision of drainage and irrigation infrastructure; provision of agriculture support services and encouraging the development of village/cottage industries since the 1980s.

In the restructuring society efforts, many inclusive policies were implemented, including the establishment of public enterprises to promote the growth of viable Malay and bumiputera commercial and industrial community. They generally focus on the following strategies: (1) direct intervention by government through the creation of specialised agencies to acquire economic interests and hold in-trust for the bumiputera until a designated time when their capabilities are ready; (2) introduction of specially designed rules and arrangements whereby the involvement and participation of bumiputeras are assisted and facilitated over a period; (3) provision of concessional fiscal and monetary support as part of the package towards entrepreneurial development; (4) programmes for education and training; (5) increasing bumiputera ownership through privatisation projects and (6) reducing progressively through overall economic growth, the imbalances in employment so that employment by sectors and occupational levels would reflect the majority of racial composition (Institute of Strategic and International Studies, 2011).

The results are overwhelmingly successful, with absolute poverty within the Malay and bumiputera community being reduced from 65% in 1970 to less than 7% in 2000. The Malays and bumiputeras have made a significant presence in various professional occupations witnessed today. The NEP has enabled the leaders and government to intervene in economy through public enterprises and trust agencies to accumulate capital on behalf of the Malays. A number of organisations have become major equity shareholders of what is now referred to as government-linked companies (GLCs) that include Khazanah Nasional, Permodalan Nasional, Petroliam Nasional (Petronas), Ministry of Finance Inc., Employees Provident Fund and many more. The success of NEP has witnessed fairer distribution of income, increased education and employment opportunities, change in economic structures and improved quality of life to create a middle class society and reduced racial disparities.

While real GDP growth has been impressive, and the standard of living of particularly the Malays and bumiputera has improved dramatically, the over-all performance of the country has not been outstanding by regional standards. In 1970, Malaysia was ranked third to Japan and Singapore in terms of GDP per capita but by 1990 it had fallen behind South Korea, Taiwan and Hong Kong. The downside of the policy also sees the phenomenon of crony-ism or redistribution of rent-seeking opportunities to companies controlled by politicians, bureaucrats and politically connected businessmen. As such political patronage led to the emergence of a group of politically influential new rich Malays, intra-ethnic inequality also grew. Dependency syndrome among the Malays makes the non-Malays dissatisfied with many aspects in the country. Thus, the success of the policy has caused detrimental effects to national integration due to its long continuing implementation till today in spite of calls for the reduction of implementation over time. Presently, the case for equality and the central importance of distributive justice has been served, at least in the perspectives of the non-Malays but much to the cha-grin, the insistence of the majority ethnic group of the Malays and the gov-ernment in still needing the policy. Racial theories will appear useful to some nationalists who will make full use of them too easily and can act to divide a nation instead of promulgation of unity in diversity.

This schism allows us to relate to Rawl and Galbraith's writings and analyses on the nature of appropriate social institutions that society may need a realistic institutional balance and the pursuit of justice. In factoring fair dimension of policies and better distribution of beneficiaries across the society, it may be well to consider Crick's (2005) writings where racialism is the characteristic perversion of nationalism. Race- and class-thinking are ideologies to claim to possess the key to history and a scheme for remedying all the defects of human condition. Racialism is a myth of the body whose mode or expression is pseudo-scientific, while nationalism is a myth of the mind whose mode of expression is cultural and historical. The hallmark of bureaucracy and politicisation tend to promote the continuation of existing policies and practices which may not anchor well in the requisite endowments of an emerging market such as Malaysia in supporting new paradigms of competition and success in tackling the challenges inherent in the creation of new competitive policies and industries. As a result, the country has been suffering from brain drain more than brain gain. Unfortunately or fortunately, one might say, leaders prefer to believe that somehow, or rather in their positions of authority, know what they are doing to continue justice/(injustice) of disproportionate power, influence and opportunity much to the dismay of powerless citizens other than during elections process.

MANAGING RISKS, SUSTAINING REFORMS AND PERFORMANCE

Relatively, the modern developed state is organised along impersonal rules, public service recruitment according to merits, and public goods in exchange for revenues and taxes collected from population. The core assumptions of the Western state model continue to relatively remain unchallenged in terms of how the state is perceived, conceptualised and analysed (Radnitz, 2011). Thus, in this respect, it is critical for realising citizen's rights and delivering efficient public services, competent leadership and efficient resource management instead of indifference to performance culture and accountability for results and weak capacity in ministries and public institutions which have long been daunting in Malaysia where politics and public administration is also divided along ethnic lines. In line with this reasoning as in the theoretical literature, the discretionary powers of public officials to administer public goods are perceived in terms of principal–agent problem in which occurs the ineffective monitoring of such discretionary powers.

While states and leaders remain powerful actors, confidence declines in their ability to adequately address the emergent challenges of a complex interdependent linkage in public administration, thus resulting in higher demands of governance from higher educated citizens. In anticipation of such demands, leaders recognise that there is a need to reform continuously to overcome many unethical and inefficient bureaucratic dysfunctions, at least to keep them at a minimum and manage the related challenges. Hence, how do leaders implement reform initiatives? And, how do leaders cope with resisting actors from inside organisations? The instrument of state power with the legitimate use of force and coercion is constantly used by the leaders. Vested interests in the economic bureaucracy are relevant and too important to leave them in the hands of say, privatisation entirely, hence the governance of strategic economic assets ultimately works in the service of the ruling party leader rather than the market (Beh, 2007a, 2007b). In developing countries, the distinction between politicians and bureaucrats tends to be blurred and an alliance between the ruling elite and high-ranking officials has often led to an oligarchy of power and privilege. As in the case of Malaysia, the post-independence period involved the extensive expansion of state functions. For example, many economic management programmes and projects were launched alongside creation of many additional public institutions and centres which then propagated its benefits to citizens through mainstream mass media. Mobilisation programmes were also established and variously labelled nation-building programmes, such as the recent 1Malaysia programme to demonstrate unity in diversity. The main goal, of course, is to involve citizens into the mainstream of economic and social development at all levels – federal, state and local governments – to overcome challenges from external environment, mainly the citizens, oppositions and non-governmental organizations. Public institutions and bureaucracy are the centre-piece of these new endeavours from time to time. Doctrines of guardianship via political parties and the executive dominated the management of public affairs to turn any possible threats into opportunities for power continuity as well as reform opportunities for better governance.

Malaysia, as a developing state, is characterised by the institutionalisation of the political economy of state and market with paternalistic authoritarian governance tolerated to some degree. State–business relations are not forged through industrial policy alone but through ethnic division in managing politics and economy, although economic labour division is more blurred today due to state-centred public administration with a majority of one ethnic who forms the majority of population. This measure also ensures that the minority will not be able to change or counter any policies that would disrupt any short- or long-term interests of leaders and population, as consociation politics is practiced in guaranteeing the socio-economic development agenda. Thus, these seemingly threats are turned into opportunities for reforms at all levels of administrative reform.

Looking back, in the civil service reform, the country was expanding rapidly for the last few decades, and in the 1970s professionals and technocrats in science, economics and other innovative fields were lacking. It was then that the development administration unit was established to train all levels of civil service and later the National Institute of Public Administration to include policy planning tasks and programme implementation since the 1980s. The on-going sustained reform equipped Malaysian officers with appropriate skills in public administration, thereby contributing to the transformation of the civil service, which further strengthens the cadres for administration (Commonwealth Secretariat, 2006).

How do leaders manage risks of potential financial losses and operational capacity from public expenditure? There was widespread view that privatisation policy then had favoured the vested interests and many beneficiaries were chosen based on political and personal connections, thus incurring losses and liabilities on many occasions. The leaders manage such risks from time to time by making public annual audit reports demonstrating the faltering process of rules and regulations compliance and transparency of governance. Owing to non-transparent selection process of contracts and suppliers, the concession agreements and government procurement led to sub-optimal outcomes, which further led to allegations of corruption during Mahathir's leadership. With reforms made on contracts above a designated huge amount, they have been made as open-tendered since Abdullah Badawi's tenure and to demonstrate that leaders were taking steps to rectify the situations and overcoming those challenges with strategies of implementation. From time to time too, civil servants were punished for criminal breach of trust and these cases were published for public consumption. More stringent audits of project financing became imperative to control the costs of infrastructure projects and public expenditure to build operational capacity.

Allegations of cronyism and preferential treatment revealed weak corporate governance practices during the 1997 Asian financial crisis, which then brought about the National Integrity Plan and Malaysian Code of Corporate Governance in 2000. More reform implementation, including administrative rules and regulations, were issued by the leaders for the purpose of policy implementation, and declaration of personal assets and liabilities of all civil servants and ministers were made mandatory till today.

Another example of achievement is the removal of ministerial control over GLCs, which further reinforce financial goals and in strengthening regulatory institutions such as Malaysian anti-corruption commission (MACC) and public accounts committee to have a balanced composition so that they can act in a non-partisan manner on public expenditures. Nevertheless, these regulatory institutions have to demonstrate the best standards of independence, integrity and professionalism, given several cases where supposedly criminal charges were expected but instead dropped due to failure of independence, at least in the citizens' perspectives. Recently, MACC advisory board identified several enforcement agencies with wide powers such as police, immigration, customs and the inland revenue board as being prone to corruption (Singh, 2017) and the public agency has been taking regular steps in nabbing and convicting senior public servants for corruption. The leaders have coped with such resisting sentiments from citizens either by a non-responsive manner or by further strengthening the power and responsibility in other exclusive public matters or raising issues with the political opposition party leader as a digression from the crux.

In overcoming challenges and managing risks from external business environment, the leaders reformed the boards of GLCs, where governance issues would be better addressed and policy makers can clarify and quantify costs of national development agenda and investment opportunities. Thus, the reconciliation strategy established the Competition Act 2010, which came into effect on 1st January 2012. It is aimed at ensuring a conducive and competitive business environment that will promote productivity and enhance innovation applicable across industries and firms. This SRI has been renamed as competition, standards and liberalisation to better reflect competition as a major component of policy and regulatory changes. The Competition Act comes under this umbrella as well as the Ministry of Domestic Trade, Cooperatives and Consumerism for competition law, the Ministry of Science, Technology and Innovation for standards, and the Ministry of International Trade and Industry for services.

It is often explicit that greater governmental transparency is crucial to enhance accountability and curb corruption. Often enough citizens and non-governmental organisations hold public office holders to account and that good behaviour always enhances the legitimacy of institutions. One of the basic assumptions upon which transparency builds upon is that exposure of corrupt individuals and institutions will produce widespread public indignation and pressure for accountability and reform. As such, if citizens believe that most other citizens engage in corruption, transparency may also erode societal accountability as such pervasive action may cause public and civic endeavours rather than induce and empower citizens to mobilise for better government (Persson, Rothstein, & Teorell, 2013). Anti-corruption reforms have largely failed, as these are based on a theoretical mischaracterisation of the problem of systemic corruption as a principal–agent problem, it much resembles a collective action problem. The key instruments to curb corruption in line with the principal–agent anti-corruption framework state that monitoring devices and punishment regimes are largely ineffective as there will not be any actors that have an incentive to enforce them. This holds true as the principled principals do not act in the interest of the society but instead pursue their own self-interests. In short, anti-corruption reforms based on the principal–agent framework will invariably fail as corruption becomes the rule rather than the exception even if everyone else condemns corruption. Nevertheless, public agency such as MACC has demonstrated its seriousness in bringing many corrupt senior officials to court for conviction (Beh, 2011), especially of late since the second half of 2016 till today in implementing reforms and overcoming challenges.

Having said that, the challenge for successful public administrators is to create space within government where trust resonates and flourishes. When the foundation of trust is authentic, it will enhance the consolidation of state institutions with well-functioning state apparatuses. For instance, the current prime minister is alleged to be involved in the state-owned investment fund 1Malaysia Development Berhad (1MDB). The controversy could have ended in January 2016 when the newly appointed attorney general Tan Sri Mohamed Apandi Ali cleared the prime minister of corruption, but critics have asked how he was let off by MACC on financial irregularities. Nevertheless, the MACC's independent operations review panel has recommended (as at the end of February 2016) that the commission continues to pursue its investigations on the RM2.6 billion donation received by the prime minister and the alleged discrepancies of SRC International Sdn Bhd, a former subsidiary company of 1MDB, in addition to global investigations from Luxembourg, Singapore, US Justice Department, etc.

Such allegations of massive corruption at the highest level of government may cause a serious crisis of confidence in the government and in its ability to lead the country forward in challenging times. Interestingly and reflecting the extent this had driven the depreciation value of the country's currency since July 2015 much to the denial of the leadership. The ringgit was the most negative towards the end of September 2015 at the time when foreign holdings of central bank bills in both conventional and Islamic financial markets fell by RM58.7 billion (about USD14.7 billion) to RM22 billion, where it was a significant factor to the ringgit depreciating by 16% against the US dollar. This may cause little faith and trust in the federal and state capacity to successfully solve important public problems and prescription for the reform as an ideology of public management where the government lacked the tools and capacity to effectively address such complex issues of gratification with much professionalism. As Newell, Reeher, and Ronayne (2008) defined trust as a foundational confidence among citizens and government agencies who will act in a reasonably consistent way to promote their shared values and interest and respond to their long-term needs and wants, thereby enhancing the lacking of trust. Newell et al.'s conception of values-based leadership may in fact be about the ethical dimensions of public service leadership as trusted leadership. Values such as accountability to society, transparency and equal opportunities known as public ethos are central to public administration to safeguard the quality of administration and service production as well as to ensure legitimacy in the population (Busch & Wennes, 2012).

Thus, the argument here is how able are these leaders in implementing reform initiatives under distrust atmosphere within the society? To begin with, leaders cope with resisting actors inside organisations by eliminating/ replacing them. For example, the deputy prime minister, Muhyiddin Yassin was sacked and replaced due to his whistle-blowing act on the alleged wrongdoings of the prime minister in the state-owned investment arm, 1MDB which has RM42 billion of debt without much cash flow to service its loans then, but its short-term debts and bank loans of RM2.83 billion have since been settled (Arukesamy, 2017) In addition, Muhyiddin was also suspended from the country's dominant party, the United Malays National Organisation (UMNO) on 26th February 2016, subsequently the post of deputy president of the party as well as his access to grassroots severed, just seven months after he was sacked from the government. The decision was made at a meeting of the UMNO supreme council; although widely expected, this sent Malaysia into another political paroxysm, and had parallels with the 1998 ouster of Anwar Ibrahim, which still divides the nation. Subsequently, Mahathir was also made to relinquish his advisory position in the national oil and gas company Petronas in March and subsequently other advisory positions in GLCs in April 2016 as he was leading the rally against Najib with cooperation from several opposition political parties to step down (although yet with much avail via Citizens Declaration). This elimination strategy is used by the leader in coping with resistance actors inside its own political party and utilising the cabinet to remove Mahathir (and other personalities) since he no longer supports the current government, and thus should no longer hold any position related to the government. Evidences of such practices were also manifested during Mahathir's tenure and may remain strong and pervasive. Hence, we see that government machinery is used by the leader to cope with any threats and resistance from within as well as denial of any wrongdoings by the leader in all capacities. Interestingly, the mainstream media have been used by leadership to cope with external forces to divert attention to other matters, although reports on debt payment of 1MDB constantly appear to show its improved financial position.

In addition, leaders also use civil service codes in raising the support where public servants and ministers would fear of repatriation and removal, as loyalty to the current government has always been emphasised with 'promiscuous partisanship'. Thus, public servants are forbidden to participate in any public rally against the government. Public servants do not stand up to their ministers even if they were to cross the line, nor does the parliamentary cabinet, as the majority comes from the ruling party, National Coalition Party. A critical point when analysing this development is the rapid pace of change in the world that demonstrates otherwise a shifting environment. For instance, information data leak from Panama-based law firm showed that prime minister of Iceland, Sigmundur Gunnlaugsson, was the first leader casualty who had to resign on 5th April 2016 over offshore assets scandal belonging to his wife after failing to dissolve parliament (Ahmad, 2016). This further demonstrates many possibilities of other current and former world leaders along with the elites of super-rich businessmen, celebrities and sports stars who may have stashed away their wealth in shell companies for tax evasion or from any other source of misappropriation. Given the strong democracy of the citizens of Iceland, such act is intolerable and the leader deemed a hypocrite in the country. Hence, we see that the role of the state and leadership is deeply integrated, and only interdependence of global technological information constitutes a highly differentiated and interdependent landscape if we are to believe that direct reflection of the current forces can define a better political and socio-economic landscape. It would be better than pinpointing the importance of individual elements such as the state or the society (high-trust society in developed states). In emerging market nation and low-trust society (using Fukuyama's term) such as Malaysia, it is based on more or less functioning formal rules and regulations due to localised mind-sets and traditional culture (often as a propaganda or control strategy used by leaders) emanating from informal institutions, which then means that the role and involvement of the state and leaders is relatively high, commonly referred to as an interventionist state or developmental state.

A commitment to integrity among political leadership is the basis for effective anti-corruption policies. However, such political will is usually absent because powerful players benefit from corruption and play a role in its perpetuation (Fritzen, 2005; Johnston, 2005). It is not just the way in which interests are masked but also the means by which interests and identities are formed. As commonly known, state-building is a continuous process. Framed in this manner, a well-functioning state with capable impartial institutions and a solid capacity to develop, legislate and implement effective policies is fundamental. Apparently, as Carothers (2007) argues, most dictators are inherently unsuited to contribute to the second stage of state-building with effective state bureaucracy, as the case in Gaddafi's Libya. State-building is likely to be affected by the state's monopoly on the use of force and the effectiveness of its basic administrative framework. In this respect, we have seen many incidences of such conventional practices throughout the leaderships of the country. As of late, we have seen the National Security Council Bill 2015 passed in December 2015; it is targeted at terrorists/(anyone) and maintaining national security but unlimited sweeping powers are given to the prime minister and (to be) appointed director of operations on grounds of their preference to act without being subjected to any judicial scrutiny at any later point of time. This is to ensure that there is little room as possible for any interpretation of the law that may limit the vast powers vested in the government by this Act. Such unlimited power is highly undesirable as it is open to serious abuse, if any. History has shown that there had been no hesitation in the past to use laws (e.g., Internal Security Act) to crush the remnants of democracy. Even of late, a statement was issued on 28th March 2016 that the authorities under the Malaysian Communications and Multimedia Commission Act could act on those citizens caught circulating any messages deemed to be seditious and defamatory on the country's leaders or royalty even if they were not created by the sender. Many citizens see these as additional measures to curb legitimate dissent and a threat to a parliamentary democracy system by the leader in managing its own threat and political survival. Leaders would turn these personal threats into instituting further legislation in the name of national security threat. Yet, democratisation and state-building are key issues for many developing countries and recognising that corruption is a misuse of entrusted power for private gain because of weaknesses in institutional infrastructures (Kaufmann, Kraay, & Mastruzzi, 2010). Thus, the ability of the government to implement rules and regulations will very much depend on the leadership and quality of regulatory environment, growing international pressures and serious intensification of reforms.

Notably, in managing risks of reform initiatives, leaders have by and large followed policies based on sound policies and principles.

THE RIGHT LEADERS AND POLICIES MATTER

The role of leadership in advancing good governance and capacities needed for leading change in government is evident. Leaders must make the case for change more so for emerging economies. Malaysia prides itself on being a multiracial and multicultural country, and to a certain extent it is true, but look deeper, one may find a fractured nation. Race relations have regressed with more polarisation as well as rural–urban divide. To achieve sustainable high administrative performance, trust-based relationships are essential. As this is necessary, the right type of leaders matter. Progress of a country always depends on a particular leader and its leadership as we have seen in the case of neighbouring Singapore as the successful example in Asia, whereby the institutional foundations are solid in capacity development to administer, deliver and renew public services concurrently with well-managed reforms. It's true that the World Bank (2012) acknowledges that not all problems can be solved in a nation but new approaches are needed to bolster positive interventions and mitigate leadership and management challenges, otherwise reform deficit is most pronounced; Malaysia has witnessed talent migration towards stronger economies in other sectors and abroad, limited retention of qualified knowledgeable citizens and inadequate leadership competencies to motivate and manage public service performance in spite of reform initiatives. There are trade-offs between security and continuity of long-term public service employment, political appointees and higher paying job opportunities in a global market.

Stewardship to meet modern challenges in mobilising talent, time and resources is critical in assuring that public resources are managed with prudence and probity. Politicians and public servants alike are the leaders who shape government of the future. With good foresight, shortcomings can be better managed in capacity-building as it is unthinkable to steer any reform without competent leadership. Citizens and researches have reinforced this point time and time again that good leaders are needed at all levels of government and management. A manager must be able to lead so as a leader who could also manage. The pressure to enhance productivity and performance around other successful parts of the world prompts the government to embark upon reform programmes and most importantly skills to sustain change. What is less clear is whether citizens are actually benefitting from these reforms. It is generally assumed that the cost-benefit analysis, community and economic development have been made, although public service competencies still inhibit much progress. A range of interventions are needed to reinforce leadership competencies, as education and training although essential are insufficient for developing many capacities. This requires value-based, selfless leadership to steer and increase capacity of resource development while culturally sensitive matters could be reduced. As grounded in the New Public Management theology that embraces transformational leadership, the focus is on the internal workings of government – leadership, employees, structure and intergroup dynamics as both process and outcome to link to innovation results.

The politicians/cabinet cannot afford to operate as commander and controller alone but to transform public servants, especially the top and senior civil servants, to become more citizen-focussed so as to obtain results that meet citizens' expectations which have been growing via collaborating and learning from every likely source as new ideas and synergies can come from anywhere. Currently, the leadership style seems to be more political instead of advancing the dynamics and challenges with more compelling national, economic and social values in meeting challenges of governance. The former premier Abdullah Badawi's achievement of allowing openness and more acceptance of criticisms in his stride for clamping corruption and be the prime minister of all Malaysians may have also caused him his continuity of premiership as he wanted to set up an Independent Police Complaints and Misconduct Commission amongst others (Oorjitham, 2016). Notably although, he succeeded in setting up the Judicial Appointments Commission and the MACC in 2009 alongside faster public service delivery across all ministries. Accordingly, he was deemed weak and pressured within his own political party as he was seen not focussing on some crucial political and communal matters and disrupting the continuity of particular projects under the previous leadership. However, if he had stayed on, according to a political commentator and previous editor-in-chief of a mainstream newsprint, 'he may have made all the changes necessary to make the country a better place' (Oorjitham, 2016). The concept of Islam Hadhari propagated during his time but not implemented to demonstrate unity in diversity with varying cultures and religious beliefs coexisting in harmony commonly fits the notion of hybridisation of religious and universal values but hindered by the expunged growth of religious advocacy organisations and political landscape. It was an attempt to redefine the role of religion as a powerful political and societal force. Of course, nothing would be more naive or misleading than to suggest that this task will be an easy solution (Phang & Beh, 2006).

In this regard, value-based leadership and ethical leadership may still be the way forward for leadership styles in the country. House (1996) holds that value-based leadership rests primarily on two leadership dimensions: (1) making values visible and meaningful and (2) creating moral engagement in organisations. This is to prevent the institution from plunging into dysfunctional processes. This value-based leadership was the emphasis during Abdullah Badawi's tenure as prime minister. He was concerned about ethics, and assumed that his concern was transparent to other public servants. He set up many commissions to oversee many public service conducts. Citizens were happy with this change as integrity and effectiveness have been associated with his style of leadership. However, his humility as well as discontinuity of certain implementation of construction projects was deemed as a weakness by his predecessor and may have caused him his position as it was more of a lone struggle.

The qualities considered important for the ability to do a good job also constitute how these leaders prioritise between different values. It is found that social discourses about the fundamental values of the public sector have influenced the organisational identity of the leaders (Busch & Wennes, 2012). This line of reasoning is supported by two of the most important values to the NPM agenda, namely meeting the needs of individuals and renewal/innovation, which are highly important but yet difficult to live up to. It is also interesting to note that the value described as 'accountability to society at large' has become less important (Busch & Wennes, 2012) as appeared by the ramifications of current leadership. This may result in more disappointments in a country of weak/moderate professional culture with low/moderate ethical standards alongside implementation of a series of reforms in public sector, which is evident more recently. Ethical leadership involves leading oneself and leading others. Ethical leaders must be sensitive to how they are perceived by others and be strong moral managers to make best ethical decisions possible. Public servants and leaders need more frequent reminders about ethical standards and ought to be part of everyday internalisation of work life and work culture, given the increasing cases of ethical scandals among employees in both private and ultimately public sector, as is our concern here, as a result of individual and contextual influences (Beh, 2011).

CONCLUDING REMARKS – SUSTAINING REFORMS THROUGH LEADERSHIP

We might say that governing becomes increasingly fraught with uncertainty and complexity. It may be said as well that public discourse in Malaysia is restricted by legislative and extra-legislative measures. For instance, the National Security Council 2015 Bill passed in December 2015 ensures that there is as little room as possible for any interpretation of the law that may limit the vast powers vested in the government by this Act. Yet, we have seen a similar Act such as the amended Penal Code, which acts against those who may threaten parliamentary democracy and legitimate dissent. There are no indications that corruption in top political institutions has declined in any meaningful way, given the entrenched conversion of public offices into private profits and other forms of pecuniary corruption in spite of inconclusive evidence and denial of such practices, enabling political and administrative officials of such incentives give many evidences of court cases. The World Public Sector Report (2015, pp. vii–viii) depicts that responsiveness and accountability are two fundamental principles of governance which are key and cross-cutting enablers of development for the state to lead and sustain. Among the highlights reiterated include responding efficiently and effectively to people's needs; meeting increasing public demands and addressing declining public trust among partners and constituents; promoting competent, diverse and ethical public servants; engaging citizens and empowering communities as well as providing for multi-channel service delivery and e-participation.

Leadership values, attributes and behaviours are closely observed and emulated. Effective leadership is widely recognised as critical to success in a country's development in view of increasing complexity and citizen expectations (Beh & Kennan, 2013). Various political parties in the country have focussed on administering their own portfolios as fiefdoms of patronage, allowing for little coordinated policymaking and given the myriad of vested interests that have blocked true reforms. Simply administering the status quo will no longer do. Given that politicians face electoral repercussions to change, policymakers are discouraged from deviating from the status quo and may be inclined to go with the flow rather than challenge the way things are done. Such reactive behaviours do become deep-seated and constrain renewal in achieving the best possible outcomes with efficiency and effectiveness in public institutions. Thus, leadership development needs to change not just primarily due to citizens' expectations but as a result of more globalisation and transparency within volatile economic conditions.

In building support for reforms and managing risks in programmes, the programmes ought to be more encompassing of all ethnics. Ethnic groups marginalised from the government decision-making process are more likely to express their distrust in the legislature which contradicts the fundamental role of legislature in representing various interests of the society as a whole. It may not appear so as the perspective changes accordingly with different communities and societal institutions depending on the preferences, constraints and threats or opportunities. Much publicity is constantly communicated to citizens on the success of policies and continuation of transformation programmes which have been or currently being implemented in supporting economic growth. Citizens recognise that change requires more than the current in strengthening and sustaining the nation in socio-economic terms and more so on trust and governance that would be the ultimate transformation in search of innovation and competitiveness in both citizenry and public entities. In managing risks of sovereign trusts and funds, regulatory reforms of institutions must be more frequent and independent in nature from executive powers.

Often, too close interdependence between public administration and politics and between government and business have resulted in reforms often becoming a platform for the pursuit of political interests, further strengthening the state and leader power instead of democratisation of reform initiatives in the long-term benefits of the country although undeniably such economic benefits are reaped by many citizens. True reforms in the long term have benefitted countries in Westminster systems (Aucoin, 2012) as well as South Korea, Japan, Singapore and also China, just to name a few in the region of Asia, and these could be modelled after in its holistic approach of state performance.

It could be argued that politics is fused with religion in this country, and as Lewis (1993) reinforces, there is no clear boundary between politics and religion. In the Malaysian political discourse, the hegemony of religion and spirituality is constantly being harped upon as the basis for support and legitimacy of the government. Hybridisation of politics and religion is welcomed when practiced with sanctity. Unfortunately, the hope for the ability of religions to solve problems plaguing contemporary Malaysia such as corruption, conflicts and terrorism has been minimal. Ultimately, only an improvement in the critical aspects of governance would make the Malaysian politics a real watershed, given those pertinent points by the World Public Sector Report, 2015. What does the future hold in the myriad of cultural contexts? It remains to be seen whether any leadership in the country can break out of this tradition of inclusivity cabinets and truly exercise fewer political compromises. As large literature commonly suggests that change is particularly difficult in the public sector and many of these are of heavily politicised programmes (Politt & Bouckaert, 2004). Leadership qualities should include the ability to embrace different cultures and diversity of thinking as well as the ability to change. It is important that leaders show political maturity by avoiding extremism or parochialism but strive towards the sustainable growth of a harmonious society and advancing good governance that has moved beyond the challenge of mere subsistence in shepherding public service renewal, sustaining reforms and reputations of public institutions in addition to mobilising the diversity of talents to serve the country's evolving needs.

REFERENCES

Ahmad, R. (2016). Action against any firm named in Panama papers. *The Star*, April 7, p. 5.
Arukesamy, K. (2017). 1MDB short-term debts, bank loans cleared. *The Sun*, March 31, p. 4.
Aucoin, P. (2012). New political governance in Westminster systems: Impartial public administration and management performance at risk. *Governance, 25*(2), 177–199.

Beh, L. (2007a). *Administrative reform: Issues of ethics and governance in Malaysia and China.* Copenhagen discussion papers 2007-23. Copenhagen Business School, Denmark.

Beh, L. (2007b). Malaysian Chinese capitalism: Mapping the bargain of a developmental state. In P. K. Voon (Ed.), *Malaysian Chinese and nation-building: Before Merdeka and fifty years after* (Vol. 1, pp. 223–267). Kuala Lumpur: Centre for Malaysian Chinese Studies.

Beh, L. (2011). Public ethics and corruption in Malaysia. In E. M. Berman (Ed.), *Public administration in Southeast Asia* (pp. 171–191). New York, NY: CRC Press, Taylor & Francis.

Beh, L., & Kennan, W. (2013). Leadership in the East: A social capital perspective. In J. Rajasekar & L. Beh (Ed.), *Culture and gender in leadership: Perspectives from the Middle East and Asia* (pp. 9–36). UK: Palgrave Macmillan.

Busch, T., & Wennes, G. (2012). Changing values in the modern public sector: The need for value-based leadership. *International Journal of Leadership in Public Services, 8*(4), 201–215.

Carothers, T. (2007). How democracies emerge: The 'sequencing' fallacy. *Journal of Democracy, 18*(1), 12–27.

Chitose, Y. (2003). Effects of government policy on internal migration in Peninsular Malaysia: A comparison between Malays and non-Malays. *The International Migration Review, 37*(4), 1191–1219.

Commonwealth Secretariat. (2006). *A profile of the public service of Malaysia.* Kuala Lumpur: MDC Publishers Sdn Bhd.

Crick, B. (2005). *In defence of politics* (5th ed.). London: Continuum.

Fritzen, S. (2005). Beyond political will: How institutional context shapes the implementation of anti-corruption policies. *Policy & Society, 24*(3), 79–96.

House, R. I. (1996). Path-goal theory of leadership: Lessons, legacy and a reformulated theory. *Leadership Quarterly, 7*(3), 323–352.

Institute of Strategic and International Studies. (2011). *Malaysia-policies and issues in economic development.* Kuala Lumpur: Institute of Strategic and International Studies Malaysia.

Johnston, M. (2005). *Syndromes of corruption.* Cambridge: Cambridge University Press.

Kaufmann, D., Kraay, A., & Mastruzzi, M. (2010). *The worldwide governance indicators: Methodology and analytical issues. World Bank policy research working paper series.* Policy Research Working Paper No. 5430. The World Bank Development Research Group, Washington, DC.

Lewis, B. (1993). *Islam and the west.* Oxford: Oxford University Press.

Lim, T. G., Gomes, A., & Rahman, A. (Eds.). (2009). *Multiethnic Malaysia: Past, present and future.* Petaling Jaya: Strategic Information and Research Development Centre.

Malaysian Government. (2014). *Government transformation programme annual report, 2014.* Kuala Lumpur: Prime Minister's Department.

Newell, T., Reeher, G., & Ronayne, P. (2008). *The trusted leader: Building the relationships that make government work.* Washington, DC: CQ Press.

Oorjitham, S. (2016). Frank talk about Pak Lah's years in office. *The Star,* April 1, p.13.

Persson, A., Rothstein, B., & Teorell, J. (2013). 'Why' anti-corruption reforms fail – Systemic corruption as a collective action problem. *Governance, 26*(3), 449–471.

Phang, S. N., & Beh, L. (2006). Rearticulating spiritual hegemony and reconceiving divinity: Malaysia's Islam Hadhari. In D. Schirmer, G. Saalmann, & C. Kessler (Eds.), *Hybridising east and west: Tales beyond westernisation – Empirical contributions to the debates on hybridity* (pp. 241–256). Berlin: Lit Verlag.

Politt, C., & Bouckaert, G. (2004). *Public management reform: A comparative analysis.* Oxford: Oxford University Press.

Radnitz, S. (2011). *Informal politics and the state. Comparative Politics*, *43*(3), 351–371.

Singh, R. (2017). Agencies with wide powers prone to graft. *The Sun*, March 29, p. 5.

Wain, B. (2009). *Malaysian maverick: Mahathir Mohamad in turbulent times*. London: Palgrave Macmillan.

World Bank. (2012). *The World Bank's approach to public sector management 2011–2020: Better results from public sector institutions*. Washington, DC: World Bank.

World Public Sector Report. (2015). *Responsiveness and accountable public governance*. Publication No. ST/ESA/PAD/SER.E/187. New York, NY: United Nations. Retrieved from https://publicadministration.un.org/publications/content/PDFs/World%20Public%20Sector%20Report2015.pdf

CHAPTER 10

LEADERSHIP AND PUBLIC SECTOR REFORM IN AUSTRALIA

John Halligan

ABSTRACT

Australia is one of the Anglophone countries that readily adapted to a public management approach. Reforms since the 1980s have shown remarkable breadth, longevity and significance. The reforms acknowledge failure of existing approaches and the need to address management deficiencies, fiscal stress and increased complexity. This chapter discusses four cases, reflecting leadership from core agencies as well as executives. Financial management reform was initially led by Finance, and then a broader agenda was pursued through a senior management committee under the Department of the Prime. However, devolution of responsibilities from central agencies did not appear to make managers more accountable. Finance was weakened by devolution and unable to exercise appropriate leadership, and agencies did not integrate performance management reform with internal planning processes. By contrast, a one-stop shopping service for welfare was successful, although later folded in the Department of Human Services. DPMC also launched reform process in the 2010s, although not a priority of the prime minister, some recommendations, such as leadership development and talent management, were implemented

Leadership and Public Sector Reform in Asia
Public Policy and Governance, 231–255
doi:10.1108/S2053-769720180000030010

that increased public service capacity. The case of Australia shows that in spite of variable political support and leadership by central agencies, a relatively stable environment (governments serving multiple terms) allowed implementation to proceed in the mid-term, including incentives to ensure responsiveness at department levels.

Keywords: Financial management; devolution; welfare; public service capacity; Australia; leadership

Leadership has undergone substantial change in the era of public sector reform with new management thinking about how public service systems should operate, and how roles and relationships should be defined. The environment that was once relatively stable for public organisations has become more competitive and dynamic, and the constraints and rules that once dictated the character of public organisations have less importance as they have sought to adapt (Brookes & Grint, 2010; Halligan, 2012).

Leadership and reform are inextricably related and have developed symbiotically with continual public sector change. Reform is necessary for leaders to sustain the effective delivery of public policy in complex and rapidly changing environments, while reform is unlikely to be successful without effective leadership. However, it is also clear that leadership issues continue to arise, and the reforms have failed to achieve proper traction for various reasons, including the limitations of leadership.

The analysis of leadership in the public sector has also advanced considerably over the last decade or so, reflecting in large part the rapidly changing subject matter and more eclectic and creative theorising and analysis (e.g., Boin & Christensen, 2008; Brookes & Grint, 2010; Raffel, Leisink, & Middlebrooks, 2009; Rhodes & 't Hart, 2014; Van Wart & Dicke, 2008).

Four cases of reform leadership have been chosen to demonstrate different experiences of leadership and reform. The first and second reforms were led by the Department of Finance (Finance), one relatively successful, the other less so. The third, initiated by the Department of the Prime Minister and Cabinet (DPMC), produced mixed results in part because political leadership undermined progress, although one lead central agency could accomplish change at the departmental level. In the first and third cases, departmental secretaries played pivotal roles. The fourth case examines the politics of leadership in welfare coordination and the transformational leadership of a chief executive in developing a large new delivery agency.

The chapter reviews the changing approaches to public service leadership and reform and several of the factors involved in change. The four cases examined are drawn from different phases of reform and involve different types of leader and lead agencies. The concluding discussion addresses propositions from the Australian experience about factors that are important for the implementation of reforms.

LEADERSHIP AND REFORM IN AUSTRALIA

The Australian structure of government is a federation comprising six states and two territories. Another central feature is responsible government based on a Westminster-type of parliamentary system, which means that the government is formed from members of parliament to which it is accountable. The central government has major responsibilities for national policy, governance and funding in the federation, but the main service delivery occurs at the state and territory levels. Employees in the national public sector account for 16 per cent of the workforce, but that of the Australian public service (APS, at the federal level) is less than 1 per cent. There were 152,430 APS employees in 2016 of which about 1.8 per cent were in the senior executive service.

Leadership

The main types of leaders in public service reform are the political executive (prime minister and ministers) and the senior public service. Within the latter, central agency leaders are highly significant for initiating and driving major reform, and departmental leaders are integral for implementation. Third parties (e.g., think tanks) may also be important for initiating reform ideas and programmes. The focus in this chapter is on the public service leader, although the role of political leadership must be acknowledged as often fundamental to the success of reform.

The lead central agencies in public sector reform are the DPMC, Finance and the Australian Public Service Commission (APSC). The 19 departments of state range over the standard central government functions (e.g., defence, immigration and foreign affairs) and service delivery (e.g., education, health and human services), and are critical for the implementation of reform. Responsiveness to ministers has become the standard mode of operating (Edwards, Halligan, Horrigan, & Nicoll, 2012).

As for the notion of leadership, this used to be largely unarticulated (cf. Talbot, 2010). Clearly, there were formal leaders but leadership was not actively pursued on the forefront. Under the twin exigencies of the reform era, the political ascendancy of political leaders and the managerialist reinvention of public Organisation, the notion emerged and progressed through several stages. Following the establishment of the senior executive service as generalist managers in the 1980s, the focus was on the development of this executive core (Halligan, 1992). Over time, the management focus shifted to leadership and its development (Baker, 1989). Leadership became a primary concept following devolution to line departments under the Public Service Act 1999, and one that in practice required systematic development. A leadership capability framework was developed and has continued to be refined (Halligan, 2015a).

The strongest signal that leadership was now central became apparent with capability reviews, which were used to provide systematic assessments of departments' capability. Leadership was one of the three core components of the evaluation template, as discussed later (Australian Public Service Commission [APSC], 2013).

The increasing prominence given to leadership can also be interpreted in terms of the changing relationship between senior public servants and ministers. Of importance was the ascendancy of a political leader, which involved the displacement of traditional mandarins, and redefined formal public service leaders' positions (Halligan & Power, 1992). According to one argument the 'leadership discourse' was appropriated by the public service because it was 'safe' and management jargon was insufficient (Althaus & Wanna, 2008, p. 126). The political executive didn't initiate this agenda, but the relegation of the public service under managerialist reforms was partly countered through leadership programmes (Althaus & Wanna, 2008, p. 127).

Public Sector Reform

Australia was one of the Anglophone countries that readily adapted to a public management approach in part because of its administrative tradition. The distinctiveness of the administrative tradition was reaffirmed during the reform era (dating from the 1980s), when Anglophone systems adhered more to precepts of new public management than other Organization for Economic Cooperation and Development (OECD, 1995; Pal, 2012) countries. The emergence of this distinctive set of reforms was facilitated by instrumentalism and pragmatism that have been features of this administrative tradition. It also reflected patterns of interaction that accorded legitimacy and relevance to initiatives within the group (Halligan, 2010). Endogenous communication patterns have been influential through networks based on relationships developed between Britain and its one-time colonies, which have been a prime source for circulating ideas and documenting experience.

The Australia experience has been characterised by waves of reform that first surfaced in the early 1980s. The reform era has been remarkable for the magnitude and breadth of the reform, the longevity of the process and the significance of changes. The second feature was that reform was comprehensive in its application, rapidity and systemisation. The range of changes covered the gamut of possibilities: philosophy, operational style, structure, personnel and culture. Thirdly, what differentiated the 1980s from the 1970s were the rejection of traditional administration and its replacement by a package of reforms based on management. Fourthly, reform was sustained. From the outset of reform there was one government in power at the federal level (five terms until the 1996 election), and which was followed by a four-term government (until 2007). In addition, reform has been constant for over more than 30 years, sometimes involving major programmes, and at other times partial agendas and implementation.

Seven factors contributed to change in the public service (although their relative significance varied over time). The first was the failure of existing approaches. This was apparent in the 1970s and 1980s when it became clear that traditional administration was not adapting sufficiently to handle the demands being placed on it. The failure of the 1970s experiments and processes, which included a royal commission into government administration (Royal Commission on Australian Government Administration [RCAGA], 1976), indicated the need for a new and more effective reform package. The managerial approach was crystallised as consensus emerged about the deficiencies of public service (Halligan & Power, 1992).

The second was management deficiencies. The failure of management in specific agencies was exposed through public inquiries. A bipartisan view emerged that the management skills of the senior public service were deficient in general and undervalued relative to their policy and administrative skills. This condition was a product of a system that viewed managing implementation and delivery as a secondary matter for public servants recruited and acculturated to support ministers. The notion of the public manager did not exist under traditional bureaucracy. The weakness of public service was regarded as a product of a system which placed too much emphasis on inputs and due process. The emerging management orthodoxy was linked to growing pressures within the public service for a reduction in centralisation: for managers to have greater freedom from procedural constraints and departments to be able to operate more independently of central agency control.

Third, fiscal stress and economic crisis have been central, and invariably provide rationales for leader's reform agendas and contraction of government. The intensification of fiscal austerity produced the need for tighter resource use that could not be satisfied by a process-oriented approach. Australia emerged in the 1980s from a long period characterised by a regulated economy and a commitment to using the public sector for providing the services of a welfare state. Economic difficulties in the 1970s had included stagflation, oil crisis and economic recession, but governments had failed to respond effectively. Economic liberalisation and financial deregulation of the economy in the 1980s intensified pressures for public sector reform. The impact of global financial crisis on the Australian public sector in the late 2000s was highly significant for the budget when combined with significantly lower commodity prices. Under governments committed to reducing the role of the state, while confronting budget issues, there were major implications for capacity and public management in addressing complex problems.

The fourth factor was the ascendancy of neo-liberal thinking. Neo-liberalism assumed more direct significance once the first neo-conservative government of the reform era had been elected. Its National Commission of Audit (1996) operated within a neo-liberal framework, and budgets and public sector reforms were driven ideologically (Kemp, 1998a; Wanna, Kelly, & Foster, 2000). This applied also to a further National Commission of Audit in 2014.

The fifth consideration was political control of public service to obtain implementation of government programmes. Reform programmes were driven by the concern of governments with political control, which came to be regarded as both an end in itself and a means to implementing party policy. To achieve this required a redistribution of power between the bureaucracy and politicians. Other reforms either conformed to political objectives (e.g., top-down management) or were simply subservient to them.

The sixth factor was reform diffusion. The Australian reform programme has been influenced by the experience of other countries (although other forms of borrowing and from other sectors whether sub-national or the private sector needs to be acknowledged) (Halligan, 2015c). Policy transfers of reform have been significant between Britain and Australia and other Anglophone countries.

Finally, more demanding environments, both global and national, have placed more complex demands on governments and public management.

Overall, the Australian experience can be summarised with reference to three phases of reform each associated with a generation and coinciding with the decades 1980s–2010s. Managerialism best reflects the first phase in which management became the central concept and reshaped thinking (see case 1).

This was succeeded by a phase that for a time came close to the mainstream depiction of new public management, in which the market element was favoured and features such as disaggregation, privatisation and a private sector focus were at the forefront (see cases 2 and 3). In turn, NPM was followed in the 2000s, although not displaced, by an emergent governance model, which initially emphasised reintegration (Halligan, 2006). Fiscal austerity in the 2010s produced a return to efficiency issues and rationalisation of the public service that had already embarked on a modernisation programme (case 4 is about the latter).

1. MANAGEMENT REFORM IN THE 1980S

The management improvement programme was a joint initiative of two central agencies, Finance and Public Service Board (PSB), which was designed to produce more efficient and effective strategic planning, policy formulation and programme management, and greater emphasis on resource use. A third central agency, and the most powerful, the DPMC, supported this agenda. The Financial Management Improvement Programme (FMIP) was essentially an umbrella concept for the standard managerial line up: corporate and programme management, corporate planning, programme budgeting and performance evaluation. Departments and agencies were to devise new organisational structures, set programme objectives, develop corporate plans in line with government policies, set priorities for effective resource allocation, shift from focussing on inputs to outputs and develop performance indicators (Public Service Board/Department of Finance [PSB/DoF], 1986, p. 3, 11).

The implementation of FMIP occurred through three broad spheres of activity (DoF, 1988, pp. 5–27): changing the budgetary regulatory environment by establishing a flexible environment for managers, improving budgetary processes through programme budgeting and forward estimates, and rewarding good performance and penalising poor performance (although it was unclear how that was pursued). Secondly, there was improving management systems. The third dimension was improvement of standards and practice. Finance conceived FMIP in terms of two complementary strands: 'Letting managers manage' by facilitating devolution of management control; and 'requiring managers to manage', for the purposes of effectiveness and accountability (DoF, 1987; Keating, 1989).

Most departments had generally adopted some form of corporate structure and corporate planning by the end of the 1980s, and programme management was ubiquitous, although it did not necessarily correspond to organisational structure. These attempts were not without difficulties. Nevertheless, the official consensus was that FMIP had made a significant impact because it was relatively comprehensive, promoted an overall framework based on letting and making managers manage, freeing up unnecessary constraints (e.g., procedures) and emphasising performance reporting (Shand, 1990, p. 4).

The centrality of Finance in the reform programme was important for its content, particularly in the second half of the 1980s. The department pursued financial management improvement objectives assiduously under the leadership of Keating (1989, 1994), monitoring and exhorting change from departments. This was both strength and limitation. By maintaining its resource management focus, the department made substantial progress in changing the Commonwealth public service by refining the budgetary and resource allocation processes, and championing the need to place greater emphasis on managerial skills. On the other hand, the narrowness of this perspective was a constraint on the realisation of goals. The larger objectives that required resource constraints had centralising effects, while micro issues of management reform were meant to be decentralising. Could one organisation be expected to handle both functions effectively? (Halligan & Power, 1992, p. 112).

Finance pronounced evaluation to be the 'crucial element' in managing for results, performing the essential function of linking policy development and programme implementation, and completing the loop in the management cycle. All programmes had to be reviewed every five years and evaluation plans produced annually for central scrutiny by Finance. According to two key reform leaders, evaluation was 'the most difficult element of a "managing for results" approach', the problems reflecting 'its multiple, but linked objectives – improving programme performance, assisting government decision-making and as a quid pro quo for the devolution of authority to managers, thus contributing to accountability' (Keating & Holmes, 1990, p. 174). The amount of evaluation activity increased but varied among portfolios, and was costly. While it was now incorporated into the management culture, most members of the senior executive service were not making much use of evaluation information in their work tending: 'to focus on satisfying the requirement for evaluation … rather than learning to use evaluation to improve programme outcomes' (Task Force on Management Improvement [TFMI], 1993, pp. 363, 378–379). Mandatory evaluations were subsequently terminated in the 1990s.

Towards the end of the 1980s the main impact of FMIP had passed. However, Finance continued to sponsor managerialism and argued that the initial period of FMIP represented only the first stage of a longer programme (DoF, 1988, p. 83).

In examining developments, two leadership processes were important: the move towards a management framework that would break with the past and offer something workable for the future, and the search for machinery and principles that would serve the framework. These processes were not as clear to the reform leaders as they became with hindsight, neither did a framework emerge as full-blown in a single flourish but over several years. After a decade of intensive change, public service leaders undertook possibly the first extensive evaluation of the new management reforms in one country. The 10-year evaluation of reform by TFMI (1993) supported the overall direction of the reforms. The nature of the reforms was described as 'a combination of broad policy objectives, long-term strategies and specific one-off or ongoing changes acted upon in all parts of the APS' (TFMI, 1996, p. 6). Nevertheless, broad directions could be discerned and the early objectives were explicit and achieved substantially. A one-time advocate and leader of managerialism acknowledged problems with the approach:

> Despite devolution of responsibilities from central agencies, there has not in all cases been adequate devolution of responsibilities within agencies.... Performance measurement remains inadequate, as does the overall quality of programme evaluation ... criticism has been made that the management system has been freed up without really making managers more accountable. (Shand, 1990)

Reform leaders argued that the reform programme sought balance between the centre and the parts, policy and implementation, and strategic policy and supporting management systems (Holmes & Shand, 1995, p. 569), and that the management framework had a structure that was 'consistent, logical and integrated' (Sedgwick, 1994, p. 341). The development of management framework could also be judged as a product of leaders balancing principle and pragmatism, and combining a strategic focus with experimentation (Halligan, 1996).

A distinctive leadership instrument, the senior management committee, was established under the aegis of the DPMC as a means of furthering management reform by conducting specialised inquiries. It resided either in or under the regular meetings of departmental secretaries, which is now known as the Secretaries Board. The committee has taken several forms since it was first established in 1987 as the Management Advisory Board (MAB) to advise the government on significant management issues and act as a forum for consideration of major management activities (in 1999, it was replaced by the Management Advisory Committee (MAC)). An operational arm comprising senior public servants and the Management Improvement Advisory Committee (MIAC), subsequently aided it.

The MAB/MIAC produced numerous reports between 1991 and 1998 had a collective basis consisting of departmental secretaries and members of the senior executive service (Campbell & Halligan, 1992; Keating, 1994; MAB/MIAC, 1997). MAB reports ranged from programme evaluation to management of change (Halligan & Power, 1992, p. 99–100). The successor MAC (2001) addressed inter alia performance management and organisational renewal (MAC, 2003). Implementation was through central agencies and line departments. The significance of the reports varied between the highly influential Connecting Government report (MAC, 2004) to the marginal impact of the 2007 red tape report (the subject of which had to be confronted again in the mid-2010s).

2. PERFORMANCE MANAGEMENT REFORM IN THE 2000S

In the first phase of reform, as outlined in the previous section, the elements of performance management were developed within a centralised approach lead by a central agency, Finance. The second performance framework (from 1997) was based on an outcomes/outputs framework, devolution to agencies, principles instead of formal requirements, and an emphasis on performance information.

The framework introduced in 1999 changed financial management and reporting through budgeting on a full accrual basis; implementation of outputs and outcomes reporting; and extended agency devolution for inter alia budget estimates and financial management. Departments were expected to identify explicit outcomes, outputs and performance measures, and their heads were assigned responsibility and accountability for performance. Reporting occurred through budget plans (portfolio budget statements) and financial year results (annual reports). In linking a planning and reporting cycle to a yearly budget cycle, performance management was seen as tangible.

The limitations of the new performance framework were soon apparent. The reform environment changed in the 2000s, in large part as a reaction to the deficiencies of NPM (e.g., fragmentation and weaker central agencies resulting from devolved responsibilities to line departments), producing a disjunction between the performance management system and the new reintegrating agendas. The process was one of desultory tinkering with the system despite a sustained and trenchant critique over a decade until a major review by Finance in 2010–2012. The most significant adjustment was the reincorporation of departmental programmes because ministers argued that their omission under the outcomes/outputs framework meant that they lacked the information required for making decisions (Halligan, 2007b).

A ministerial review exclaimed that: 'The outcomes and outputs framework was intended to shift the focus of financial reporting from inputs ... to outputs and outcomes i.e. actual results. While this is worthy in theory, it has not worked. Basic information on inputs was lost in the changeover, and reporting of outcomes is seriously inadequate' (Tanner, 2008, p. 4). A multi-year review was conducted by Finance (Department of Finance and Deregulation [DoFD], 2012a, 2012b). The authoritative diagnosis includes insufficient integration of the components of the resource management cycle, lack of coherence in performance management, the role of outcomes in appropriations and weaknesses in performance monitoring and evaluation (DoFD, 2012a). Moreover, capability reviews of departments at this time (see later discussion) indicated that insufficient attention was being given to outcomes.

Why was the performance framework not implemented properly by departments? The first reason was the issue of engaging with performance information. The non-use of performance information has attracted a variety of interpretations internationally for the common findings that politicians' use of performance information was often poor, and that managers' use was variable (van Dooren, Bouckaert, & Halligan, 2015, pp. 144–145). In the Australian case, the quality of financial information is regarded as having improved because of the outcomes/output framework and explicitly identifying performance indicators (DoFA, 2006). However, performance measurement of outcomes provided difficulties in spite of its centrality to the resource management framework. Output performance measures were generally more appropriate and measurement more reliable. Performance reporting in departmental annual reports needed improved information with respect to specification of the performance framework and the quality of measures, and the reporting of results. The auditor-general reported that performance information was being used by decision makers for policy development and allocating resources but the actual 'influence of outcomes and outputs information on decision making was mixed' (McPhee, 2005, pp. 3–4). A series of studies raised serious questions about the efficacy of aspects of the existing performance management system and the need for significant renewal (e.g., Australian National Audit Office [ANAO], 2011, 2013; Hawke, 2012; Hawke & Wanna, 2010).

Leaving aside the challenges of implementing performance measurement, there were two interrelated reasons for the failure of the second framework. The first was central agency leadership and the standing of Finance; and the second was the departments' use of the framework.

For the first framework the elements of performance management were developed within a centralised and top-down approach driven by Finance. The second framework was part of broader devolution from central to line agencies. As a consequence, Finance was downgraded in status without the capacity or expertise to exercise influence over the operation of the system. Finance had not necessarily retained the role of policy adviser on budgetary and performance matters (Mackay, 2011). The central agency failed to exercise appropriate leadership in the implementation phase of the second framework. In addition, ministers were not particularly concerned about the quality of outcomes as expressions of their objectives. New initiatives in the 2000s somewhat enhanced Finance's roles and its capacity to oversee financial management and information, and to provide advice to government.

The second area was the response of department leaders and organisational incentives. The performance framework did not require departments to integrate internal planning process where they had ownership, with the performance process, which was an external imposition. Consequently, the two processes often ran in parallel in departments. Priority was given to external reporting, while performance information was not necessarily made use of internal purposes. The incentives did not exist for departmental leaders to apply the framework for their own purposes, and Finance's power to require compliance was constrained under a system of devolved departmental responsibilities.

There is now a third performance management framework because of the limitations of the second framework. Outcomes remained as a focus with augmented features to several dimensions of the framework to connect more effectively intentions and reporting and integrate planning and performance management. The new framework under the Public Governance, Performance and Accountability Act 2013 was implemented in the mid-2010s by Finance. The public service supported the consultation on the change process but fealty to the reworked system has yet to be demonstrated.

3. REFORMING THE COORDINATION OF SERVICE DELIVERY

The third case addresses the coordination of welfare administration and how different leaders were mobilised and transformational leadership was central. Unlike the other cases, this does not entail comprehensive and systemic reform of the public sector. However, it was highly significant as the organisation involved was responsible for 30–40 per cent of expenditure, and therefore had great political salience.

The reform of service delivery unfolded over two decades, and covered questions about the advantages of departmental versus agency delivery, how to handle relationships between departments and agencies and levels of autonomy and integration. All three are susceptible to changing fashions and agenda. Changing leadership agendas and the roles of political and public service leaders were important.

The original context was shaped by political leaders with a neo-liberal agenda that were seeking to rationalise the provision of services based on welfare transfers, and were casting around for options to reduce costs through the consolidation of national delivery networks and whether the provider should be public or private organisations. Two departmental secretaries engaged in a pre-emptive action to meet the new government's expectations for staff savings in the public service by proposing the concept of an agency that would merge two departments' networks for social security and employment, which then became its two major clients. The concept became a one-stop shop delivery agency designed to provide services to purchasing departments but with the potential to serve others (Halligan, 2008).

Centrelink was formally established in 1997. The agency acquired the delivery of government services to recipients of social welfare benefits and services from the Department of Social Security. The Department of Social Security's other responsibilities were transferred to a new Department of Family and Community Services (FaCS). By 2005–2006, Centrelink accounted for $63.5 billion, or about 31 per cent of total commonwealth expenditure, and employed approaching 27,000 staff spread across over 1,000 service delivery points across Australia.

The agency was located within the FaCS portfolio and therefore within the core public service, but was a separate entity from the FaCS department with its own legislation, accounting and reporting requirements. In contrast to the standard departmental model, Centrelink was responsible to the Minister for Family and Community Services through an appointed board of directors, which gave strategic direction and set the overall objectives and business rules. The client departments were the purchasers of services detailed in negotiated agreements with the agency. Each client – usually a policy department – negotiated a purchase price for specified services that Centrelink agreed to undertake.

In its formative years, Centrelink was led by the chief executive, Sue Vardon (1998, 2002), who established a delivery model of international significance (Halligan, 2008). There were powerful incentives to achieve successful integration of delivery networks to produce significant savings for the government. The alternative, floated by politicians in the initial years of the organisation, was the use of other networks (e.g., those of the post office or the private sector). In managing transformation in the new organisation, Vardon made use of Kotter's (1996) well-known principles for leading change, in particular the 'guiding coalition'. This large top team of executives had to address a number of initiatives concurrently, such as formulating strategy, managing performance and stakeholder expectation and renewing talent pools (Halligan, 2008, p. 73).

In terms of the positioning and legitimising of the agency, the core agenda was evolving the service delivery system; consolidating, protecting and enhancing the concept of the one-stop shop; and expanding business through agreements with new clients (Halligan, 2007a). The advocacy of Centrelink's position was important for defining roles and registering its place. Several themes were consistently promoted: the holistic conception of the individual and how the service delivery agency should respond; intra-agency integration of responsibilities and the one-stop shop concept; dealing with numerous clients simultaneously; competing for work; pushing relevant policy agendas as a delivery agency; and provision of choice through channel management. Much depended on Centrelink's capacity to define long-term objectives and to be able to achieve them (Halligan, 2008).

The broader reform agenda of integrated governance in the 2000s included resurrecting a more comprehensive ministerial department through absorbing agencies or extending controls as a result of a review into the corporate governance of statutory authorities and office holders. The review included two delivery agencies, one being Centrelink (Uhrig, 2003). The impact of this agenda on Centrelink was comprehensive: the relationship to ministerial direction, stronger ministerial departments in relation to policy leadership and control over devolved public bodies enhanced central agency's capacity for monitoring service delivery and implementation and clarification of corporate governance models. Two agendas were operating: one addressed agency governance and ministerial accountability, and the other tempering devolution in the public service.

Centrelink made effective use of internal capacity – a product of scale of operation, the allocation of resources and strategic decisions about agenda setting – to produce and advance policy and service delivery ideas and innovations in public management. As a large agency with the capacity to take policy initiatives, Centrelink was a challenge to policy-focussed departments, which had experienced a contraction of their responsibilities, and inter-departmental tensions arose where the agency appeared to be dictating reform agendas to ministerial departments (Halligan, 2007a, 2008).

Centrelink was subsumed under a new parent department in 2004, and its board was disbanded. The Department of Human Services (DHS) was created as a small agency with responsibility for strategically directing, coordinating and brokering improvements to service delivery for six agencies operating under direct ministerial control and one advisory board. The rationale was to improve the delivery of services within a whole-of-government approach that involved better collaboration and performance, and to strengthen the vertical (ministerial and departmental control) and horizontal dimensions (delivery network across agencies). Centrelink was subsequently integrated within the DHS, although retaining its identity through the brand and business line.

The creation of DHS and the demise of Centrelink's independence were mainly a matter of corporate governance (Edwards et al., 2012) focussed on strengthening the vertical dimension of ministerial and departmental control. The DHS subsequently became a portfolio department in its own right. The cycle moved from integrated department to multipurpose delivery agency to an integrated delivery department, suggesting that strong path dependency provided the underlying explanation for the choice of organisational form. The circular process was completed when Centrelink was absorbed within the DHS, demonstrating the Commonwealth's preference for leadership by the ministerial department (Halligan, 2015b).

4. REFORM AGENDA IN THE 2010S

The fourth case involved leadership by two central agencies. The head of DPMC, Terry Moran, drove the initial reform exercise.[1] The implementation of much of the agenda fell to the APSC led by Steve Sedgwick. Unlike the previous phases of reform, the 2010s have been characterised by greater environmental instability as governments contended with high fiscal stress. The Australian reform process on government administration was unusual in that it occurred amidst the global financial crisis but was not essentially a product of it (for details of the process see the analysis by Lindquist, 2010). The combination of crisis and falling commodity prices converted a budget surplus into a deficit, which impacted the implementation of reform.

Australia's *Ahead of the Game: Blueprint for the Reform of Australian Government Administration* (Advisory Group on the Reform of Australian Government Administration [AGRAGA], 2010) posed as a case of comprehensive reform even though many of the constituent elements were not inherently significant. In terms of the reform era, it was unusual in that an extensive document was produced to channel reform.

Why did Australia have an explicit and full-fledged reform process? One interpretation is that the party out of power for 11 years wished to launch a reform agenda in order to differentiate itself from the previous regime (Halligan, 2010). Of relevance were the expectations of an activist government, and a prime minister with a highly ambitious policy and reform agenda. The expansive programme was already making demands on the public service that exceeded capacity and exposed implementation weaknesses. According to the Prime Minister, 'the next stage of renewal of the APS requires more than just piecemeal change. We need a more sweeping reform driven by a long-range blueprint for a world class, 21st century public service' (Halligan, 2010; Rudd, 2009, p. 12).

Two features defined much of the character of the report: the coherence and focus of the narrative, and the mode of implementation. The Australian report picked up several matters already the subject of discussion, debate and reports. The specific diagnosis suggested lack of capacity and accountability, a series of deficits (e.g., a shortfall in capability), a lack of high performance and creeping bureaucratisation and compliance issues (termed 'red tape') (AGRAGA, 2010; Rudd, 2009). The 28 recommendations were organised under four themes: citizen needs, leadership and strategic direction, capability, and efficiency at a high standard. The catalogue of items compiled in the report included efficiency dividends, revising APS values, reducing red tape, stewardship, weaknesses in policy-making and the consequences of different conditions of employment in agencies. Reform areas included a strengthened APSC for driving change and expectations for agencies (e.g., agility and capability). Recommendations addressed roles and responsibilities of secretaries, strengthening leadership and assessing the senior executive service. They also reflected the emerging importance of collaborative relations internally and with other governments and non-governmental actors (AGRAGA, 2010).

A number of ideas were new to APS but based on practice elsewhere. The UK capability reviews were adopted for departments, but the concept was adapted to Australian needs. The lack of a distinctive and unifying core issue or theme added to the mixed acceptance of the reform agenda overall within and beyond the public service. Without an 'urgent, politically "hot" reform trigger, the Moran group clearly found it difficult to weave a coherent narrative that holds the disparate activity clusters together' ('t Hart, 2010).

There were clear comparisons to be made with the 1980s when the shift from administration to management was underway (Halligan & Power, 1992). A different model emerged during each of three decades reflecting the tone and content of the then reform agenda: managerialism in the 1980s, new public management in the 1990s and integrated governance in the 2000s. International trends suggest that collaborative governance provided a benchmark, if hazy, for official aspirations for public governance in the 2010s, but to what extent could it be addressed in a formal agenda? Specific areas identified in the Blueprint – citizen engagement, joined-up government, shared outcomes and more generally cultural change – in combination had the potential to redefine much of public governance, but a great deal remained to be spelt out and institutionalised (Edwards et al., 2012).

The ultimate aim of the Blueprint for reform was cultural change presented as a culmination and enveloping product of an ongoing reform process (Moran, 2010). The question of sustaining cultural change, long an Achilles heel of reform, depended on whether the rigidities of an existing system can be breached or bridged by tangible requirements that affect behaviour. However, the recommendations were mostly 'single-loop learning: technical, managerial solutions to soft spots in the machinery of government. What the review does not do much is to lay down truly "double-loop" learning ambitions; that is, fundamentally re-examining and redesigning some of the key underlying assumptions, values and design principles' ('t Hart, 2010).

The Blueprint provided the agenda for an extended reform process managed by the public service leadership. This rolling agenda had a large range of elements that encompassed many players (in particular, two leadership groups, a new secretaries board and APS 200, a senior leadership forum for supporting the secretaries). Implementation was divided between the three key central agencies: the DPMC, Finance and Deregulation and the Public Service Commission with the last being assigned a more prominent role because of the nature of the recommendations.

Prior to the 2010 elections, several processes were under way to implement the *Ahead of the Game* recommendations (AGRAGA, 2010). The most significant was the augmentation of APSC's powers by government endorsement of the report. It was made the lead agency for around half the recommendations with $39 million being allocated under the 2010 budget.

The impact of the fiscal crisis on the Australian public sector had consequences for public management with the reform agenda being subjected to significant cuts. With the displacement of Prime Minister Rudd by his own party in 2010, the implementation of public service reform was disrupted. The funding was heavily cut by the new Prime Minister Gillard when projecting fiscal rectitude during the election campaign, and the funding was reduced for a succession of budgets (Sedgwick, 2011). The reform agenda was not a priority for the prime minister as indicated by the inattention to it in her 2011 Garran Oration to the Institute for Public Administration (Gillard, 2011).

As the chief adviser to the prime minister (and the leader of the public service) reaffirmed, the role of the DPMC has been shaped by the prime ministerial styles and preferences (Watt, 2012, p. 2). Without explicit support from political leadership, and given some ambivalence towards the overall reform exercise, the implementation of *Ahead of the Game* was constrained.

Nevertheless, agendas derived from *Ahead of the Game* were pursued, and claims were subsequently made that the recommendations were either implemented or in progress (Joint Committee of Public Accounts and Audit [JCPAA], 2012). Of significance were those associated with a reconstituted APSC, which became the lead agency for reform. The commission's new approach was to engage collaboratively with departments in pursuit of common outcomes. The departments funded the commission to provide a range of services covering leadership and skills, talent management, workplace planning and standards and a range of staffing matters affecting public service capacity. The Strategic Centre for Leadership, Learning and Development was established in 2010 within the APSC to give effect to reform recommendations (Sedgwick, 2011). The Centre developed a leadership development strategy using a human capital strategic approach, which involved identifying capability gaps through analysis of drivers in the external environment and the business needs of the public service. The strategy had the imprimatur of the secretaries' board, the steering and coordinating unit of the APS. The Centre was perceived to have strengthened the Commission's contribution.

Capability reviews were used by the APSC to provide systematic assessments of departments' capabilities. The technique was modelled on reviews undertaken in the United Kingdom. In each case an independent review panel of former senior public servants and consultants reported on a department or agency with a rating system that combined indicators, traffic light assessments and back-up judgements.[2] There were 17 Australian reports on departments published by early 2015. These reports were relevant in three respects: they provided an indication of departments' willingness to respond to the reform agenda by the time of their review; leadership was one of the three core components of the evaluation template (APSC, 2013) and as a medium-term reform tool for exacting change. The capability review reports indicated that many departments had not voluntarily acted on key recommendations to enhance collaboration and to become more focussed strategically.

The overall coordination and review of the results of reform was the responsibility of the DPMC with a departmental network being important for both systemic agendas and agency-specific reforms. The secretaries' board provided a formal central mechanism, chaired by the head of the DPMC, although the efficacy of the board in comparison with the previous MAB was questioned (Podger, 2013, p. 79).

One further result of note was the specification of the roles of departmental leaders. The ambiguous status of the role of departmental secretaries was such that it required legislation to clarify their formal responsibilities (Halligan, 2013). Politicians' lack of strategic focus and 'short-termism' indicated that an alternative was needed to rely heavily on political direction. The 2013 amendments to the Public Service Act distinguish four roles of secretaries – policy advice and manager – and two centred on stewardship, one being within their department, the other public service-wide, which is to be 'discharged in partnership with other secretaries and the APS Commissioner' (AGRAGA, 2010, p. 47). The stewardship role is designed for the public service to have 'the capacity to serve successive governments … regardless of the style of any one Minister or government', and covers 'financial sustainability' and efficient resource management as well as 'less tangible factors such as maintaining the trust placed in the APS and building … integrity in policy advice' (AGRAGA, 2010, p. 5).

LESSONS FROM LEADERSHIP AND REFORM

What are the lessons from leadership in reform from the Australian experience? Three factors were particularly important for the initiation and implementation of reform: the support and drive of public service leaders in both central agencies and departments; the role of political leaders in endorsing and supporting reform; and a relatively stable environment that allowed for implementation to proceed.

Public management reform gives scope for the public service leaders to take the lead (provided of course that the relevant minister has signed off on major agenda). The role of leaders in central agencies in initiating and leading major reform was pivotal. Having moved from top-down control to a more devolved model, central agencies had to be more creative with the provision of inducements. In other words, there were limits to what could be imposed from the centre,[3] which allowed departments considerable discretion in how they interpreted reform agendas, but also facilitated inattention.

There was resistance to significant change at times. This could be played out at the macro level as when senior public servants, who were reluctant to accept the new management culture in the 1980s, were given the opportunity to demonstrate fealty when their positions were abolished with departmental mergers, and they had to apply for them. Micro level dynamics were also important as when Vardon sought to make the 'guiding coalition', mentioned earlier, a large and inclusive body to buy off staff opposed to major change in Centrelink. Public service opposition could also lead to the fashioning of compromises: mandarins' resistance to the Labor government's proposal to make political appointments to the upper ranks of the public service led to the creation of contract consultants in ministers' offices; the coalition government elected in 1996 was considering the radical options for the handling of benefits mentioned earlier until two departmental secretaries conceived a specialised service delivery agency that became Centrelink (Halligan, 2008).

The continuity of office holding was a major factor in allowing reform to advance and be sustained during the first two decades. The collective basis to such reform activity is evident from the work of the senior committees on dimensions of reform, in particular the role of the secretaries' board and its predecessors. The Public Service Commissioner's engagement of departments in funding key dimensions of the 2010 reform agenda signalled a collaborative approach.

A relatively stable environment is necessary to allow implementation to proceed in the medium term. The disruptions come either from the environment (the most notable recent case being the global financial crisis) or from political instability and succession. In the reform era, there have been two periods of steady reform due to parties retaining office for extended periods.

Sustained implementation also requires the support and drive of public service leaders, and much depends on the incentive systems in place to ensure responsiveness at the department level. The implementation of comprehensive reform is contingent on conditions being in place. The public service leadership must be both equipped to handle a large reform agenda and believe in it as a whole. Clear imperatives for reform must exist, either in the environment or because of internal dysfunctions, and be reflected in a thematic core of issues that can be readily communicated and provide focus. The combination of these factors makes the difference between success and failure.

The third factor was the support of the political executive with major reform. Conventional wisdom once regarded the lack of political support and the failure of politicians to sustain their commitment as key factors in reform failure (March & Olsen, 1989). Australian experience indicated that major change requires the intervention of politicians even if they do not actively manage the process (Halligan & Power, 1992). The political executive can be the key factor in the success of major reform, at least at certain strategic points in the reform process, because fundamental change means new approaches and leadership, and the existing senior public service may not support change of this order if it undermines their positions and values. Contrariwise, where governments are divided and reliant on special interests for support, or lack of tenure in office, there are greater obstacles to achieving change. More significant management reform has been achieved by governments serving multiple terms.

The non-implementation of Australian proposals in the 1970s was attributed to the neglect of political factors. The enhancement of political executive's power since then has resulted in new political mechanisms for influencing and directing the public service. Political leaders have sought greater responsiveness to government policies and priorities, which allowed ministers greater influence and changed the roles of the public service leadership (Campbell & Halligan, 1992; Halligan & Power, 1992). However, there has been a downside to the heightened role of politicians. The last decade in Australia has been characterised by unstable government and turnover of political leaders. Political interventions are more common and sustained reform more challenging.

CHANGING APPROACHES TO PUBLIC SERVICE LEADERSHIP AND REFORM

The more than three decades of reform have seen the formal recognition and evolution of new concepts of leadership (Halligan, 2015a). There is acceptance of a more collaborative, stakeholder-oriented and politically responsive public service leader. The opportunities for public service leadership have, however, become more constrained where there are hyper-active political executives who dictate policy and implementation. This makes for tensions between responsiveness to ministerial preferences and stewardship of public policy that are not of high political priority. The exigencies of new political governance (Aucoin, 2012) promote short termism, which had an effect on implementing reform over time. Major reform has however become more difficult beyond the 'hard' efficiency-centred programmes that cut across other agendas. The major challenges for leadership are therefore two-fold: finding a balance between the roles of political and professional leaders; and discerning new ways of responding to complex public policy issues in increasingly volatile environments.

NOTES

1. Terry Moran spent his early career in a Commonwealth central agency, and later ran the Victorian state government's Premier's Department before becoming secretary of the DPMC. He had a strong mandate, and an understanding of how to manage a large and complex public sector, the systemic requirements and the interplay between components. Note that Finance does not feature here because it was running a relatively self-contained agenda on performance and accountability.

2. Main sources are http://www.apsc.gov.au/priorities/capability-reviews and APSC (2013).

3. The authority of Finance remains constrained. The Finance secretary observed that individual departments retain responsibility for developing their performance indicators, and Finance will try 'to assist and monitor – and cajole – but we ... do not have the big whip' (JCPAA, 2014, p. 6).

REFERENCES

Advisory Group on the Reform of Australian Government Administration. (2010). *Ahead of the game: Blueprint for the reform of Australian government administration.* Canberra: Commonwealth of Australia.

Althaus, C., & Wanna, J. (2008). The institutionalisation of leadership in the Australian Public Service. In P. 't Hart & J. Uhr (Eds.), *Public leadership: Perspectives and practices,* (pp. 117–132). Canberra: ANU Press.

Australian National Audit Office. (2011). *Development and implementation of key performance indicators to support the outcomes and programs framework.* Audit Report no. 5. Commonwealth of Australia, Canberra.

Australian National Audit Office. (2013). *The Australian government performance measurement and reporting framework, pilot project to audit key performance indicators.* Report no. 28, 2012-13. ANAO, Canberra.

Australian Public Service Board/Department of Finance. (1986). *Financial Management Improvement Program: FMIP Report.* Canberra: AGPS.

Aucoin, P. (2012). New political governance in Westminster systems: Impartial public administration and management performance at risk. *Governance, 25*(2), 177–199.

Australian Public Service Commission. (2013). *State of the service report 2012-13.* Commonwealth of Australia, Canberra.

Baker, J. (1989). From management to leadership: A comparative perspective on leadership in the Australian Public Service. *Australian Journal of Public Administration, 48*(3), 249–263.

Boin, A., & Christensen, T. (2008). The development of public institutions: Reconsidering the role of leadership. *Administration & Society, 40*(3), 271–297.

Brookes, S., & Grint, K. (Eds.). (2010). *The new public leadership challenge.* Basingstoke: Palgrave Macmillan.

Campbell, C., & Halligan, J. (1992). *Political leadership in an age of constraint: The Australian experience.* Pittsburgh, PA: Allen and Unwin, Sydney/University of Pittsburgh Press.

Department of Finance. (1987). *FMIP and program budgeting: A study of implementation in selected agencies.* Canberra: Australian Government Publishing Service.

Department of Finance. (1988). *1988 FMIP report.* Australian Government Publishing Service, Canberra.

Department of Finance and Administration. (2006). *Australia's experience in utilising performance information in budget and management processes.* Report for the 3rd annual meeting of the OECD senior budget officials network on performance and results. DoFA, Canberra.

Department of Finance and Deregulation. (2012a, March). *Is less more? Towards better Commonwealth performance.* Discussion paper on Commonwealth Financial Accountability, Australian Government, Canberra.

Department of Finance and Deregulation (2012b, November). *Sharpening the focus: A framework for improving commonwealth performance*. Discussion paper on Commonwealth Financial Accountability, Australian Government, Canberra.

Edwards, M., Halligan, J., Horrigan, B., & Nicoll, G. (2012). *Public sector governance in Australia*. Canberra: ANU Press.

Gillard, J. (Prime Minister), (2011). Garran Oration, Institute of Public Administration Annual Conference, Hobart, 26 August.

Halligan, J. (1992). A comparative lesson: The senior executive service in Australia. In P. W. Ingraham & D. H. Rosenbloom (Eds.), *Promise and paradox of civil service reform*, (pp. 283–302). Pittsburgh, PA: University of Pittsburgh Press.

Halligan, J. (1996). Learning from experience in Australian reform: Balancing principle and pragmatism. In J. P. Olsen & B. G. Peters (Eds.), *Lessons from experience: Experiential learning in administrative reforms in eight democracies*, (pp. 71–112). Oslo: Scandinavian University Press.

Halligan, J. (2006). The reassertion of the centre in a first generation NPM system. In T. Christensen & P. Lægreid (Eds.), *Autonomy and regulation: Coping with agencies in the modern state*, (pp. 162–180). Cheltenham: Edward Elgar.

Halligan, J. (2007a). Advocacy and innovation in interagency management: The case of Centrelink. *Governance, 20*(3), 445–467.

Halligan, J. (2007b). Performance management and budgeting in Australia and New Zealand. In P. de Lancer Julnes, F. Berry, M. Aristigueta, & K. Yang (Eds.), *International handbook of practice-based performance management*, (pp. 341–360). Thousand Oaks, CA: Sage.

Halligan, J. (2008). *The Centrelink experiment: An innovation in service delivery*. Canberra: ANU Press.

Halligan, J. (2010). Australian public service: New agendas and reform. In C. Aulich & M. Evans (Eds.), *The Rudd government* (pp. 35–54). Canberra: ANU E-Press.

Halligan, J. (2012). Leadership and the senior service from a comparative perspective. In B. G. Peters & J. Pierre (Eds.), *Handbook of public administration*, (pp. 115–129). London.

Halligan, J. (2013). The evolution of public service bargains of Australian senior public servants. *International Review of Administrative Sciences, 79*(1), 111–129.

Halligan, J. (2015a). Australia. In A. Hondeghem & M. Van Wart (Eds.), *Leadership and culture: Comparative models of top civil servant training*, (pp. 25–40). Basingstoke: Palgrave Macmillan.

Halligan, J. (2015b). Coordination of welfare through a large integrated organisation: The Australian department of human services. *Public Management Review, 17*(7), 1002–1020.

Halligan, J. (2015c). Anglophone systems: Diffusion and policy transfer within an administrative tradition. In F. M. van der Meer & J. C. N. Raadschelders (Eds.), *Comparative civil service systems in the 21st century* (2nd ed., pp. 57–76). Basingstoke: Palgrave.

Halligan, J., & Power, J. (1992). *Political management in the 1990s*. Melbourne: Oxford University Press.

Hawke, L. (2012). Public sector governance in Australia – Success of performance? *International Journal of Productivity and Performance Management, 61*(3), 310–328.

Hawke, L., & Wanna, J. (2010). Australia after budgetary reform: A lapsed pioneer and decorative architect? In J. Wanna, L. Jensen & J. de Vries (Eds.), *The reality of budgetary reform in OECD countries: Trajectories and consequences* (pp. 65–90). Cheltenham: Edward Elgar.

Holmes, M., & Shand, D. (1995). Management reform: Some practitioner perspectives on the past ten years. *Governance, 8*(4), 551–578.

Joint Committee of Public Accounts and Audit. (2012). *Report 432: APS – Fit for service.*
    Parliamentary Paper 205/2012. House of Representatives, Parliament of Australia, Canberra.
Keating, M. (1989). Quo vadis? Challenges of public administration. *Australian Journal of Public
    Administration, 48*(2), 123–131.
Keating, M. (1994). A MAB/MIAC perspective. In *Public service reform* (Vol. 1). Report from
    the Senate Standing Committee on Finance and Public Administration, Department of
    the Senate, Canberra.
Keating, M., & Holmes, M. (1990). Australia's budgetary and financial management reforms.
    Governance, 3(2), 168–185.
Lindquist, E. (2010). From rhetoric to blueprint: The Moran review as a concerted, compre-
    hensive and emergent strategy for public service reform. *Australian Journal of Public
    Administration, 69*(2), 115–151.
Management Advisory Board/Management Improvement Advisory Committee. (1997). *Beyond
    bean counting: Effective financial management in the APS – 1998 and beyond.* Report of
    the Public Services and Merit Protection Commission, Canberra.
Management Advisory Committee. (2001). *Performance management in the Australian public
    service: A strategic framework.* Canberra: Commonwealth of Australia.
Management Advisory Committee. (2003). *Organisational renewal.* Canberra: Commonwealth
    of Australia.
Management Advisory Committee. (2004). *Connecting government: Whole of government
    responses to Australia's priority challenges.* Canberra: Commonwealth of Australia.
March, J. G., & Olsen, J. P. (1989). *Rediscovering institutions: The organizational basis of politics.*
    New York, NY: Free Press.
McPhee, I. (2005, May 20). *Outcomes and outputs: Are we managing better as a result?* CPA
    National Public Sector Convention, Melbourne.
Moran, T. (2010). Presentation to APS Staff by Terry Moran, Secretary of Department of the
    Prime Minister and Cabinet, Canberra, 21 May.
National Commission of Audit. (1996). Report to the Commonwealth. Department of Finance,
    Canberra.
National Commission of Audit. (2014). Towards responsible government: The report of the
    National Commission of Audit Phase One. Commonwealth of Australia, Canberra.
Organisation for Economic Co-operation and Development (OECD). (1995). *Governance in
    Transition: public management reforms in OECD Countries,* Paris: OECD.
Pal, L. A. (2012). *Frontiers of Government: The OECD and Global Public Management Reform,*
    Palgrave Macmillan, Basingstoke.
Kotter, J. P. (1996). *Leading Change,* Harvard Business School Press, Boston: Mass.
Podger, A. (2013). Mostly welcome, but are the politicians fully aware of what they have done?
    The Public Service Amendment Act 2013. *Australian Journal of Public Administration,
    72*(2), 77–81.
Raffel, J. A., Leisink, P., & Middlebrooks, A. E. (Eds.). (2009). *Public sector leadership:
    International challenges and perspectives.* Cheltenham: Edward Elgar.
Rhodes, R., & 't Hart, P. (2014). *Oxford handbook of political leadership.* Oxford: Oxford
    University Press.
Royal Commission on Australian Government Administration. (1976). Report. Australian
    Government Publishing Service, Canberra.
Rudd, K. (2009). John Paterson oration, Australia. *New Zealand School of Government annual
    conference,* Canberra, 3 September.

Sedgwick, S. (1994). Evaluation of management reforms in the Australian public service. *Australian Journal of Public Administration, 53*(3), 341–347.

Sedgwick, S. (2011). Commissioner's overview. *Australian Public Service Commissioner*. State of the Service Report 2010-11. Commonwealth of Australia, Canberra.

Shand, D. (1990). Management reform – A strategic approach: Lessons of the previous decades. *Background paper for conference on public service performance*, Canberra, 27–30 August.

Talbot, C. (2010). Central government reform and leadership. In S. Brookes & K. Grint (Eds.), *The new public leadership challenge* (pp. 19–32). Basingstoke: Palgrave Macmillan.

Tanner, L. (Minister for Finance and Deregulation). (2008, December). *Operation sunlight: Enhancing budget transparency*. Australian Government, Canberra.

Task Force on Management Improvement. (1993). *The Australian public service reformed: An evaluation of a decade of management reform*. Canberra: Australian Government Publishing Service for the Management Advisory Board.

't Hart, P. (2010). Lifting its game to get ahead: The Canberra Bureaucracy's reform by Stealth. *Australian Review of Public Affairs*, July.

Uhrig, J. (2003). *Review of corporate governance of statutory authorities and office holders*. Canberra: Commonwealth of Australia.

van Dooren, W., Bouckaert, G., & Halligan, J. (2015). *Performance management in the public sector* (2nd ed.). London: Routledge.

Van Wart, M., & Dicke, L. A. (Eds.). (2008). *Administrative leadership in the public sector.* Armonk, NY: M.E. Sharpe.

Vardon, S. (1998, September–December). Creating a responsible service delivery agency: Centrelink Australia. *The Innovation Journal, 3*(3). Retrieved from http://www.innovation.cc/volumes-issues/vol3-iss3.htm

Vardon, S. (2002). Centrelink, changing culture and expectations. In E. M. Milner (Ed.), *Delivering the vision*, (pp. 39–62). London and New York, NY: Routledge.

Wanna, J., Kelly, J., & Foster, J. (Eds.). (2000). *Managing public expenditure in Australia.* Sydney: Allen and Unwin.

Watt, I. (2012). Reflections on my first year as secretary of the Department of the Prime Minister and cabinet and thoughts on the future, Great Hall, parliament house. Canberra, 5 October.

CHAPTER 11

LEADERSHIP AND PUBLIC SECTOR REFORM IN NEW ZEALAND

Caroline Rennie and Evan M. Berman

ABSTRACT

New Zealand is a small country with a rich history of pioneering administrative reforms. This chapter describes administrative reform processes emanating from the 'core agencies' of the State Services Commission (SSC), Treasury and the Department of the Prime Minister and Cabinet. It describes the famous New Public Management reforms of the late 1980s–2000s, led by the Treasury that restructured ministries (creating more agencies that are single-purpose agencies), rewrote policy rules (e.g., the same laws for public and private sector employees) and created accountability from agency heads to ministers as well as SSCs who evaluate and re-appoint agency heads. It should be noted that in this Westminster system, ministers provide policy leadership but not executive leadership of ministries. The chapter describes in detail two reform processes led/administered by the SSC since the mid-2000s to increase accountability for ministry mid-term policy and organizational capability targets (performance improvement framework) as well as

Leadership and Public Sector Reform in Asia
Public Policy and Governance, 257–285
Copyright © 2018 by Emerald Publishing Limited
All rights of reproduction in any form reserved
doi:10.1108/S2053-769720180000030011

cross-ministry goals (better public services). These efforts have been evaluated over time as being quite effective and are noted for their sustainability and improvement.

Keywords: New public management; accountability; policy leadership; state services commission; sustainability; New Zealand

INTRODUCTION

This chapter is focussed on public sector reforms in New Zealand and the nature of the leadership that facilitated these reforms. There are two significant periods of reforms that are discussed, the New Public Management (NPM) reforms of the late 1980s through the mid-1990s, and the more recent reforms starting in 2009, which can be linked to New Public Governance (NPG). The organizations that lead both reforms are the three core agencies in New Zealand's central government.

Within this centralized public sector, the three core agencies, viz. the NZ Treasury (Treasury), State Services Commission (SSC) and the Department of Prime Minster and Cabinet (DPMC) are self-named the 'corporate centre', a term adopted in the most recent reforms. This chapter discusses how these agencies acting as the 'corporate centre' has been at the heart of leading key public administration reforms since the late 1980s. The corporate centre terminology comes from the organization structure of using core departments of finance, human resources and a chief executive office. These three departments have system-wide oversight over state sector and provide key advice to senior ministers on the performance of the sector and changes required to get the sector to work more efficiently and effectively.

This chapter starts with a short outline of the New Zealand public sector and the role of these three agencies within the system. Included is a discussion on the leadership roles of these three agencies as individual entities and as a corporate centre for central government.

The chapter then discusses reforms of the late 1980s providing an important case study of the leadership role played by Treasury, and how Treasury was supported by SSC and DPMC during those reforms. Treasury sought to incorporate fundamental private sector theories of efficient and effective management of entities into the public sector and the agency had the key leadership role on advising ministers about these reforms.

The third part of the chapter discusses the reforms of the late 2000s in some detail and reflects on the role that SSC played in these reforms, providing the central leadership role supported by Treasury and DPMC. The collaborative approach sought the inclusion of senior officials across several government agencies to ensure their buy-in, and therefore effectively implement the reforms. In part this was because the reforms included the introduction of functional leadership in areas such as information technology, which required this buy-in to be effective. In spite of the need for a collaborative approach to lead these public sector reforms, these latest reforms still highlight the importance of the leadership role of the core agencies of Treasury, SSC and DPMC in public sector reforms.

The final part of the chapter is to consider the changes envisioned for the reforms that are still unfolding in New Zealand. One key area of development by the SSC is the focus on a system-wide adoption of a leadership framework. This framework is designed to promote and support the development of effective leaders throughout the individual's careers as they gain more seniority in the New Zealand public sector system.

THE NEW ZEALAND CONTEXT

New Zealand is an island nation in the South Pacific, roughly the size of the United Kingdom in area but sparsely populated, with approximately 4.7 million people (Statistics Department, New Zealand, 2016), and geographically remote from other countries (Australia lie almost 2,000 km to the west, across the Tasman Sea).

The two major islands are North Island and South Island, stretching some 1,700 km in combined length, but narrow across, as no locality is more than 110 km from the sea. The climate is temperate, and much of the terrain is mountainous, with the greater part of the agricultural land on North Island. A significant proportion of the population lives in cities, the largest being Auckland, then Wellington, the capital, which are both on North Island, and Christchurch is on South Island.

A former British colony and a member of the Commonwealth, New Zealand is a democratic nation with a parliamentary system of government. New Zealand has no formal constitution, rather the constitution is derived from a few key documents. The New Zealand constitution is to be found in formal legal documents, in decisions of the courts and in practices (some of which are described as conventions). It reflects and establishes that New Zealand is a monarchy, it has a parliamentary system of government and is a democracy. The documents include the Treaty of Waitangi, which is often considered the founding document of the government in New Zealand, the New Zealand Bill of Rights Act 1990 and the Constitution Act of 1986, which sets out the essential provisions relating to executive, legislature and judiciary (Governor General, New Zealand Government, 2016).

Parliament, under the Constitution Act, consists of the Sovereign in right of New Zealand and the House of Representatives. The House of Representatives is elected by universal suffrage every three years. Prior to 1993, New Zealand followed a 'first past the post' or simple plurality electoral system with single-member constituencies. In 1993, a referendum held concurrent with the 1993 election resulted in the adoption of a modified form of proportional representation. It is based on a 120-seat House, increased from 99 seats. Under mixed-member proportional representation, electors have two votes: the first vote for one of the 60 constituency seats, and the second vote to determine the remaining seats and the party standings in the House of Representatives.

The responsibility for choosing the cabinet is handled differently by the National and Labour parties. The National Party assigns the responsibility exclusively to the prime minister. However, the Labour Party's cabinet selection involves both the parliamentary caucus and the prime minister; the whole caucus elects the ministers, and then the party leader (prime minister) allocates the portfolios among those selected.

The structure of the public service is used in a Westminster system, with a politically neutral public service, accountable to the political executive and open on a competitive basis to suitably qualified persons who are recruited and promoted on the basis of merit. The organization, structure and functions of the public service are determined by legislation, namely the State Sector Act (1988) and the Public Finance Act (1989). A state services commissioner also known as the head of state services oversees this apolitical public sector. This role, which operates under a warrant from the Crown, is responsible for the appointment and performance of chief executives, allowing these appointments to not be politicized, and thus giving effect to the notion of an apolitical system.

Under the New Zealand State Sector Act (1988)

- The DPMC was reorganized combining the cabinet office with the advisory side of the prime minister's office and leaving separate the prime minister's private office.
- The Treasury advises the minister of finance and the cabinet on fiscal policy, financial management, macroeconomics and regulatory policies that have a major influence on economic performance.
- The SSC is headed by two statutory officers – commissioner and deputy commissioner – appointed by the governor general in council on the recommendation of the prime minister for a term not exceeding five years, and eligible for reappointment.
- Chief executives are hired on contract to head government departments by the state services commissioner. They sign performance agreements with the state services commissioner in consultation with the relevant minister/s that specify the targets they and their departments are expected to meet.

THE ROLE OF CORE AGENCIES

The New Zealand public administration is a very centralized system by international standards; with most key policy delivery agencies administered by ministers in the central government rather than being delegated to local government authorities. New Zealand's small size, use of one house in parliament, its democratic political system and well-established central government public administration supports this centralized approach. The central government is responsible for a wide range of public services, including everything from defence and security to welfare and education.

Core to this public administration are three key departments. The Treasury, which is responsible for fiscal control, allocating the government's budget, economic advice on the economy and public sector management. The SSC is responsible for monitoring and assessing the performance of the chief executives of the government departments, infrastructural design of the system and providing advice on supporting and growing the skills of the key resource of the public sector and its people.

The DPMC has several roles, including a policy advisory role to the prime minister. While policy advisers in DPMC will rarely agree to the recommendations of other departments on policy matters, including recommendations for public sector reforms, they will nearly always acknowledge that they have been informed (e.g., better public service (BPS) results: 2015 mid-year progress report cabinet paper). While DPMC may not explicitly support policy recommendations, it is critical, they signal they are aware of it. This ensures that ministers can have some confidence in presenting a policy initiative to their cabinet colleagues and that the prime minister is aware of the proposal. Of course, depending on the significance of the policy initiative, this will gain greater or lesser attention. Public sector reforms are considered significant because of the impact they have on how the system runs and how accountability is determined between ministers' responsibilities and those of senior public sector officials. Therefore, the role of DPMC, although seemingly passive in the 1980s account of the reforms, was in fact critical to the success of those reforms. The presence of DPMC as a key member of the corporate centre has increased subsequently to the BPS reforms and their endorsement of initiatives such as the performance improvement framework (PIF) is now clearly evident (State Services Commission [SSC], 2016).

New Zealand Government operates with a separation between political leaders and those employed in public service. A state services commissioner also known as the head of state services oversees this apolitical public sector. This role, which operates under a warrant from the Crown, is responsible for the appointment and performance of chief executives, allowing their appointment to occur without political determination; however, it does require considerable political consultation, which gives effect to the notion of an apolitical system. The separation was formalized in 1913 after the opposition party campaigned strongly on the need to get rid of the patronage occurring in the state services, and against the wasteful spending of public money. The party called itself the Reform Party and came to power in the 1912 election.

Within months, the government established the Public Service Act 1912, which enshrined a professional, politically impartial, career public service based on strict and systemized rules and regulations. Key to this was the establishment of SSC, which was led by the predecessors to the role of state services commissioner. This model means the public sector officials supporting the government of the day did not change depending on the public party in power, thereby allowing for consistency of experience and knowledge. It also means career public sector officials can invest into their skills and abilities without threat of losing their position every three years. A key part of the central agencies, and particularly the SSCs, role is to develop and support system-wide initiatives that encourage and maintain the required skills for a high performing state sector.

The tripartite relationship between ministers, chief executives and commissioner exists within this system with both formal and informal allocation of responsibilities between the parties. These responsibilities cover policy development, policy delivery and the performance of the entities. The relationships are managed in part through formal statutory arrangements, some requirements as set out in cabinet manuals (Cabinet Office New Zealand Government, 2016) and informal discussions and negotiations held between chief executives, ministers and the state services commissioner. The development of a political authorizing environment is critical for public sector officials to present recommendations for change and have confidence to proceed with implementation of policy agendas. It is instrumental to the success of public sector reforms to be able to understand, advise and implement the programmatic political agenda of the party in power, which has been elected through a democratic process. A critical part of the senior officials' leadership role in these core agencies is to steer the policy agenda, so it reflects the political intentions while also influencing these political intentions. These senior officials of the core agencies draw from their own experiences as well as the experiences and insights of their colleagues and staff to inform the discussions between themselves and ministers. The effective teamwork between senior ministers and senior officials allows for reforms that are and continue to be beneficial to New Zealanders and the public sector.

NPM REFORM – TREASURY'S LEADERSHIP

After the first oil shock, in 1973, New Zealand's economic growth reduced significantly for a decade, with combined private and public sector foreign debt rising from 11 per cent of GDP to 95 per cent between March 1974 and June 1984. Net public debt rose from 5 per cent of GDP to 32 per cent during the same period. Annual inflation remained in double digits for the entire, December 1973 to March 1983, period, which was subsequently controlled only through an extensive wage–price freeze (Evan, Grimes, Wilkinson, & Teece, 1996). When a snap election was called by the prime minister in June 1984, the combination of a likely change in government and devaluation of the exchange rate lead to a rapid outflow of foreign exchange in relation to available reserves that the Reserve Bank ceased converting New Zealand dollars into foreign currencies. This created a foreign exchange and constitutional crisis during the interregnum until the outgoing prime minister agreed to implement the instructions of the incoming government (Evan et al., 1996).

Following the foreign exchange and constitutional crisis of July 1984, the New Zealand government embarked comprehensive programmes of economic reform, including changes in financial markets, privatizations and deregulations, liberalizations to international trade, deregulation to labour markets and reforms in public finance and public sector. The success of institutional and organizational changes delivered by the reforms, called NPM, implemented in the late 1980s has been well recorded and assessed by several authors (Scott, 2001).

Scott (2001) observes the following:

> In October 1987, a group of four concerned ministers and some of their senior officials held several long meetings at the SSC to discuss the personnel and industrial relations arrangements for the New Zealand public service. They sought way to improve the effectiveness of government department by initiating changes in the management framework for the public sector. Over the next 18 months, a radical new public sector management framework was put in place based on the State Services Act 1988, the Public Finance Act 1989 and related legislation.

The 1987 reforms sought to achieve changes to the economy, the way government managed the economy and changes to the way public sector managed its self. By adopting private sector management theories and techniques it aimed to achieve greater efficiency and transparency. Scott (2001) notes further:

> These reforms occurred in an environment of significant privatization of some state assets (airlines and railways) and corporatization of others such as the electricity sector. The objectives for the reforms for state sector were to reduce the rigidities in the public sector so that there could be greater responsiveness and greater flexibility.

McKinnon (2003, p. 357) observes that Treasury leadership was instrumental in these reforms.

> Treasury had secured, via a circuitous route most of the economic reform agenda set out in the Economic Management Strategy of 1984. The new economic constitution with the Reserve Bank Act and the Fiscal Responsibility Act represented how the Government signed up to Treasury's economic strategy, with its strong focus on liberalization and deregulation of microeconomic policies.

These Treasury-led economic reforms were significant reforms and are explored in greater details by the authors such as Scott (2001). This chapter focusses on the public reforms that occurred at the same time, which were also lead by Treasury and supported by SSC and DPMC. These reforms themselves were extensive and revolutionized the way the public sector operated and the way it has been held to account for both its fiscal and performance management.

The Treasury officials advising the ministers stressed the importance that direct accountability between chief executives and their ministers could make to a new and effective public service management system. In doing so, they were continuing to promote the ideas first set out in 1984 in *Economic Management*, the Treasury briefing to incoming Labour Government, subsequently published as a book. Scott (2001) notes the concepts that were expanded and developed in the future published briefing to the government after the 1987 election that was titled *Government Management*. In that brief, the Treasury argued that a well-managed government should have the following six characteristics:

- Clear objectives that inform managers what is expected of them and enable their performance to be monitored;
- Transparency in setting out those performance objectives and the means by which they are to be pursued;
- A structure that minimizes the potential for 'capture' of policy by people and organizations that are providing services;
- Incentives for managers and staff to achieve the goals of the government rather than their own goals;
- Effective use of relevant information to promote effective performance; and
- Contestability of both policy advice and service delivery.

Greater discretion and authority was sought for managers, which was matched with effective accountability for clearly specified results. As part of these reforms much greater use was to be made of formal arrangements to clarify roles and performance requirements.

Scott (2001) observes the following:

Specific changes recommended by the Treasury included:

- the establishment of a clear, unbroken line of accountability from ministers to their departmental heads and from departmental heads to the staff in their departments;
- greater involvement by cabinet in appointment and other employment decisions about the heads of departments, and by heads of departments in employment decisions about their staff;
- the dismantling of external controls over inputs; and
- the introduction of a robust performance management system based on specified performance requirements that would feed into the performance assessment and career development for staff and into employment decisions about the departmental heads.

The Treasury also advocated for new approaches to the structure of government and to budgeting, and accounting such as accrual accounting and financial management. These were subsequently adopted by the government and led to some profound changes in the way in which the public service was organized and did its business. The reforms provided increased understanding about the cost of government policies and the value of government's investments as well as formalizing the accountability framework for both fiscal control and performance management. These changes created building blocks from which subsequent reforms, including the reforms in 2011, could occur.

Officials from the SSC, who were advising the ministerial committee, supported the directions of the reforms. They promoted the alignment of public sector labour law with the private sector labour law, which was being revised at the time. The procedures for negotiating wages and the resolution of disputes were the focus of attention. The officials also stressed the need in any new arrangements to retain the key values of the old system, such as its non-political character and its fundamental ethics and values. The officials favoured the retention of at least some measures of effective central control in order to promote these values and characteristics; consequently the SSC promoted the concept of senior executive service (Scott, 2001).

McKinnon (2003) observes the reform and asked basic yet fundamental questions regarding what governments could and should manage in the economy and the public sector:

> Two fundamental ideas questions had been asked throughout the life of the idea: Who should do the managing – what should be the balance of power and influence between ministers and officials, politicians and officials and what should managing involve – what kind of management of what kind of economy?

While the directive leadership approach adopted by Treasury was necessary and expedient for senior officials, there were, however, dissenting voices as to the wisdom of Treasury adopting such an approach. McKinnon (2003) notes:

> 'During the reforms years [between 1984 and 1993] the conventional relationship between elected government and bureaucratic advisors in a Westminster system was to a great extent reversed. The Treasury became the principal initiator to know what governments would do; one read the Treasury's briefing papers, not the party programs.

The role of Treasury in the 1980s came under scrutiny and was subjected to criticism for Treasury's involvement in decisions over policy changes as opposed to just advising on the best policy approach. McKinnon observes:

> The document titled *Government Management* that led to major reforms in the public sector was also viewed as 'a failure on the part of this government department to recognize its true role in New Zealand Society'. Treasury staff seem to have forgotten that are policy advisers and instead they have become politicians...

However, as McKinnon (2003) points out that 1987 was different from times before and its minister supported Treasury's advice. Although he notes that the nature of the way the arguments were framed in the government management:

> 'a sense that Treasury had crossed the boundary separating the official from the political, the official from the theoretical and certainly the digestible from the indigestible. Even, given Treasury's determination to provide only what it saw as the best advice, however unpalatable, a different kind of production might well have enhanced – and would not have limited – Treasury's ability to get policies it favoured adopted.

In subsequent reforms, senior officials took a more collaborative approach, particularly the significant public reforms of 2011 creating the BPS agenda. This meant ministers clearly lead the policy agenda and provided the justification and rationale for the reforms. In addition, because of the introduction of mechanisms such as functional leadership buy-in from other senior officials was required and this necessitated a more inclusive and collaborative approach rather than directive. Both approaches did deliver results and reflected not just different styles but a different sense of urgency and judgement about how changes to the public sector could be achieved.

The reforms of the late 1980s and subsequent work in the 1990s created the backdrop for the reforms from 2009. The changes achieved created for the system a good understanding of the balance sheet and the fiscal performance of the entities. It also created accountability within entity structures and between the commissioner and the chief executives. However, the commentators and critics pointed to the weaknesses in the reforms. 'Structural reorganizations within departments have brought improvements in productive efficiency and standards of service, greater contestability of advice and clearer organizational focus and mission. But there have been problems ... more generally; while it is desirable to have broad principles of organizational design, they should be applied with circumspection and concern for evidence. The authors note the possibility of a shift in time away from a managerial paradigm of structure to one reflecting 'holistic governance'. (Scott (2001) referring to Boston et al. (1996)). Perhaps, some of these weaknesses have subsequently sought to be amended in BPS reforms.

BPS REFORMS – THE CORPORATE CENTRE'S LEADERSHIP

The BPS reforms place greater emphasis than the NPM on how the government operates as a system to design policy solution and implement effective change. As part of this is a recognition of the multi-year nature of government intervention, with intergenerational criteria in policy-making, to effect sustained changes. Consistency in government investment to these policies is required to get the results. This means a change in the way accountability was understood and used in the public sector. Recognition of concepts such as stewardship and functional leadership to ensure senior officials are accountable not just for their entities but also for policy agendas that require system collaboration and long-term investment of assets and resources.

The Government was keen to operate as a more cohesive system to enable better results. The need for focus on the leadership required implementing change and developing a culture of stewardship to view initiatives over multiple years and even generations to get long-term benefits from the investment'. (Rennie, 2013)

The SSC, Treasury and DPMC have historically provided leadership as core agencies. This arrangement is now being recognized as the Corporate Centre, acknowledging the departments' role for system-wide consideration of financial and personnel management. This leadership role is particularly important when adopting centralized system-wide approaches such as the PIF.

The three central agencies – the State Services Commission, Treasury, and Department of Prime Minister and Cabinet (DPMC) - are working together as a *Corporate Centre* to lead a state sector that New Zealanders trust, and that delivers better public services, including outstanding results and value for money. This requires the *Corporate Centre* to take an active role across the sector, and provide system-level coordination, a clear focus and strong leadership. The Corporate Centre works together, and uses the three agencies' respective strengths and collective expertise to support the state sector to deliver better outcomes for New Zealanders. (Rennie, 2013)

How the Reforms Started?

The global financial crisis of the mid 2000s motivated several reforms internationally, including New Zealand. New Zealand's reforms were started in an environment of austerity, where the Government was focussed on requiring value for money from agencies, where budgets were capped but improved productivity was sought. The BPS reforms were in response to the need to get better government for less and viewed as 'the next stage of reforms' (Key, 2012). The direction and focus of BPS is also like the themes found in the NPG paradigm (Osborne, 2010). NPG focusses on how government works as a system and the recognition that public sector entities can't just concern themselves with the efficiency, effectiveness and sustainability of their own organizations. NPG argues that entities within the state sector are part of a complex public service delivery system where their mission-critical objectives require the successful negotiation of relationships within these systems, including policy makers, other PSOs, service users, citizens and indeed a range of service system elements and stakeholders (Osborne et al., 2015). The BPS reforms recognized the significance of government operating them as a system and designed changes to facilitate the achievement of system-wide objectives.

Important to these reforms was the commitment of ministers to find solutions that had the potential to lift performance by improving the way resources were used rather than just applying more resources. An authorizing environment was created through the leadership of senior officials in SSC and Treasury, working closely with their colleague in DPMC to secure the mandate necessary from the prime minister, deputy prime minister, associate finance ministers and state service minister to implement the reforms.

The reforms recognized the opportunity to rely on the strength of the system to solve policy problems. They realized that policy problems, for instance in social welfare, were multidimensional and complex and often included a number of government agencies in providing a solution. However, getting better results would require an agreement across senior ministers and officials as to the critical results worthy of attention and the changes to the system needed to enable different agencies, each with their independent responsibilities to share accountability to get results. The BPS lead to a shift in approach to managing these issues.

In 2009, PIF was introduced to provide diagnostic tools for understanding the needs of individual agencies.

> The Performance Improvement Framework (PIF) was developed six years ago by a team from across the state services, including chief executives, to support continuous performance improvement across the state services. The team took the best of the *United Kingdom's Capability Review Programme* and the best of the organizational improvement models from the New Zealand private sector, as well as methodologies from other jurisdictions, and adapted them for the New Zealand public management system (SSC, 2015)

It was because of gaining this improved understanding that system solutions proposed in the BPS became more self-evident to the senior leaders in the core agencies of SSC, Treasury and DPMC.

> Performance Improvement Framework (PIF) in 2009 essentially started New Zealand on the pathway of reform as this diagnostic tool helped to uncover some of the failings within the agency approach to policy development and delivery. PIF is governed by the three central agencies and delivered by the SSC. It was launched in 2009 and aims to help senior leaders in the state services improve their agencies' performance in the face of continuously evolving and increasing complexity. PIF does this by enabling Ministers, chief executives and Crown entity boards to respond with agility and purpose to the opportunities and challenges presented.(SSC, 2015)

Specifically, The PIF framework has been used in three distinct ways (Victoria University of Wellington, 2017):

- As a diagnostic tool to drive improvements in agency and cross-agency performance by helping 'senior leaders lift the performance of the agencies they lead'.
- As a tool for central agencies to ensure improvement in overall system performance.
- As a tool to provide ministers, the public and other stakeholders with the assurance that improvements in agency performance and across the system are occurring.

Through the PIF, the SSC, Treasury and DPMC aimed to develop a very comprehensive understanding about whether the state service agencies were doing well. After a PIF review, senior teams should be clearer about their roles and know how to add maximum value for New Zealand; they can enlist, engage and enrol their people – and others – in the delivery of that value. The assessment leading up to PIF was that agencies were very good at responding to the demands of ministers here and now. The departments were also very good at responding to crisis and mobilizing response. Now, cross-agency and systemic perspectives were needed as well as deepening of public sector capabilities and leadership.

The PIF reviews revealed that agencies were weak at focussing on policy issues that the government would need to tackle within five to 10 years; ministers received limited support as to how to address these issues and the timelines required delivering the policy solutions that would affect good results. The PIF reviews also revealed that departments were not good at issues such as succession planning and talent management. Finally, capital management of system-wide assets struggled to get attention it desired with comprehensive planning approach without a long-term system-wide approach to capital management. These agencies, acting as individual agencies, were much less good at thinking about the long term, creating a stewardship culture and mobilizing across agency solutions to long-term goals. So, a fundamental shift from the short-term to the long-term planning was required to achieve the objective of having a high performing state service.

PIF has four key elements:

- *Four-Year Excellence Horizon* – What is the agency's performance challenge?
- *Delivery of Government Priorities* – How well is the agency responding to government priorities?
- *Delivery of Core Business* – In each core business, how well does the agency deliver value, increase value and exercise its stewardship role over regulations?
- *Organizational Management* – How well is the agency positioned to deliver now and in the future? (SSC, 2015).

The reports were published and used to highlight good and strong practice as well as to ensure accountability and transparency. PIF uses system-improvement research to promote system-wide understanding. A combination of seminars, workshops and master classes were to share what has been learnt and to stimulate conversations and good practice.

The heart of the programme is the PIF review. It looks at the current state of an agency and how well placed it is to deal with the issues that confront it in the medium-term future. It then proposes areas where the agency needs to do the work to make itself fit for purpose and fit for the future. It is not an investigation. It is not an audit. PIF is unique in the sense that it is inspirational and future-focussed. It asks an organization about its greatest contribution to New Zealand, and how well placed it is to deliver on that.

Reviews are conducted with agencies as required or when incoming chief executives and boards who want to use PIF to set a strategic agenda and create change. PIF reviews are completed by experienced, independent and trained lead reviewers. The lead reviewers use a mix of co-creation, appreciative enquiry and peer-review to create future states, also known as four-year excellence horizon, for senior teams.

The four-year excellence horizon can be tabled in parliament. Ministers and senior leaders oversee the delivery of the four-year excellence horizon via the four-year plans, letter of expectations and chief executive performance agreement. Self-reviews are offered alongside PIF reviews. Crown entity boards often use self-reviews to reset strategy or monitoring agents to better understand sector and system performance.

For ministers, the PIF provides assurance that the agencies they are responsible for are constantly looking for ways to improve how they do business and deliver value for the taxpayer's investment in them. Ministers also get independent assurance, as external expert parties undertake PIF reviews.

The four-year excellence horizon is strategic narrative written by lead reviewers as a way for senior teams to understand and stay ahead of emerging opportunities and to respond quickly to unexpected issues. The approach was adopted as it was recognized that strategic planning with departments was at risk of becoming very transactional and only compliance-focussed. Consequently, medium-term planning around finances and workforce were being detached from each other or overlooked entirely in the strategic planning discussion.

For the corporate centre, the PIF provides a good picture of what is good about the New Zealand public management system and what needs to improve. The PIF process ensures that senior leaders in a department are having a regular strategic conversation where they look both at their future spending and future workforce needs. This conversation means that they are thinking about what resources they will need in both terms of people and money. For the corporate centre, the four-year plans help identify pressures or gaps in the system, and allow these core agencies to prepare system-level interventions. Ultimately, it provides good information that allows officials to give assurance to ministers that departments are taking a robust approach to change processes, and that leaders have a good understanding of any risks or gaps.

The four-year excellence horizon was developed in 2011 as a separate 'summary' section at the front of PIF agency review reports and self-review reports. It provides a distillation of the findings, themes and conclusions about the priority areas for performance improvement, given the contribution New Zealand needs from the agency and its current and medium-term context, issues, risks and opportunities. The important role of the four-year excellence horizon is made explicit in this refresh of the framework. Government agencies that are required to produce a four-year plan need to ensure that the plan shows how the agency is responding to the four-year excellence horizon and the commitment the agency made in its response to its agency review. (SSC, 2015)

The performance of the agency is judged against this future narrative, not just on its previous performance. The four-year excellence horizon is a distillation of the critical shift that an agency needs to make to be successful in four years' time. It does this by focussing on the following areas:

- Leadership and direction
- Delivery for customers and New Zealanders
- Relationships
- People development
- Financial and resource management.

This four-year excellence horizon connects directly to the departmental planning during the annual budget cycle. SSC and the Treasury work with departments in the production of four-year plans prepared by the department on behalf of the minister. These plans create a strategic document that

- provides a clear and integrated view of an agency's medium-term strategy and intentions;
- shows how agencies will manage their resources to deliver their strategy and
- identify the risks to delivery.

These are central components of the budget process, incorporating both budget planning and workforce strategies. The workforce strategy elements ask departments to articulate

- the broad workforce capability they want to develop,
- information on any specific skills gaps,
- a firm four-year prediction of staff numbers and
- a signal of their expected medium-term people costs.

Four-year plans are increasingly being seen as a key strategic planning exercise by departments, helping senior leaders clarify challenges, drive change, align thinking of diverse business units and better tell their departments' performance and management story to engage staff or ministers. The maturity and quality of four-year plans has increased, particularly in the areas of more specific strategic direction, consideration of operating models, increased awareness of customers and the importance of partnerships.

The PIF review framework has been upgraded thrice since its launch to keep step with changing environment. In December 2015, the framework was refreshed to better reflect how agencies are delivering on the reform agenda of BPS that calls for agencies to build and deliver their services around a clear understanding of their customers. Four-year plans are reviewed, and best practices shared. The SSC published in April 2013 *Core Guide 3: Getting to Great; Lead Reviewers Insights from PIF*, which identifies good practice from the individual PIF reviews. The following key themes for further improvement were drawn from the 21 PIF reviews in the guide:

- Providing clear purpose and clarity on how the organizations' strategy will best achieve its goals.
- Ensuring strong internal leadership that attracts talented people and inspires them to dedicate themselves to working with integrity to deliver the outcomes that the agency has identified as mattering most to New Zealand.
- Investing in talent by providing challenging, interesting and important work to do, while also managing poor performances to either improve or exit.
- Enlisting the active support of all those outside the agency who are necessary to the agency's delivering.
- Demonstrating that learning, innovation and continuous improvement are valued.
- Engaging corporate support areas such as finance, information technology, organizational development, strategy, risk and human resources as business partners (Biswell, 2013).

An independent review of the PIF finds broad support for the above (Victoria University of Wellington, 2017). A systematic survey of 430 respondents in 35 agencies 'shows that respondents felt that benefits accruing from PIF were worthwhile and endurable'. The review finds that lead reviewers are credible, free from bias and upholding public service standards. The self-review is also seen as becoming increasingly important and contributing to organizational narrative and awareness of organizational roles and strategic mission. Following the PIF process, organizations are also perceived as having strengthened their contributions to New Zealand and having increased their organizational stewardship for mid-range goals. Positive PIF reports are also seen as increasing ministers' confidence in their organization's performance. Overall, the PIF process is helping to improve clarity of an organization's purpose, providing a clear and detailed understanding of what to focus on, and improving the organization's strategic framework.

However, the independent review also notes areas for further improvement. Whereas the four-year excellence horizon was very helpful to many people, at least one-third of survey respondents felt that this was too short. Ministers were said to have shorter horizons. PIF is also not well regarded for enhancing organizational values or culture. Just over half the survey respondents felt that PIF had helped to strengthen the organization's commitment to core values or improve its organizational culture. The case studies further find tensions between PIF as a compliance exercise and as a tool for improvement, suggesting that fear of negative results (accountability) could drive out improvement. Some recommendations for improving PIF include considering the role of PIF relative to other accountability and performance reviews; strengthening post-PIF processes and support to ensure sustained momentum for change and demonstrable operational improvements and demonstrate cases where PIF reviews have led to operational improvement.

BETTER PUBLIC SERVICES AGENDA

In 2011, the Better Public Services Advisory Group was established and it produced recommendations that lead to BPS reforms. The reforms were and continue to be informed by the work of PIF reviews. The reforms themselves included the introduction of the following:

- A set of challenging goals or targets, framed as 'results' to be achieved within a timeframe.
- A programme of legislative, organizational and process reforms aimed at facilitating more across-organization approaches to improve services, creating a different style of public sector leadership and to allow innovation to thrive so that 'more and better services can be achieved with less' (resources) (Eppel, 2013).

These reforms were regarded as 'a focus on getting better results, and greater efficiency, from the public sector' (Rt Hon John Key, 2012). Speech from Seven years on the reforms have been imbedded through legislative changes achieved in 2013 and through ongoing changes lead by the core agencies of SSC, DPMC and Treasury.

The BPS advisory group recommended changes focussed on delivering policy results in complex, cross-boundary areas such as education, welfare and health. The institutional and operational changes to the New Zealand public sector involved designing and delivering value-for-money services to meet the rising expectations of citizens, stronger whole-of-government leadership and capability. An overview of legislative and related policy proposals points to three primary reform themes: results focus, citizen focus and performance focus.

Better Public Services Reform Themes (N.D.)

Results focus: Getting traction on the results that matter most
This entails:

- Defining results that matter;
- Specifying ministers to lead results and chief executives to deliver on results;
- Funding departments for results;
- Reporting on results; and
- Consolidating/organizing agencies and resources to deliver on results.

Citizen focus: Better services and value for money
This entails:

- Engaging with citizens and business;
- Focussed reporting;
- Leveraging expertise and scale;
- Best sourcing; and
- Continuous improvement and innovation.

Performance focus: Strengthening leadership, culture and capability
This entails:

- Tasking state services commissioner with overall responsibility for state sector performance and reform;
- Refocussing accountabilities (e.g., functional leadership);
- Improving leadership development; and
- Having a culture built process across the state services.

These reform themes translated into a strengthened role for the state services commissioner to become the head of state services, so creating more enhanced and effective leadership of the reform programme, including, for example, more flexible deployment of senior leaders across the public sector. In addition, the changes added additional tools to support results and allowed work across agency boundaries. Finally, the reforms included a focus on better quality and less volume reporting to parliament to enable improved quality output from departments.

Results Focus: Getting Traction on the Results that Matter Most

In 2011, as part of the BPS reforms, the 'Results' programme was launched. '*Results* is not just about the 10 results of the better public services. It is about a new way of working' (Rennie, 2013). The programme sets out to drive results, improve quality, responsiveness, the value-for-money of public services and strengthening leadership. There is strong government commitment to result areas and resourcing, and staff is allocated to enable Results to be achieved.

The 2011 programme focusses on 10 results across the following five areas:

• Reducing long-term welfare dependence;
• Supporting vulnerable children;
• Boosting skills and employment;
• Reducing crime; and
• Improving interaction with government for business and the public.

BPS results were chosen for their importance to citizens and businesses. They are designed to strengthen public accountability and signal our commitment to transform performance in the areas that matter most to New Zealanders.

Setting specific and measureable targets for the BPS results is intended to:

• reinforce the government's commitment to a new results-driven approach;
• demonstrate public's high expectations for public services;
• spur innovation and encourage the adoption of new approaches; and
• accelerate the pace of state sector reform (SSC, 2013).

New Zealand public sector have had mixed results in achieving the proposed targets. Officials note that the targets are designed to be difficult to achieve in full because of the high expectations set in agreement between ministers and the public sector and the desire to lift public service performance.

> Both individually and collectively, the BPS targets challenge departments and contributing agencies to deliver substantial progress by refocussing and reshaping public services. In addition, we want to position the BPS results high in the public consciousness so that New Zealanders can grasp our ambitious vision for better public services and hold us to account for performance achieved.(SSC, 2013)

Citizen Focus: Better Services and Value for Money

The core agencies focus on a number of agenda items that are aimed at improving the citizen experience. The move for the PIF reviews to focus agencies on becoming more customer-centric is an important part of these reforms. Other initiatives are data improvements, better longitudinal information, more targeted use of governments' assets and resources, better investment into citizens and creating a continuous improvement culture.

The corporate centre places increasing value on being customer-centric. Previously, leaders within the public service were very good at servicing ministers, and can achieve great things in times of crisis. However, leaders in the corporate centre believe that departments need to be better at providing services to the public in a way that works best for the public. This means putting the customer at the centre of their businesses by involving them directly in the design and delivery of services. It also meant strengthening interdepartmental collaboration for the benefit of the citizen.

State Services Commission sets out the plan for improving outcomes for New Zealanders within a tight fiscal environment through state sector reforms. As with the use of PIF reviews to understand with improved clarity and insight into agencies, improvements to data analysis enables the system to better understand how New Zealanders engage with government across agency boundaries and the impact government services have on New Zealanders.

> We're bringing together key data from across a range of agencies, and making it more easily available to the public sector and external researchers. We will complete two streams of work:
>
> - Establishing a central agency *analysis and insights team*. This team will perform analysis on wider cross-agency data to identify patterns and better predict and understand the pathways, connections and outcomes of New Zealanders' interactions with government services.
> - Expanding Statistics New Zealand's *integrated data infrastructure (IDI)*. The IDI is a linked longitudinal dataset that covers an extended range of pathways, transitions and

> outcomes information. Safe and secure access for approved researchers is provided to integrated and anonymised multi-agency data. (SSC, 2013)

The information is intended to be used for better research and analysis. It enables better understanding of how sections of the population use government services and benefit from government interventions. By connecting this data, it can be used for research and policy purposes without compromising the privacy of individuals.

In a recent speech, the secretary for the NZ Treasury, on what is being done with the data that is now being collected, stated the following:

> *Social Investment Insights* is an online mapping tool providing data analysis and information about children and youth aged 24 and under who are at risk of poor future outcomes. As well as showing, right down to a suburb level, the number and ages of children at risk of poor outcomes, the tool can predict the cost to government (over time) for various interventions over a person's lifetime. This tool is an expression of an investment approach. It's not just a question of saving money it's about using data held within various agencies and technology to better understand people who need help and deciding on the best way of doing that. (Makhlouf, 2016)

Creating the social investment insights tool presented the officials with a number of challenges, including identifying the relevant agencies and resolving privacy issues related to the use of data. In addition, the core agencies had to resolve the siloed way in which central government had historically tended to operate and adopt a system-focussed approach.

> We focused on understanding their lives from the perspective of the myriad of agencies they are likely to come into contact with through their lifetime. By doing this we've been able to see what is and isn't working and what the cost to the system is as a result. Releasing this tool means government agencies *and* community organisations have rich information right at their finger-tips.(Makhlouf, 2016)

The core agencies work on generating data to inform decisions on where to invest, and improve the monitoring of projects and measuring their success. Improvements to use and access information is seen as critical to the BPS reforms.

> There is now a dedicated *government investment portfolio* team in Treasury that provides investment management support across the public sector. Part of their work is about increasing accountability through greater transparency. Last year they released the first annual report providing a snapshot of the government's overall investment programme. It covers 409 projects such as Information, Communication and Technology (ICT), new schools, defence projects and construction – with a total annual cost of $6 billion. We also released the first tri-annual *Major Projects Performance Report*, providing a comprehensive update on the 38 most complex of those 409 investment projects, and tracking whether they are delivering on expectations.

Part of the reforms recognises the importance of transparency to enhance accountability. For the first time in 2104, Treasury produced its investment statement, which details the Crown's balance sheet showing line by line what assets the government holds. So, that's the number of schools, recreational facilities, reserves – everything – publicly available for anyone to look at. Moreover, the Administrative & Support Services Benchmarking report provides performance information across agencies and gives transparency over a significant area of expenditure. The benchmarking reports are an important step towards transparency and scrutiny of government services. (Makhlouf, 2016)

The continuous improvement of the state services is another critical part of the PIF framework. PIF has helped to foster a culture of continuous improvement, enabling agencies to work more efficiently and effectively every day.

Specifically tailored to our state services, the 'better every day' approach enables agencies to design and manage services around the needs of citizens in a joined up way, so the customer experience is *better every day*. This practical approach engages staff in changing how they work and develop leadership and management capability to continuously improve performance.

Drawing on a range of methods and influences, including the work of John Seddon, W. Edwards Deming, Chris Argyris and Gerard Egan, the State Services Commission's continuous improvement centre of expertise has developed the 'better every day' approach with six partner agencies – Land Information New Zealand, New Zealand Police, New Zealand Customs Service, Ministry of Business, Innovation and Employment, Ministry for the Environment, Inland Revenue – and the Public Service Association. (SSC, 2016)

Performance Focus – Strengthening Leadership, Culture and Capability

Performance focus incorporates the idea that better more focussed leadership is critical to the success of the 'better public service' reforms. The establishment of the functional leader and the introduction of the concept of stewardship are the approaches designed to build capability and a culture that embed the reforms agenda over the long term. Senior officials in the core agencies recognized that the system was not very good at making sure the agencies were focussed on policy issues that the government would have to grapple with in five to 10 years. Therefore, the system was failing to provide advice on long-term solutions to the government so that these issues could be addressed.

Part of the solution was the performance of the system, or more specifically the performance of the public servants. The primary area of focus was to change the performance of the leadership talent, today and into the future. This meant changing expectations on current leaders, such as requiring a stewardship focus and improving issues like succession management and talent management. To develop a high-performing state service, a shift from leaders being equipped to deal with the short term to leaders skilled to consider the long term was fundamental.

The performance expectations on chief executives are increasingly being geared towards stewardship and being held to account for the stewardship agenda of their agency. The aim is to build better resilience into the system by reshaping the expectations on senior officials. The mechanism to hold chief executives to account involves Cabinet endorsing each year the stewardship obligations, which the State Service Commissioner gives to [the] chief executives. It means active planning and management. It means thinking about stewardship in a very different way. (Rennie, 2013)

FUNCTIONAL LEADERSHIP

The statutory amendments which added the role of head of state services to the state services commissioner mandate was designed to make more explicit the state services commissioners' responsibility for the performance of state services. Another role that has a similar sharp degree of accountability is that the chief executive of the department of internal affairs/chief government information officer is responsible for the ICT strategy and action plan (SSC, 2016). Government has put in place some very stretching and clear expectations around ICT performance across the system, and around this role in terms of visible assurance and leadership of the system. The leadership is being embedded into the system. In the past the system was set up so that most operational decisions in government agencies, such as decisions around procurement, accommodation and ICT, were made by individual chief executives based on the business needs and functions of their individual agencies. The use of functional leadership is aimed at maximizing the benefits and reducing the overall costs to government of common business activities, removing the need for an agency-by-agency approach.

Functional leadership as a part of the BPS change programme aims to improve the effectiveness and reduce the overall costs of common business functions to government. Functional leadership roles have been given to three chief executives to drive performance across the state services in ICT, procurement and property respectively. Following are the functional leaders:

- The chief executive of the department of internal affairs/chief government information officer responsible for the ICT strategy and action plan;
- The chief executive of the ministry of business, innovation and employment, responsible for government procurement reform; and
- The chief executive of the ministry of social development, responsible for the property management centre of expertise and the government national property strategy.

They retain their departmental roles but wear an additional functional leader 'hat' to achieve benefits for government overall (SSC, 2016).

The roles are designed to finding ways to

- drive efficiencies (through economies of scale, leveraging buying power in whole-of-government contracts, setting common standards and approaches and reducing duplication);
- develop expertise and capability (centres of expertise, coordinated professional development, deploying capability to where and when it is most needed); and
- improve services and service delivery (through sharing and coordinating activities and facilities, joined up service delivery).

The areas of procurement, property and ICT were chosen for functional leadership mandates because of their significance, as they are major areas of expenditure and management attention for agencies. In addition, there is considerable number of risks associated with these investments that can best be managed as cross-government portfolios, there are opportunities for effectiveness and efficiency gains and potential for long-term better coordination.

Head of Profession

In addition to the functional leaders are the various head of profession roles, including the secretary of treasury as the head of profession for financial, the head of DPMC as the head of profession for policy, the government chief talent officer employed in SSC as the head of human resources and the solicitor general as the head of legal profession. The expectations include more actively developing their professions, setting standards, building communities of practice and recognizing excellent performance in those professions right across the state services (SSC, 2016).

LEADERSHIP CAPABILITY DEVELOPMENT AND DEPLOYMENT

In addition to the appointment and performance management of chief executives, state services commissioner and head of the state services have the responsibility for overseeing the development of senior leaders in public service. The change means making leadership development and talent management a collective system responsibility. It also means thinking differently about the type of leaders that are recruited, developed and moved around.

The shift by SSC means senior leaders are seen more as 'system assets' rather than 'agency assets', which lines up with the need to work more collaboratively across the state services. Through chief executive lead career boards, SSC stewards the development and deployment of senior leaders to the areas they are needed most. This may means that they bring their experience to strengthen the existing team or it could be that the role is intended to develop them for more senior and complex roles. The use of career boards involves chief executives engaging with talent management across the system at a senior level. They discuss the development needs of high potential people in their agencies, and how departments can work as a system to provide for the development of these individuals while also looking to benefit from this more agile use of people resources.

The SSC is also focussed on building a strong infrastructure to allow data analytics to identify trends and predict talent risks in the future. Together with agencies and the leadership development centre, a common approach to talent management is being built. This includes redefining the leadership success profile, and assessing the senior leadership cohort against this profile so that the system can better understand where baseline of strengths and gaps exist. A mechanism to inform the decisions is the establishment of talent management information system, which is used to store and integrate data (SSC, 2016).

> The SSC is putting in place a programme that is significantly changing how the state sector identifies, develops and utilizes leaders and talented people from the start of their careers to their most senior levels. The new talent management system will provide the tools and approaches to help leaders and people reach their full potential. By maximizing our potential leadership and talent across the public system, we will achieve better results for New Zealanders. SSC is building leadership and talent across the State services by:
>
> • strengthening leadership across the system;
> • encouraging and supporting leaders to step into more challenging and complex roles;
> • supporting the move away from a Wellington-centric view, encouraging diversity within the Public Service and
> • identifying our most talented people, developing them and placing them where they are most needed. (SSC, 2016)

The SSC is also focussing its attention on those at the other end of the leadership pipeline, those that are early in their careers. To do this, the department is providing shared development opportunities for interns and graduates from agencies across the system to understand what it means to be part of the state sector and not just being in the agency.

CONCLUSION AND REFLECTIONS

These public sector reforms in New Zealand have been the focus of this chapter. Of interest has been the leadership role of core agencies in very centralized public management system. Changes to the way New Zealand public sector officials operate might require amendments to funding, reallocation of resources and/or lines of accountability will undoubtedly come to the attention of these three core agencies and consequently will involve the input of Treasury, SSC and DPMC. This chapter has not focussed on singular agency or even sector reforms but rather on the two significant system-wide reforms lead by Treasury in the 1980s and by the corporate centre (three agencies) in 2009. The driving ideology behind the first of these significant periods of reforms is commonly referred to as NPM. These reforms sought to make significant improvements to efficiency and effectiveness within public sector entities and used several private sector theories and approaches to achieve these aims. The thinking behind the current reforms, starting in 2009, is more closely linked to approaches advocated in NPG, particularly the idea that government works as a system. BPS, the name applied to these recent reforms in New Zealand, focussed on the significance of working with the government not as independent entities but rather as a whole system. In this approach the solutions sought worked to align accountabilities and resources to result areas and more recently to create leadership capability equipped to work in a system-focussed public sector.

The organizations that lead both reforms are the three core agencies in New Zealand's central government. Within this centralized public sector the three core agencies, Treasury, SSC and DPMC, are self-named as 'corporate centre'. This chapter discussed how these agencies acted as the 'corporate centre' and how they have been at the heart of leading these two key public administration reforms. These agencies are SSC, Treasury and DPMC.

The reforms of the late 1980s provide an important case study of the leadership role played by Treasury and how Treasury was supported by SSC and DPMC during those reforms. The NPM-style reforms advocated by Treasury and large respect adopted by the government of the day sought to incorporate fundamental private sector theories of efficient and effective management of entities into the public sector. At this time, notwithstanding the primary responsibilities SSC would have implementing the reforms, Treasury played a key leadership role on advising to ministers.

The reforms of the late 2000s provided a more prominent role for SSC. During these reforms a shared leadership role was evident between SSC, Treasury and DPMC as they operated together to engine the reform advice. The approach to changes in the late 2000s also included the commitment and support of senior officials across several critical agencies to give effect to changes and reforms. In part, this was because the reforms included the introduction of functional leadership, in areas such as information technology, so required the buy-in of the chief information officer to be effective. However, even more significant to the success of the reforms was the general support required across government. This was because the reforms were essentially about moving away from a focus on entities individual efficiency and effectiveness to understanding government as a system. This means that more and more efficient and effective solutions need to designed and implemented in a comprehensively collaborative way for the system to achieve results. Notwithstanding the importance of this, the latest reforms still highlight the importance of the leadership role of the core agencies of Treasury, SSC and DPMC in public sector reforms.

The final part of the chapter discusses those reforms at the early stages of implementation. One key area in the state services is the focus on a system-wide adoption of a leadership framework. This framework is designed to promote and support development of effective leaders throughout the individual's careers as they gain more seniority in the system. Further work is also taking place in improved communication across the 'system', recognizing the need for clear understanding of what is happening and its impact on shared results initiatives. Finally is the increased focus on the need for collaboration that extends beyond the public sector and even the state sector and incorporates the role of community and citizens in achieving good outcomes. Consequently, some of the key result areas are working towards improved engagement with citizens and providing access to information to improve the decision-making capacity of individuals as well as government.

REFERENCES

Better Public Services Advisory Group. (2011). *Better public services advisory group report.* Retrieved from https://www.ssc.govt.nz/sites/all/files/bps-report-nov2011_0.pdf.

Better Public Services Reform Themes. (n.d.). *Better public services: Overview of legislative and related policy proposals.* Retrieved from http://www.ssc.govt.nz/sites/all/files/bps-2325817.pdf.

Biswell, S. (2013, July). Charting the course to great public sector. *Journal of the Institute of Public Administration New Zealand,* July, 16–17. Retrieved from http://www.ssc.govt.nz/sites/all/files/pif-article-publicsector-july13.pdf.

Boston, J., Martin, J., Pallot, J., & Walsh, P. (1996). *Public management: The New Zealand model.* Auckland: Oxford University Press.

Cabinet Office, New Zealand Government. (updated 2008 and 2017). *Cabinet manual.* Retrieved from https://cabinetmanual.cabinetoffice.govt.nz/introduction.

Department of Prime Minister and Cabinet, http://www.dpmc.govt.nz.

Eppel, E. (2013). *Public sector reform: Comparing a new public management and network governance analysis with a complexity theory informed approach.* Paper prepared for COMPACT Work II: Challenges of Making Public Administration and Complexity Theory Work, La Verne CA, June 5–8.

Evans, L, Grimes, A, Wilkinson, B, & Teece, D. (1996). Economic reform in New Zealand 1984–95: The pursuit of efficiency. *Journal of Economic Literature, 34*(4), 1856–1902.

Governor General, New Zealand Government. (2016). Retrieved from http://www.gg.govt.nz/role/constofnz/intro.

Key, J. Rt Hon. (2012, March). *Better public services – Speech to the Auckland chamber of commerce.* Retrieved from: https://www.beehive.govt.nz/speech/better-public-services-speech-auckland-chamber-commerce.

Makhlouf, G. (2016, 14 March). *Trust, transparency and the facts – Driving forces behind modern government.* Speech delivered to Institute of Public Administration New Zealand (IPANZ), Auckland. Retrieved from http://www.treasury.govt.nz/publications/media-speeches/speeches/drivingforces/sp-drivingforces-14mar16.pdf.

McKinnon, M. (2003). *Treasury, the New Zealand treasury 1840—2000.* Auckland: Auckland University Press in association with the Ministry for Culture and Heritage.

Osborne, S. P. (2010). Public governance and public services delivery: A research agenda for the future. In S. P. Osborne (Ed.), *The new public governance? Emerging perspectives on the theory and practice of public governance* (pp. 413–428). London: Routledge.

Osborne, S. P., Radnor, Z., Kinder, T., Vidal, I. (2015). The SERVICE Framework: A Public-service-dominant Approach to Sustainable Public Services. *British Journal of Management, 26*(3), 424–438.

Rennie, I. (2013). *Speech of head of state services and state services commissioner Iain Rennie at the Institute of Public Administration of New Zealand (IPANZ).* Retrieved from http://www.ssc.govt.nz/sscer-speech-ipanz-30july13.

Scott, G. (2001). *Public management in New Zealand.* New Zealand Business Roundtable.

State Sector Act. (1988). Retrieved from http://www.legislation.govt.nz/act/public/1988/0020/latest/DLM129110.html. NZ Business Roundtable.

State Services Commission. (2016). Retrieved from http://www.ssc.govt.nz.

Statistics Department, New Zealand. (2016). Retrieved from http://www.stats.govt.nz/

Victoria University of Wellington. (2017). *Independent review of the performance improvement framework.* Wellington: VUW, School of Government.

INDEX

Hashimoto Administrative
    Reform, 47
Health sector, Thailand, 116–117
High economic growth period,
    Japan, 22–23
High-level policy, 7
HR accreditation, 159

Increase Fairness and Transparency
    of Government, 28
Indonesian leadership in reform
    Asian Financial Crisis (AFC), 54
    bureaucracy reform, 56–57
    central–local fiscal balance, 55
    Commission for Corruption
        Eradication, 55
    democratization process, 55
    economic recovery and
        development, 54
    government effectiveness and
        efficiency, 57
    Indonesian politico-
        administrative system, 54
    law enforcement, 55
    leaders determination
        cascading ideas, 61–64
        operational capacity, 64–67
        public values, 59–61
        reformist leadership, 57–59
    political and economic
        reform, 55
    pragmatic reform, 56
    reactionary reform, 56
    reform sustainability
        authorizing environment
            creation, 75–76
        bad governance awareness, 75
        collaboration beyond
            bureaucracy, 76–77
        education and training, 74

potential leaders and allies,
    72–74
reform-oriented executive
    training, 74
risk management
    dealing with resisting actors,
        69–70
    public distrust, 67–69
    reconciliation strategies, 70–72
Information and Communication
    Technology (ICT),
    65, 159
Innovative leadership
    complicated situations and risks,
        93–94
    decision-making, 95
    developmental approaches, 93
    factors, 93
    innovation ability, 94
    national governance, 95
    planning, 94
Inter-ministerial and inter-agency
    committees, 15
Interpersonal approach, 63
ISO certification, 159

Japanese leadership in reform
    administrative organizations, 29
    administrative reform
        advisory council, 31–32
        Central Government
            Organizations, 27
        Civil Service System And
            Management, 28
        decentralization, 28
        Deregulation And Regulatory
            Reform, 28
        efforts, 20
        E-Government, 28
        government organizations, 27